BEING HAD

Also by Donald Harman Akenson

The Irish in Ontario: A Study in Rural History

A Protestant in Purgatory: Richard Whately, Archbishop of Dublin

Between Two Revolutions: Islandmagee, Co., Antrim, 1798-1920

Local Poets and Social History: James Orr, Bard of Ballycarry, with W.H. Crawford

A Mirror to Kathleen's Face: Education in Independent Ireland, 1922-60

The United States and Ireland

Education and Enmity: The Control of Schooling in Northern Ireland, 1920-50

The Church of Ireland: Ecclesiastical Reform and Revolution, 1800-1885

The Irish Education Experiment: The National System of Education in the Nineteenth Century

BEING HAD

Historians, Evidence,
and the Irish in North America

Donald Harman Akenson

P. D. Meany Publishers

© Donald Harman Akenson, 1985

Canadian Cataloguing in Publication Data

Akenson, Donald Harman, 1941-
   Being Had: historians, evidence, and the Irish in North America

ISBN 0-88835-014-7

1. Irish — Canada — Historiography. 2. Irish — United States — Historiography.
3. Canada — Emigration and immigration — Historiography. 4. United States —
Emigration and immigration — Historiography. I. Title.

FC106.I6A43 1984   971'.0049162   C84-098627-0
F1035.I6A43 1984

47,558

Printed and bound in Canada by
T.H. Best Printing Company Limited
Don Mills, Ontario
for P.D. Meany Company Inc.
Box 534, Port Credit Ontario, Canada L5G 4M2

Dedicated to my brother

James Edward Akenson

CAMROSE LUTHERAN COLLEGE
LIBRARY

Contents

Acknowledgements

I am very happy to acknowledge the John Simon Guggenheim Memorial Foundation, the Ministry of State for Multiculturalism, and the Social Sciences and Humanities Research Council of Canada for financial support in the research and writing of this study. I am particularly grateful to the Tryone Guthrie Centre, Annaghmakerrig, Co. Monaghan and to the Virginia Center for the Creative Arts for providing an environment in which it was possible to work uninterruptedly on these and other writings.

Chapter Two of this book is an expanded version of an article which appeared in the *William and Mary Quarterly* and Chapter Three is an extension of an article that appeared in *Labour/Le Travail*. It is a heartening commentary on the tolerance and catholicity of the North American historical profession that two such journals, each premier in its own field, but based on radically opposed ideological principles, would publish the work of a heretic who subscribes to neither of their two outlooks. A portion of Chapter Four appeared in *Canada Papers in Rural History*. All of this material appears by permission of the copyright owner.

Many people read earlier drafts of various chapters. These include: Mary Akenson, James Axtell, Kathryn Bindon, John Blackwell, Ramsey Cook, Jane Errington, Klaus Hansen, Joan Harcourt, Grey Kealey, John Kelleher,

Michael McGiffert, R. Marvin McInnis, Mary Millar, H. Viv Nelles, Bryan Palmer, George Rawlyk, Peter Ward and William Westfall. I am grateful for their constructive criticism, while emphasizing that responsibility for all errors of fact or interpretation is entirely my own.

Finally, I should like to acknowledge my indebtedness to the example of two scholars. One of these is Jack Hexter, whose colleague I was fortunate to be for a time at Yale, and the other is David Hackett Fischer whose book on historians' fallacies is an enduring delight. Both of these scholars have reminded us that what is the generally promulgated opinion in the historical profession too often is a product of contemporary fashion or of logical fallacies, rather than of a proper assessment of historical evidence.

D. H. Akenson
December, 1984

Chapter One.
Introduction:
Being Had

(I)

To any one who is fascinated by human behaviour, watching historians is often more fun, and much more revealing, than is reading books of history. Amongst the things that make historians intriguing is that, as a group, we are inept con men and are adept only at fooling ourselves. In serious historical writing, all statements of historical fact that are not common knowledge, all ideas that are borrowed from somebody else, are required to be cited — "footnoted" — in a fashion that makes it easy for an interested, or skeptical, reader to check. In theory, hard evidence is assumed to determine interpretation (not the other way around), and we are all supposed to keep one another honest by checking each other's evidence, right down to burrowing into archives to find out if the primary sources were correctly read.

Actually, historians are badly fooled much of the time, and not because our trade is full of master forgers of bogus data. There are a few of those, but that level of artful uttering is not necessary to con most of us. Few historians check each other's footnotes, let alone replicate a given historical study to see if it really was done honestly. Academic historians, particularly in Canada, are a polite, indeed deferential, lot, and it is recognized as bad manners to look too keenly at the way another member of the guild uses evidence. Spats about ideology are all right, but questions of evidence — which is to say, questions of professional competence — are out. The existence of this tacit Geneva Convention amongst academic historians is illustrated by the few rows which do break out publicly: almost always a skeptic who questions the evidentiary base of a given piece of work (or of a whole school of historical thought) receives for his pains a rebuke that is phrased in terms of cultural values or of ideology. Someone who questions the data-base of a bit of Marxist social history is called an "empiricist" (read: right wing); an individual who notes that there is no basis in solid evidence for a certain piece of intellectual history is termed a "reductionist" (read: philistine); a scholar who questions the evidence on which a glossy company history is based is "naive" (read: left wing). And so on. Too rarely is historical competence, in particular the crucial question of the relationship of the fabric of interpretation to primary evidence, dealt with directly.

The chapters in this book are connected by two common concerns. The first of these is the relationship between historical interpretations and the evidence for them; and the second is that they all deal with that most engaging of North American ethnic groups, the Irish.

In a sense, I come to the topic of the Irish in North America as an outsider, for most of my work in the past has been on the Irish in the homeland. That, though, is not necessarily a disadvantage: doubtless, a Ph.D. in Fashion Technology would have prevented the little boy from realizing that the Emperor had no clothes. An outsider looking at historians of the Irish in North America sees one striking characteristic — how easily they have been had.

(II)

As a parable with which to set the tone for the essays that follow, let us look briefly at the neutral, but instructive, case of Richard Whately, an Englishman who spent the unhappiest years of his life trying to understand the Irish.

Richard Whately (1787–1863) is a useful focus of a parable because he was a first-class scholar. As a young man, Whately was elected a fellow of Oriel College, one of the few academic offices awarded on merit in the Oxford of that day. He was a natural don, a great talker, a constant critic, and a prodigious writer — he published more than two million words during his lifetime, on subjects as diverse as political economy, meteorology, and the Pauline letters, as well as several volumes of sermons, some of which are thoroughly scholarly in character. As an academic, his reputation rested chiefly on two *magna opera*: his *Logic,* which appeared in 1826 and which became the standard treatise on the subject until John Stuart Mill's great volume of 1843, and his *Rhetoric,* which dominated the field in the English language for the rest of the century (and which, indeed, today still influences the teaching in Speech departments in the United States). Whately was also one of the early devotees of the then-emerging field of political economy and from 1829–31 was the second incumbent of the Drummond Chair of Political Economy at Oxford, an office whose required lectures he gave with more enthusiasm than technical competence. Whately was not a fool for every new idea that came by, however, and he is also remembered for one of the keenest and funniest philosophic satires of the last century, *Historical Doubts relative to Napoleon Buonaparte.* This piece was published anonymously in 1819 and was into a fourth edition by 1831, when Whately finally acknowledged authorship. It "disproved" the existence of Napoleon Buonaparte by the same methods that David Hume had used to disprove basic Christian doctrines. Beneath its corrosive satire, it is an essay in the proper use and evaluation of evidence. If not a great mind, Whately was first-class by the standards of his time, a hard worker, receptive to new ideas, but well aware of the canons of evidence.[1]

In 1831 something of a tragedy overcame Whately, although at the time he viewed it merely as a perplexing event: he was appointed Protestant Archbishop of Dublin. Why Whately was nominated to this post, an ecclesiastical plum yielding £7,786 a year in net revenues, was as much a mystery to him as to his contemporaries, and, indeed, to his biographer. Equally unclear is why he accepted, for he was not greedy for money and he hated pomp. One suspects that, like a modern-day professor who receives a surprise appointment to, say, the Council of Economic Advisors, he accepted as much out of curiosity about what it was like to be a person of public affairs as for any other reason. Whatever the reasons, the appointment took Whately from Oxford to Ireland, where most of the Anglican clergy under his charge mistrusted him as being too liberal towards the Catholics and a foreigner to boot, while the Catholics saw him only as a leader of the despised Established Church. As his close friend Thomas Arnold later wrote, "it was an evil hour that took Whately from Oxford, where he was doing great and certain good, to exhaust his powers in what is an attempt to raise corn out of the sea-sand."[2]

But even while ploughing the sea-sands of Ireland, Whately tried to keep in touch with the leading intellectual developments of his time. One of these was phrenology, now viewed as an historical curiosity, but in the early nineteenth century a potential science that at least warranted open-minded investigation. In his encounter with phrenology, Whately's life becomes a parable for our own generation, for his natural hard-headedness and scholarly skepticism were overcome by a will-to-believe. Simply put, Whately was conned — and here the vernacular word is totally accurate. That Whately was a reviled English liberal amidst rock-ribbed Irish Protestants and implacable Catholic hard-liners makes his reaching out for new ideas and for new and amiable acquaintances understandable, but it does not make his gullibility any less certain.

As an excellent study by Dr. David de Guistino has shown, nineteenth-century phrenology was a complex phenomenon based upon continental philosphic antecedents, and sustained in part by its affinities to the faculty-psychology which was strong in philosophical-psychological circles throughout the nineteenth century. The father of British phrenology, George S. Combe (1788–1858) was himself a complex person: sometime Scottish businessman, philosopher, social reformer, educationalist, metaphysician, and occasional fraud.[3] For our purposes, the principles of phrenology as they existed in Whately's time can be summarized as follows: (1) that certain intellectual faculties exist as innate and independent entities; (2) that each faculty is associated with a separate portion of brain tissue; (3) that there is a direct correlation between the size of each "organ," or part of the brain, and the strength of the given faculty, and (4) that the overall contour of the skull is determined by the relative strengths of the various faculties; (5) thus external measurement of the skull indicates its internal propensities.[4]

With that as background, the steps by which Richard Whately was duped by George Combe followed a tight *schema.*

Stage One: Whately as a Mark. In many ways the Archbishop was a perfect victim. He was widely curious and, although highly logical in abstract thought, was inclined to believe whatever he was told in face-to-face conversation. As the son of his former private secretary observed, "he was very unsuspicious of dishonesty in others and owing to this cause was sometimes, perhaps, deceived."[5] In particular, like most scholars, he was highly susceptible to flattery, especially if it took the form of interest in his own writings.

Stage Two: Contact. Sometime before mid-1831, Whately and Combe began writing to each other. By mid-1832, Combe had sent Whately copies of four of his books and articles, Whately had ordered a complete backset of the *Phrenological Journal,* and Combe had written to the Archbishop regarding Whately's own writings.[6] Paying attention to Whately's writings always was the best way to capture his attention. Whately wrote to Combe in May 1832, "I wish to assure you that I have never entertained the vulgar prejudice against phrenology. I have not been able to devote myself sufficiently to physiological influences to ascertain the truth or falsity of the doctrine."[7]

Stage Three: the Bait. Whately, of course, wanted his own head read. As early as late July 1831 he was talking about sending a cast to Combe, but he did not get around to doing so until about a year later. Despite his professed agnosticism about phrenology, Whately clearly wanted to be convinced that it was a genuine science. In one letter he referred to having encountered a phrenologist who interpreted a cast of a Mr. Arney, a Cambridge mathematician, with great accuracy. In a later letter, the Archbishop added that he was struck with the coincidence of several phrenological doctrines with those which he himself had developed.[8]

Stage Four: the Hook. In late August 1832, Combe sent to Whately a long analysis of a cast of the Archbishop's head. This was supposedly a preliminary scientific analysis by Combe, but actually was an exercise in flattery and dissimulation. Here are some of Combe's phrases:

> large size of the organ of moral sentiments [certainly a safe thing to say to an archbishop] . . . a fine balance in the proportions of the feelings . . . organs of domestic affection are strong. Your grace knows full well the delights of an attachment in which the mind reposes with fullest confidence in its object. I do not allude exclusively to love between the sexes; I do not know whether your Grace is married. ["Do not know"?! Whately's appointment to the Dublin Archbishopric had made him the subject of widespread gossip, and anyone reading a newspaper would have learned that he was married.]

The flattery continued without stint.[9]

Stage Five: the Twist. In the same letter quoted above, Combe said that he would send the cast of his Grace's head to a Mr. James Simpson, "who is now in the country and has not the least idea that the cast is coming; and I shall transmit his report and shall give no hint of the character or individual." Whether or not Mr. Simpson ever had anything to do with the Whately cast is not clear and is irrelevant. Subsequent events indicate that Combe was simply creating a spurious air of scientific objectivity.

Stage Six: the Full Con. With extraordinary gullibility, the Archbishop took Combe at his word and took no steps to ensure that a truly blind analysis of his cast took place. Instead, he played into Combe's hands. On 2 September 1832 he wrote to Combe saying that, "as Mr. Simpson [the supposed phrenological analyst] is left in genuine ignorance of all circumstances respecting the owner of that skull . . . I think you had better be put in the possession of as many [facts] as possible that you may compare the character with his judgement of the cast." Thereupon the Archbishop proceeded to give an analysis of his own character which is of some interest in its own right, but in the present narrative is useful for comparison with the analysis which Combe later returned to Whately. Of his own childhood the Archbishop said: "He was a prodigy in one and only one point: calculation, in which from about 5 to 8 he was [two illeg. words]. But his tendency was never encouraged . . . At about 8 the talent left him and he has been below par in calculation ever since."[10] That was written 2 September 1832 and Combe probably received it the third or fourth of September. On 6 September Combe wrote to Whately enclosing the supposed analysis from Mr. Simpson, which Combe claimed he was sending before Simpson "shall have seen your Grace's remarks." Further, Combe added his own observations, which should be compared to Whately's words above: "The organ of number is now only moderately developed in your Grace's head and it is a curious circumstance that the power of calculation after having been great, should have disappeared. At the present time the manifestations and development are in harmony."[11] So much for scientific analysis! The Archbishop was being gulled; yet so involved was he with discussing his own mind that he played into the same trap when, on 11 September 1832, he sent Combe a further exposition of his own character compiled by intimate friends.[12] He received by return post another letter from Combe which simply re-phrased Whately's own description of his mental make-up.[13]

Stage Seven: the Result. The Archbishop never became a zealot of phrenology, but it did become a part of his intellectual system. This, however, was not a personal mental revolution because Whately already had rejected the Lockean view of the mind as a passive unit and had adopted a faculty-psychology. After having his own skull read, Whately was sufficiently convinced of the validity of the study to tell Combe that, if the object of science would be served, the analysis of his own head and the evidence of the accuracy of that analysis could be shown about — provided that nothing should be said that would lead anyone to suspect the identity of the original subject. A perpetual polymath, by early December 1832, Whately was sending Combe a set of suggestions for a nine-sign system for more precisely describing head size.[14]

What did Combe gain by his efforts? Not merely an enthusiast, which would have been self-discrediting in any case. Instead, he gained a man of high position and intellectual reputation who believed that phrenology was worthy of investigation (although not necessarily credence) by men of open mind. The only direct personal use Combe made of Whately was in 1836, when he applied for the professorship of moral philosophy at the University of Edinburgh. Whately then wrote for him a public letter of recommendation, stating that, even if all connections between the areas of the brain and specific functions turned out to be a perfect chimera, phrenology still was of value for its employing a mental nomenclature far more logical and accurate than that of Locke and associated writers.[15]

Actually, Whately's use to the phrenological school was mostly internal to the movement. Although chiefly a pseudo-scientific system, phrenology under Combe's hegemóny also was an ambitious amalgam of social reformisms. In particular, Combe and his followers favoured the education of the masses, and Whately's position as a champion of the Irish system of national education provided a useful experiment and example. Also, Whately as a writer of a widely used set of school texts provided an important plank in the phrenologist's platform of education.[16]

Only after having been so badly gulled by Combe did Whately begin to think somewhat critically. In early 1833, he wrote to Combe concerning a story that was going the rounds in Dublin, that Combe had examined the unidentified cast of the skull of a professor of astronomy, a famous mathematician, and had declared it the skull of a mental incompetent. Was there any truth in the story? Combe argued fulsomely that there was not. Although Whately later wrote for Combe the letter of recommendation for the Edinburgh chair, the relationship between the men cooled. Combe kept sending copies of his books and articles to Whately, but now, on occasion, Whately had his wife acknowledge them, rather than responding personally. Yet he was still sufficiently credulous to write to Combe in 1837, saying that Mrs. Whately had a strong suspicion that the shape of his own head had considerably altered since taking up his new episcopal duties and so, to gratify her, he would like to find someone competent in "craniology." Finally, in 1838, the Archbishop posed some sharp critical questions to Combe and complained that the phrenologist was evasive in reply.[17]

Despite his cooling towards Combe, Whately maintained a generalized belief in phrenology. In 1847, for example, he wrote a cloying letter to the wife of his close friend Thomas Arnold, couched in phrenological language:[18]

> My Dear Mrs. Arnold — I cannot forbear expressing the high admiration I feel for the justice of your character . . . Other virtues depend in some degree on several tendencies, but the proper function of what the Phrenologists call the organ of conscientiousness, is to decide what is right, simply for that reason. And the formula for calling this organ into play, is that which is furnished us by the highest authority; — to put oneself in another's place, and consider what we should think fair then.

However, the Archbishop's acceptance of phrenological concepts was essentially a private belief and he kept expression of them out of most of his published works. Given the public skepticism about the pseudo-science, his reticence was prudent. It has also been suggested that he was alive to the delicacy and awkwardness of avowing himself a phrenologist in view of his own peculiarly shaped head.[19]

(3)

Modern scholars are never had so easily as was Richard Whately, or at least so we believe. But, simply for the sake of discussion, let us conjecture that we can be fooled rather more easily than we think. Continuing to use as a parable Archbishop Whately's falling for George Combe's scam, we can infer the circumstances under which a scholar is most likely to be fooled. Whether we are acting as producers or consumers of history — as professionals writing or reading history — we seem to be most vulnerable when: (1) the subject at hand is close in some way to our personal life and belief or sense of individual identity. Whately was the more easily fooled because Combe's "analysis" of the cast of Whately's head was an evaluation of Whately's mind and personality. Similarly, historians are most vulnerable to weak or virtually faked, evidence on subjects that deal with their own ethnic group, their personal religious beliefs, or their ideological commitments. (2) Whether or not the evidence we find reflects on our beliefs as private persons, we are apt to credit more easily evidence that confirms a particular intellectual position that we already have assumed, and we are more apt to ignore or discredit evidence that does not confirm our position. Whately illustrates this nicely, for it was easy to perceive phrenology as a natural extension of his earlier rejection of Lockean psychology. One of the hardest, perhaps *the* hardest, pieces of discipline to incorporate into one's everyday life is to remember, constantly, that, merely because a piece of evidence apparently fits with one's previous intellectual position, it is not inherently more likely to be accurate than another piece of historical evidence that undercuts one's position. (3) We are less apt to evaluate evidence shrewdly when we are unhappy. In part, Whately was less shrewd than usual in evaluating the case concerning phrenology because he was very unhappy in Dublin. Amongst present-day historians, the parallel situation occurs amongst those who perch uncomfortably on the margin of academic society (those young scholars who, through no fault of their own, have become a virtual academic proletariat) or who are dissatisfied with what they perceive as an unjust and unjustifiable social structure in general. (Usually, these individuals are identified as left-wing, but a few are right-wing.) Unhappy people are easily fooled. (4) The closer the personal contact one has with another scholar, the less likely one is to be critical of the evidence supporting his viewpoint. Undoubtedly Richard Whately was the more easily fooled by George Combe because their correspondence was not merely an intellectual interchange, but a personal one as well. Such exchanges almost always are implicitly flattering. When one receives a letter from another scholar, asking for advice or respectfully begging-to-differ, it strokes one's ego. Sometimes, as in Combe's dealing with Whately, the flattery is laid on with a trowel. But, even if overt flattery is not involved, it is still very hard to be truly skeptical of the evidence and argument of someone with whom one shares a common passion for a subject and with whom one has had dinner, joked, had a few drinks, and exchanged complaints about the inequity of an academic system that insufficiently rewards both of us. This is particularly true of the avuncular godfather figures that exist in most historical specialities, men of a senior generation who are kind, generous, and helpful, but whose own work often is terribly weak. It is easy to let pass in silence the sloppy use of evidence by these kind old uncles. (5) As scholars, we are the more vulnerable to being fooled by inadequate or bogus evidence, the more august the personages involved are, whether they be the producers or the consumers of the shoddy goods. Whately was particularly vulnerable because of his high position, and I suspect that senior scholars in our trade are particularly susceptible to being fooled, especially because anyone approaching one of them usually adopts a deferential manner that is disarming to their powers of skepticism. More important, though, we as lower-level consumers of historical evidence, are most apt to accept at face value the statements and evidentiary citations published by individuals, or groups of individuals, who head the various professional associations, who hold endowed chairs, or who direct well-financed collective research projects. (6) Finally, we are particularly vulnerable to being conned when alleged evidence is presented in the vocabulary of scientific-chic. The pseudo-science of Combe's system appealed to Richard

Whately, and why not? Even in the third decade of the nineteenth century, advanced scholars had adopted the attitude — implicit but pervasive — that, if something seemed scientific, it probably was right. Noting this is not to imply that a modern historian should not use tools acquired from the social sciences: indeed, one can scarcely claim to be a competent social historian without a middling knowledge of micro- and macro-economics, of statistics, and of basic sociology and ethnology. However, once one has acquired these minimal tools, if one finds that a "scientific" presentation of some body of evidence still requires the zeal of an intellectual ferret to uncover its meaning, then one probably is being had. The temptation, though, is to accept the opaque as being meaningful. It rarely is.

In the chapters which follow, the vulnerability on each of these six counts of historians of the Irish in North America is illustrated. Most of the essays discuss the massive misreading of the available evidence that has taken place, although one piece — on the possible impact of Irish precedents upon the culture of Ontario — is not a discussion of mistakes in assessing evidence, but rather of the difficulties of evaluating evidence in certain historical situations. In that particular essay, Richard Whately will reappear, not as a mere parabolic character, but as a direct causal influence on the outlook of the people of nineteenth-century Ontario, Irish and non-Irish alike.

Chapter Two.
The Accepted Estimates of Ethnicity of the People of the United States, 1790

(1)

In an important article in the *William and Mary Quarterly* of April 1980, Forrest McDonald and Ellen Shapiro McDonald called attention to problems relating to the accuracy of the standard authority on the ethnicity of Americans at the close of the colonial era.[1] This authority, the "Report of Committee on Linguistic and National Stocks in the Population of the United States," was drawn up by a committee of the American Council of Learned Societies (ACLS) and published by the American Historical Association.[2] The ACLS committee was chaired by Walter F. Willcox, former president of the American Statistics Association, and had four other members: Max Farrand, director of the Huntington Library, Robert H. Fife, professor and head of the Department of Germanic Language and Literature at Columbia, Joseph A. Hill, sometime chief statistician of the U.S. Census Department, and J. Franklin Jameson, chief of the manuscripts division of the Library of Congress and former head of history at the University of Chicago, president of the American Historical Association, 1906–07, and managing editor of the *American Historical Review*, 1895–1901 and 1905–28.[3] This committee of elite academicians was responsible for the final report, but the bulk of the work was done by two consultants, Howard F. Barker, an internationally recognized authority on family names, and Marcus Lee Hansen, at that time one of the two or three leading scholars in American immigration history.

In a general sense, the ACLS report was occasioned by the federal government's attempts in the 1920s to control the size and character of the stream of migrants into the United States. The Immigration Act of 1924 had provided that, beginning in 1927, the flow of immigrants should be related to the "national origins" of the existing population. This posed a particular problem, because the United States censuses had not begun to ask where people were born until the 1850 enumeration. How then did one arrive at some approximation of the pre-1850 population? The answer was that one used the best pre-1850 census — that for 1790 — to determine the ethnicity ("national origin," as it was then termed) of the entire *white* population, and then one employed the rudimentary data available on immigration in order to bring matters up to 1850. So, fundamental to a determination of who would be let into the United States from the late 1920s onward (and, in the actual event, until 1965 when the system was radically altered) was an analysis of the ethnic character of the American population in 1790.

The proximate cause of the ACLS's becoming involved was that the government had done a study of the 1790 census that most competent scholars believed dubious at best. This was *A Century of Population Growth,* published by the Bureau of the Census in 1909, under the supervision of W. S. Rossiter. The fundamental assumption of Rossiter's estimates — one accepted by the ACLS committee — was that in the absence of direct data on ethnicity, surnames provided the most accurate of all possible informational surrogates. This decided, Rossiter assigned experienced clerks to rework the 1790 data and to assign the family name of each head of household amongst the white population to a specific national background. Rossiter's work involved, not a sampling procedure, but a method that potentially was much more accurate: he studied the entire population, something even his critics never essayed. Rossiter's results were as follows concerning the ethnicity of the *white* population of the United States in 1790:

Ethnicity	Percentage
English and Welsh	82.1
Scottish	7.0
Irish	1.9
German	5.6
Dutch	2.5
French	0.6
All others	0.3
	100.0

Given that Rossiter's fundamental assumption concerning the usefulness of surnames as an index of ethnicity was acceptable to the ACLS and, further, that his "sample" was nothing if not adequate, what went wrong? According to the investigating scholars, Rossiter's clerks had not understood how, in the process of anglicization, certain European names became indistinguishable from English names. Names that sounded English, even though preceded by a non-English first name, were tallied as English.[4] Manifestly, a restudy of the 1790 data was necessary, both for reasons of historical accuracy and for the guidance of U.S. federal immigration policy.

The ACLS study started from the same assumption that Rossiter's work had rested on, namely, that family names were a valid surrogate for ethnic data. But, lacking the large staff that Rossiter had had at his disposal, the ACLS authorities developed a sampling procedure. This procedure was *not* a random one, but one should not reject it out of hand for that reason: in certain instances non-random samples can produce more accurate results than random samples. Instead of dealing with all the surnames that existed in America in 1790, the ACLS committee and its consultant on surnames, Howard Barker, dealt only with those they believed could be identified unambiguously as being attached to a specific and discrete ethnic group. The ACLS's rationale underlying this method was perfectly sensible: they decided that they would get farther dealing with what they knew (certain unambiguous denominators) than with what they did not (whether an ambiguous name, such as "Smith," was English, German, Scottish, or Irish).[5]

Of course conclusions derived from a sample of any sort have to be reconstituted if they are to apply to the larger population from which they are drawn. In cases of random samples this is done virtually automatically, for an un-spoken equation is accepted, as follows: whatever happened to the sample population equals whatever happened to the entire population from which the sample was drawn (within certain limits of possible error, determined by sample size, etc.). But this study of the 1790 census was not to involve randomly generated data, but data produced from the conscious selection of certain surnames that were believed to be ethnically denotative. This non-random sample, therefore, was not automatically representative of the larger population, the 1790 census, from which it was drawn.

Here arises one of the problems with the report, for the ACLS committee and its consultants described their methods in such a fashion as to make critical examination of their work difficult. The committee, in the body of its report, explained the statistical procedure as follows: "The occur-rence of names distinctive of a mother country in a popu-lation largely drawn from that country measures roughly the proportion of the population coming from that source. For example, if bearers of distinctive English names were nine-tenths as large a proportion of the population in Maryland in 1790 as they were in England, it is inferred that the population of Maryland was nine-tenths English."[6] The arithmetic here is correct, but the explanation is not of much value, because the committee talks in terms of derived numbers (proportions of two populations) rather than in the terms that the researchers had to use: direct data concerning actual individuals with the various surnames.

But this formulation, non-operational though it was, was clearer than Barker's thirty-eight page explanation of his general methodology.[7] For some reason, Barker preferred to express himself indirectly, even when presenting his tables of calculations. One example will suffice. In a table showing his calculations of persons of English ethnicity in the U.S. in 1790 he presented three facts and a conclusion concerning the surname Parker:

(a) In England and Wales in 1853 there were 39,100 persons named Parker.
(b) The name Parker numbered 2.12 per 1,000 population in England and Wales as of the same date.
(c) The name Parker occurred 1,120 times in the 1790 U.S. Census.
(d) Therefore, if one relied solely on the basis of the occurrence of the surname Parker, one would conclude that that there were 528,300 persons of English ancestry in the U.S. in 1790.[8]

Why should one bother at all to interpolate the number-per-1,000 as an intermediate step in the calculations? It introduces minor errors, involving as it does, the rounding off of important numbers and more significantly, obscures what really was being done.[9]

Actually, a very simple formula, a ratio, lay behind Barker's work on surnames and the ACLS report that assimilated it. This was that the number of persons with certain distinctive names found in the population of England and Wales, would bear the same proportion to that population as would the number of persons bearing the same distinctive names to the persons of English and Welsh ancestry in the population of the United States. To take the surname Parker again, the ACLS committee's formula was as follows:

$$\frac{\text{Number of persons named Parker in the U.S. (1,120)}}{\text{Total number of persons of English and Welsh ancestry in the U.S. (``X'')}} = \frac{\text{Number of persons named Parker in England and Wales (39,100)}}{\text{Total population of England and Wales (18,404,421)}}$$

Naturally, one uses as many names as possible, for the more names one has that are unambiguously associated with English or Welsh ancestry, the more apt the sample is to be representative of the total population involved, and, therefore, the more accurate the final results.

Primarily by this method the ACLS committee derived a complex table, state by state, ethnicity by ethnicity. The general conclusion concerning the ethnicity of the white population in 1790 was as follows:[10]

Ethnicity		Percentage
English		60.1
Scottish		8.1
Irish: Ulster	5.9	9.5
Free State	3.6	
German		8.6
Dutch		3.1
French		2.3
Swedish		0.7
Spanish		0.8
"unassigned"		6.8
TOTAL		100.0

These estimates are still accepted by American historians as the most accurate available.[11] Even the most significant attempt at revising them, that made recently by the Mc-Donalds, assumes that the approach taken by the ACLS committee was sound and that only minor adjustments need to be made to change the ACLS conclusions into an acceptable depiction of historical reality.[12]

The McDonalds, along with the host of much less sophisticated social historians who have accepted the ACLS study at face value, are wrong. The ACLS study, like the one by Rossiter that preceded it, is so full of errors, ranging from the minor to the fundamental, that it is beyond rehabilitation. It must be abandoned, erased from the historical literature, and forgotten.

The stakes here are high. Not only does the ACLS report supply the only ethnic summation we have of the American colonial experience; it also provides the only extant ethnic base line for the study of American social history in the nineteenth century. The importance of the ACLS report is magnified by the extraordinary fact that the U.S. government did not begin collecting data on ethnicity until 1969! Granted, beginning in 1850, authorities asked information on where immigrants came from, and, beginning in 1880, on where one's parents came from.[13] However, the grandchildren of immigrants and those of succeeding generations were all deprived of ethnic identity and simply labeled "native of native parentage." Ethnicity, of course, cannot be measured by dealing only with the immigrants and their offspring, for it is a perduring attribute, with characteristics that survive, muted and subtle but real, much longer than merely the generation that steps off the boat and their children. In 1969–70, when the federal authorities finally attempted a study of the ethnic origins of the entire United States population, it was a happy idea with an unhappy ending: the analysis lumped all individuals who expressed a dual or multiple ethnic identity (Swedish and Danish, for example) into the "other" category and thus invalidated all their results. The 1980 census contained a direct question on each individual's perception of his own ethnicity, and these, if processed properly, would provide, at last, a direct and accurate ethnic census of the United States.[14]

(II)

What the paucity of U.S. ethnic data says concerning the 1790 study is that *if* the ACLS work were reliable we would have at least one trustworthy datum-point on ethnicity before the late twentieth century.

The conceptual framework for the ACLS analysis had

one very important virtue, namely, that *if* the method of using surname samples as ethnic surrogates were valid and *if* the method were applied systematically to each ethnic group, *then* the derived total of all ethnic groups would equal the known total white population of the United States. In other words, all the parts would add up to 100 percent. Thus, in a very elegant manner, the results of the work would be not only a conclusion but the validation of the assumptions and methods under which it had proceeded.

Because the technique used by the ACLS committee was unique to its enterprise, there is no standard method for assessing what degree of variance from the known total white population would have been acceptable. Surely, few scholars would cavil at a variance of 2-3 percent, but, equally surely, had their results added up to, say, 75 percent of the known white population, or to 125 percent, few could have defended the method as successful. The method, then, held the seeds of its own disproof.

One is fascinated to discover that instead of facing this Damoclean test, the ACLS committee applied its formula *only* to the Irish, Scottish, and English elements in the American population. When dealing with the Germans and with "minor stocks" (the Dutch, French, and Swedish) the ACLS introduced two additional methods of bookkeeping, which precluded the use of internal consistency as either a validation or a disproof of the report's methods. In the case of the Germans, there was no reliable list of surnames for the old country, so the formula applied to the surnames of the British Isles could not be used. Instead, Barker made a study of the most common family names in Pennsylvania and then treated Pennsylvania as if it were a foreign country. That is, he used the ratio:

$$\frac{\text{Number of persons in Pennsylvania with certain German names}}{\text{Total population of German-Americans in Pennsylvania}} = \frac{\text{Number of persons in the U.S. with certain German names}}{\text{Number of persons of German ethnicity in the U.S.}}$$

Manifestly, this is not only incompatible with the method used to calculate the English, Irish, and Scottish proportions of the population, but works only if one knows independently what the total population of German-Americans in Pennsylvania actually was before one begins. With very little direct evidence, Barker declared that about one-third of the population of Pennsylvania in 1790 was of Germanic origin. Using this as his "hard" datum, he came to the conclusion that 8.1 percent of the white population of the United States in 1790 was of German stock. But certain patterns in his name analysis led him to believe that 8.1 percent was too low, so, for reasons not adequately explained, he redid the data to produce 8.7 percent as the proper number. The ACLS committee finally settled on 8.6 percent.[15]

Then a third method of bookkeeping was introduced, this time by the committee's other main consultant, Marcus Lee Hansen, who was in charge of estimating the numbers of persons of Dutch, Swedish, and French ethnicity. Using a variety of sources, ranging from names on the 1790 census to church records, local genealogies, and county histories, and injecting a large dollop of his own intuition, Hansen produced state-by-state totals for each of these ethnic groups. It well may be that his estimates are correct, but his discussion of them is of such a nature as to make verification impossible.[16]

Conceivably, the estimates produced by these three methods of ethnic bookkeeping are accurate, despite their being methodologically incompatible. One can recognize that the German and other continental European data could not have been handled like the Irish, Scottish, and English data and therefore commend the ACLS committee's approach for flexibility. But one must simultaneously recognize that the use of three different bookkeeping methods destroyed the research design that had been the integral undergirding of the study. Now the project was no longer automatically validated if everything added up to 100 percent. Indeed, one at least has to consider the possibility that the Germans, Swedes, Dutch, and French may have served as an "account-rectifying residual." That is, potentially they served the same purpose that the "miscellaneous" category does on the expense account sheet of a free-wheeling salesman: a residual that includes everything that cannot be adequately accounted for and is always set at the exact number required to make everything add up to 100 percent.

(III)

Did the ACLS people need such a fudge category? Consider: when Barker first applied his ethnic-name formula to the people of North Carolina, he found that 100.5 percent of them were English. Then he combined English and Welsh names and found that only 98 percent of the residents of North Carolina in 1790 were English. Finally, he decided that 66 percent was about right.[17]

The fact is that the ACLS report, elegant though it was on the outside, was eaten away by several massive intellectual carcinomata. These were as follows.

(1) The fundamental data basis for the study of the English, Irish, and Scottish was invalid. The 1790 census itself was acceptable within certain broad limits; the problem is that for the report's set of surname ratios to operate, one has to have accurate data both on the various surnames as they appeared in the British Isles and on the aggregate population of each nation within the British Isles. In practical terms, one needs (a) a tally of the surnames' occurrence in the U.S. in 1790; (b) a comparable tally for the relevant foreign country; and (c) similar aggregate population data on the U.S. in 1790; and (d) data on the relevant overseas nation involved. But (b) and (d) cannot just be picked up for any date; information on surnames and aggregate population in England in the year 1500, or in 1980, would be of no use, in part because of orthographical changes and in part because the selective nature of migration makes the surnames of either the earlier or the later populations incompatible with the population of the U.S. in 1790. For the ACLS formula to operate, a valid overseas data base is imperative. To be valid, this base must be roughly

coterminous in time with the U.S. data, and the two data sources must not pollute each other.

Consider this first requirement. No one could reasonably argue that if the English, Scottish, and Irish comparative data had been gathered in 1780 or 1800, they would have been chronologically incompatible with the U.S. material for 1790. But the farther in time one goes from 1790, the more apt are the British Isles data to have been distorted by exogenous events. Remember that the ACLS committee's principal model was that of the simulacrum. Were anything to affect the British Isles data that did not similarly affect the 1790 U.S. data, then the simulacrum would be no more and the entire project would fail. The farther in time the two sets of data are separated, the more likely is such an event.

For what period were the basic British Isles data compiled? The answer is: at various dates up to 1890. The English (and Welsh) surnames distribution was derived from a basic list begun in 1837 by William Farr and completed as of 1853. The Scottish material was collected as of 1860 by James Stark, and the Irish material as of 1890 by the Irish registrar-general, Robert E. Matheson.[18] Manifestly, this is unsatisfactory, for too much had happened between 1790 and 1853 (for the English material), between 1790 and 1860 (for the Scottish) and between 1790 and 1890 (for the Irish) that would influence frequency of surnames in the British Isles for comparisons to be made with the United States in 1790. One scarcely needs to be reminded that the nineteenth century, particularly after 1815, was the era of the great diaspora from Great Britain and Ireland; that migration out of the British Isles was not random but selective by class, region, and occupation; that the surnames of the British Isles were not randomly distributed but were localized by region and by class.[19] To compare name-frequencies in the early United States with those obtaining in England and lowland Scotland after the human displacements of the industrial revolution and with the names predominating in Ireland and the Scottish highlands after the Great Famine of the late 1840s is so outlandish as to be ludicrous.

(2) The second requirement of a valid data base connects with the first — that the U.S. and the British Isles data cannot be permitted to pollute each other by any distortional interaction. Pollution would have been prevented if either (a) the two populations being compared, that of the U.S. ethnic group and the respective national group in the British Isles, were hermetically sealed, the one from the other, or (b) the interactions between them were completely random so that there was no bias towards the existence of certain surnames in one population but not in the other.

Obviously, condition (a) could not be met by the ACLS committee because the U.S. surname population being studied was directly derivative from the British Isles population being used for comparison. This is easily seen if one makes the almost otiose observation that when someone named, say, Sterling, left England and migrated to America, there was one more person named Sterling on the American side of the ethnicity formula and one fewer on the English side.

So condition (b) had to be assumed by the ACLS group. And "assumed" is the proper word, for the ACLS people admitted their ignorance in a footnote declaring that "the committee has found little evidence on the questions whether name patterns are or are not permanent and are or are not materially influenced by mass migration."[20] (They noted, though, that the proportion of the first letters with which surnames began had not changed much in England and Wales between 1854 and 1929, a fact of virtual irrelevance to the assumption they were making.) So, having little evidence, the committee implicitly postulated that the interaction between the U.S. and the British Isles data sources was random.

To understand what they thought was happening, visualize two bell jars, one large, one small, sitting side by side and filled with several gases, amongst them helium. Now, if the two jars were connected, the random character of atomic action would assure that with the passage of time, the mixture of gases in the jars would be identical. Therefore, the proportion of helium atoms in the small bell jar would stand in the same relation to the total number of atoms in that small jar as would the number of helium atoms in the large jar to the total number of atoms in that jar. To bring the example back to surnames, the number of Frasers in the U.S. would be to the number of persons of Scots ethnicity in the U.S. as the number of Frasers in Scotland to the total population of Scotland.

This holds only if the whole process of migration from the British Isles had been entirely random. But the single fact agreed upon by all serious students of migration is that migration is a highly selective process. To return to the analogy of the bell jars, migration has the same effect in the social world that a semi-permeable membrane has in the physical world. Were a semi-permeable membrane interposed at the point where our two jars joined, the gases in the small jar would not have been the same in proportion as those in the large, and no conclusion concerning the composition of one of the jars could automatically be transferred to the other.

Which is to say: *even* if the ACLS had not attempted the unacceptable task of comparing the 1790 U.S. population with that of the British Isles of sixty-three to one hundred years later — even if it had used surname data from the British Isles and the U.S. for the same year, 1790 — the exercise still would have been invalid. The two populations did interact, but did not do so randomly.

That the selectivity of migration — especially the tendency for migration to affect some families more than others — could be relevant to the study's validity did occur to Barker. In particular, he had trouble with the name Forbes. His calculations showed that on the basis of that name, there should have been 96,000 Scottish families in the U.S. in 1790. Other surname projections, though, indicated that 33,500 was a more likely number. Instead of taking this discrepancy as a hint of the real situation — that the entire method was invalid — Barker dealt with the problem with a flourish: he simply threw out all the data on the Forbeses![21]

(IV)

Given that the entire process the ACLS committee and its consultants used was invalid, it seems almost supererogatory to go farther and indicate that even within their own erroneous conceptual framework they made some remarkable errors. This is a useful exercise, however, first, as an illustration of how early historians of ethnicity in America operated, and, second, as a prophylactic against any attempt to reclaim the 1790 ethnic estimates from the detritus of scholarly follies.[22] Consider then that

(1) the ACLS committee actually worked with a very small number of family names thought to be ethnically distinctive. The number of names used to identify persons of "Celtic-Irish" extraction (read: Irish Catholics) in the United States was quite high: 126. The numbers for the English and Welsh (22), the Scottish (17), and the "Scotch-Irish" (14) were much less impressive.[23] When one uses fewer than two dozen names, as in the cases of the Scottish, English, and Ulster-Scots (to use the current term in Irish studies for the Scotch-Irish), one is open to a great deal of bias in one's conclusions, the more so because migration to the New World often was familial.

The ACLS committee accentuated this problem by subdividing their surname data into even tinier cells, state by state, and in the case of Ireland, by provincial origin in the Old Country. Can anyone think that the discovery of sixty-nine heads of families in Connecticut having one of seventeen Scottish surnames gives an adequate basis for projecting the total number of persons of Scottish ethnicity in the state?[24] Or, if that is not sufficiently striking, note that the committee confidently presented an estimate of the proportion of persons in Rhode Island who were of Irish Catholic ethnicity and from the province of Munster, on the basis of exactly *two* heads of family bearing a designated Irish name.[25]

(2) Moreover, by their own admission, the committee's surname list actually was not ethnically exclusive. Ideally, each of the names used would have been a perfect discri-

minator: that is, the name existed in the Old Country only as an English, Irish-Catholic, Scottish, or Ulster-Scots name, and thus every time it occurred in the New World it could be ascribed unambiguously to a specific ethnic background in the British Isles. But the English, Scottish, and Ulster-Scots names were only partial discriminators. Three of the names employed in the study as being exclusively English were also used by Irish-Americans, and at least seven of the "English" names occurred in Scotland. All of the Ulster-Scots names also had some currency in Scotland, and the best that could be claimed for the distinctly Scots names were that they had "practically" no Irish usage.[26]

Consider a simple example of what this did to the committee's basic formula. Take the name Robinson. If Robinson is a perfect indicator of English ethnicity, then

$$\frac{\text{Number of persons with the name Robinson in the U.S.}}{\text{Persons of English and Welsh ancestry in the U.S.}} = \frac{\text{Number of persons with the name Robinson in England and Wales}}{\text{Total population of England and Wales}}$$

We know, however, that Irish-Americans bore the name and that it also was used in Scotland. Therefore, the number of Robinsons in the United States must be compared with the number of Robinsons in the entire British Isles, not just in England. The only valid equation would be

$$\frac{\text{Number of persons with the name Robinson in the United States}}{\text{Population of the United States of English, Scottish, and Irish ethnicity}} = \frac{\text{Number of persons with the name Robinson in the British Isles}}{\text{Total population of British Isles}}$$

That, though valid, is useless if what one really wants to know is how many people were Scottish or Irish or English.

To escape this impasse, the ACLS committee took the remarkable decision to count as exclusively English (or

Scots, Irish, or Ulster-Scots) all those persons who had any of the "distinctive" names. They made strenuous efforts to correct for the most obvious errors this procedure induced, but none of these got to the heart of the matter. The sad fact is that unless one has precise discriminators, one perforce has a set of erroneous equations. Instead of abandoning their effort, the committee and its consultants created false ratios, whereby certain surnames of people in the U.S. that stemmed from several sources in the British Isles were placed on one side of an equation and were compared with the same surnames as they occurred only within a single nation in the British Isles. Obviously, without a great deal of fudging of the calculations, the resulting estimates for each ethnic group would have been inflated (because the numerator on the left-hand equation was inflated, its denominator, the "result," necessarily would be). Indeed, had this method of surname calculation been applied to all ethnic groups in the U.S. in 1790, the results would have added up to well over 100 percent of the population.

(3) In a quixotic attempt to distinguish amongst the Americans of "English" ethnicity what proportion was of Welsh ancestry and what part was English in the narrow sense of the word, the ACLS committee, under the tutelage of their expert on names, adroitly combined several of the fallacious ways of proceeding as illustrated previously. They first divided the twenty-two English names that they were using into two groups: twelve "Cambrian" (read: Welsh) and ten "Anglican" (read: everyone else in England and Wales). Let the ACLS report explain what was done next:

> A study of the population of England and Wales in the seventeenth and eighteenth century shows that those counties in which Anglican names were dominant contained about eighty-two per cent and those in which Cambrian names were dominant about eighteen per cent of the population. If in an American state Anglican names were eighty-eight per cent as common and Cambrian names fifty-five per cent as common as in England, the prevalence of English-Welsh blood would be estimated as follows:

$$88 \times 0.82 \ldots\ldots\ldots\ldots 72$$
$$55 \times 0.18 \ldots\ldots\ldots\ldots \underline{10}$$
$$82$$

indicating that English blood was about seventy-two per cent and Welsh about ten per cent of such a population.

By methods of this sort the proportion of the population of the several States and of the United States in 1790 which originated in England and Wales has been estimated.[27]

"By methods of this sort," indeed. Note that (a) an (uncited) study of English surnames of the seventeenth and eighteenth centuries is (b) related to total population of England and Wales at some unspecified point; (c) this point either was the "seventeenth and eighteenth centuries," which long antedated the first accurate English census of 1801, or it was "1853," the date whereat the ACLS people collected most of their English census material;[28] (d) in either case, this was to be the basis of determining the pattern in the United States in 1790. And (e) most important, the names that were being used in the old country were very imperfect discriminations of the English-Welsh split (names such as Jones, Morris, Phillips and Roberts, for example, were used as Welsh discriminators by the ACLS even though they often belonged to Scots and to many people of English ethnicity, in the narrowest sense of the word). Thus, just as occurred in the case of the committee's handling of the other imperfect discriminators described above, the number of persons of English and Welsh ethnicity in the United States in 1790 was improperly magnified. "The result is too large," the report admitted and back-pedalled furiously before deciding that the English and Welsh total in the U.S. white population in 1790 was "not more than seventy per cent."[29]

(V)

When the ACLS committee and its consultants turned to dealing with the Irish, they did almost nothing right. Even for the coolest heads, Ireland presents a problem, for it contains three distinct ethnic subgroups, which for practical purposes can be identified as the Catholics (of "Celtic-Irish" descent), the Presbyterians ("Scotch-Irish" or "Ulster-Scots") and the Anglo-Irish (English by descent and mostly Anglican by religion). The ACLS scholars, however, did not remain calm but thrashed about and, like flies in a spider's web, became ensnared to the point of fatality:[30]

(1) Least important, but useful as an indication of their confused state, the committee prefaced their historical work with some very modern history. Ireland had recently been partitioned into Northern Ireland and the Irish Free State, and U.S. immigration policy would have to distinguish between independent Ireland and the part that remained in the United Kingdom. The committee simply declared that Ulster was "now Northern Ireland"![31] It was nothing of the sort. Northern Ireland, roughly, consisted of only six of the nine counties of the historical province of Ulster, and *all* of the data which they collected and calculated concerning the population of Ulster was for the nine, not the six, counties. (Significantly for eventual U.S. policy, the ACLS report artificially increased the immigration quota for the United Kingdom and reduced that for the twenty-six counties of the south of Ireland, but that is another matter.)

(2) Given that the fundamental problem was to distin-guish the respective populations of Ireland's three major ethnic subgroups, the ACLS committee decided to deal first with the "Celtic Irish" (that is, the Irish Catholics). It did so by identifying, province by province, certain distinctive Irish Catholic names and proceeding by methods already discussed in detail, thereby incorporating the errors in the use of imperfect discriminatory processes. Incredibly, a further layer of error was introduced in the Irish Catholic material by an inexplicable decision to merge the 1890 surname data with population figures for the 1821 Irish census![32] Recall here that despite all their problems, the English-Welsh and Scottish formulae each at least had possessed the virtue of internal consistencies. The right hand side of the equation had been, for England:

$$\frac{\text{Number of persons with certain surnames in England and Wales in 1853}}{\text{Estimated total population of England and Wales in "1853"}}$$

and that for Scotland[33]

$$\frac{\text{Number of persons with certain surnames in Scotland in 1860}}{\text{Total population of Scotland in "1860."}}$$

But for Ireland the equation was as follows:

$$\frac{\text{Number of persons with certain Irish Catholic names in the U.S. in 1790}}{\text{Total number of persons of Irish Catholic ethnicity in the U.S. in 1790}} = \frac{\text{Number of persons in Ireland with certain Irish Catholic names in 1890}}{\text{Total population of Ireland in 1821.}}$$

Questions of wrong method aside, the effect was significant. Because the population figures for Ireland were considerably higher in 1821 than in 1891 (6.8 million as compared to 4.7 million) the number of Irish Catholics estimated to have been in the 1790 U.S. population was considerably augmented and, consequently, any U.S. immigration policy based upon the ACLS report would set an artificially high ceiling on the number of immigrants from the Irish Free State. (This offset to some extent the opposite error mentioned above.)[34]

(3) All this was being done for the Irish Catholics province by province, probably because of requirements of U.S. immigration policy that Ulster and the Free State be dealt

with separately. Barker next went through the motions of making surname calculations for both the Anglo-Irish and the Ulster-Scots. The problems, though, were so great that he could not keep up the pretence of scholarly confidence: the fourteen names used as distinctive of Ulster-Scots all were very common in Scotland and thus presented complex problems; so too did the Anglo-Irish names that, by definition, were found in England as well. In the heel of the hunt, Barker made two massive guesses and one crucial admission. The guesses were, first, that in 1790 the Ulster-Scots "may be reckoned as equivalent to about a third of the population of Ulster."[35] That figure he then used as the basis for determining what proportion of ambiguously named migrants should be assigned to Scotland and what proportion to Ulster. This guess was made without recourse to the nearest piece of relevant data, the 1834 study of Irish religious persuasions done by the commissioners of public instruction in Ireland. That commission found that only 22 percent of the inhabitants of the ecclesiastical province of Armagh — roughly, but not exactly, equivalent to the geopolitical province of Ulster — were Presbyterians,[36] that is "Scotch-Irish" in Barker's vocabulary. Thus his guess almost certainly was high, with the outcome that the eventual results magnified the number of Ulster-Scottish migrants to the United States.

Barker's second guess also magnified the non-Catholic figure eventually derived for the U.S. In the absence of any direct evidence about the Anglo-Irish in Ulster, he guessed "that the migration rate of bearers of English names was intermediate between the rate of bearers of Celtic and bearers of Scotch-Irish names." The closest he came to giving a reason for this guess was that, concerning the Anglo-Irish in Ulster, "their very heterogeneity suggests as the rate of their migratory activity, one between that of the Celts and that of the other unassimilated element, the Scotch-Irish."[37] Since the Ulster-Scots flow had been raised by Barker's earlier excessive guess about the total Ulster-Scots population, the Anglo-Irish migration flow also perforce was raised as well.[38]

The admission that Barker made in a footnote to his discussion of Ulster-Scots names was this: "The Scotch-Irish give evidence of factional migration of such marked character as partly to destroy the validity of Matheson's data on 1890 conditions as indicative of those in the eighteenth century . . . The exodus of most of the members of certain groups . . . gives their names more than the normal representation in the New World and leaves the population of the motherland with an unusually small proportion of bearers of these names."[39] In so writing, he had taken a first step towards a conclusion that he and the ACLS committee could not face: that the entire project was a fool's errand.[40]

(VI)

Must the discussion end on a purely negative note? No. There are a number of research strategies that are potentially promising if one wishes to determine the ethnic proportions of the late-eighteenth century U.S. population. Most of these involve accepting the basic idea that names can indeed be a valid surrogate for ethnic data.

That surnames are related to a person's ethnic origin is a notion we all accept from our everyday experience, and, therefore, it is exactly the kind of fundamental assumption that we are likely to accept uncritically. That is where the trouble begins. Let me give one example as a metaphor for the difficulties involved. Everyone acquainted with English history knows the name Oates. As a surname it fits on any list of pure-English names, or so one would think. Professor John Kelleher one time told me of some acquaintances from Roscommon who were quite innocent of any connection with the late little-lamented Titus Oates, but who proudly bore the surname. He investigated the matter, and discovered that their name originally was "McQuirk." McQuirk in Irish is Mac Cuirc, "son of Corc," and *Corc* in Old Irish is an heroic epithet meaning "purple light." The Old Irish word does not exist in modern Irish, however, and would not be understood by Irish speakers. So McQuirck became Oates from a mistaken popular etymology which derives from the modern word *coirce,* meaning "oats." Historical and etymological investigation would produce cases of this sort by the thousand. Thus, the operative issue becomes the need to escape from bondage to the often-fallible lists of "distinct" national names drawn up in the Old World.

This can be done empirically for all ethnic groups but only by precisely specifying the geographic boundaries for which surname-data will be collected and the precise time period involved. What one wants to know is the ethnicity of the holders of various names who (a) lived *within the boundaries of colonial America* in (b) the years, say, 1750–90. Forget entirely all the surname lists for England, Scotland, and Ireland. Instead, one should be empirically deriving a bank of relevant names that are ethnically-distinctive based on (a) the names actually existing in colonial America, and (b) whose links to the Old Country have been established and (c) whose variants in spelling and form have been historically documented. The only persons presently doing this kind of work are the much-maligned geneaologists. Through the collection of thousands of individual family histories, each well documented in linkage to the Old Country, it should be possible to develop a name-bank that is reasonably reliable as a surrogate for ethnic data. Crucially, this name-bank must give data on both first and last names, for in many instances, even when a surname was anglicized, the Christian name still indicated ethnicity (e.g. Helmut Smith).

Once such a name-bank is in place, a variety of research-designs are possible. The following is one practical way to proceed.

First, acquire a copy of relevant raw data. There are ample sources at hand. In particular, the Bureau of the Census's twelve-volume *Heads of Families at the First Census of the United States taken in the Year 1790*[41] are an extraordinarily rich starting point. These give the first and last names of the head of each white household along with ancillary details that include information on family structure.

Second, decide that only a single method of bookkeeping

will be used in the analysis of the raw data (not two or three as was done in the various name-ratio studies).

Third, do not take any short-cuts, especially not those of the name-ratio approach or those used in the lists of names found in the Bureau of the Census's *A Century of Population Growth from the First Census of the United States to the Twelfth, 1790–1900*,[42] especially 11, Table III, wherein names have been aggregated in ways that mix together distinct ethnic groups. Instead, adopt the approach taken by the much-maligned W.S. Rossiter and deal with each and every name of a head of household recorded in 1790. In the era of large-memory computers this is not as difficult a task as it sounds, for there were only 27,337 surnames on the schedules that survived from the first census.

Fourth, comes the hard part. The method must be checked for validity against an external standard. Specifically, one must take a sample of the individuals to whom one has ascribed ethnicity through their names and trace them geneaologically back to their European roots. Geneaologists know how to do this. Most historians do not, but it is an acquirable skill.

Fifth, that accomplished, the ethnic-ascription program can be rewritten to correct for its having had any deviations from reality.

Sixth, then a "semi-final" run of the data can be made.

That run is only semi-final, because a seventh step is necessary: there will be a residuum of heads of families who had unique, or nearly unique names and which for various reasons are not included in the bank of ethnically-distinctive surnames. These will probably be about 12,000 surnames, representing only one-half of one percent of the population. (Of the 27,337 surnames on the 1790 schedule, 15,403 represented 99.5 percent of the white population). This residuum needs to be distributed amongst the ethnic categories either by scrutiny by name experts and geneaologists or by an appropriate statistical technique.

The very rough research design presented here may appear daunting, but larger projects have been successfully completed and this one is certainly not beyond the capacity of a research team at any good university. The real question is whether or not any foundation or government agency is willing to bear the costs. Considering that so little solid data exist on ethnicity in the United States, the first census would be an excellent place to start to get the story right.

Chapter Three.
The Historiography of the Irish-Americans

(I)

In history, as in mathematics, elegance is an attribute that distinguishes an humdrum exposition from one of real excellence. The presence of this quality is contingent upon the veracity of the proof or exposition being presented, but mere accuracy is not enough to produce real elegance. In the field of American social history there has developed, through the individual works of several score, indeed hundreds, of scholars, a generally-agreed explanation of the behaviour of the Irish in America. When viewed as a synthesis of their work, this agreed explanation seems elegant indeed.[1]

"The history of the Irish in America is founded on a paradox. The Irish were a rural people in Ireland and became a city people in the United States."[2] Thus, in an often-quoted summation of the Irish-American experience, does William V. Shannon pose what has been taken as the central problem of Irish-American social history: why did they become an urban people? Lawrence McCaffrey observed in a lapidary phrase, that the Irish "had the painful and dubious distinction of pioneering the American urban ghetto. . . ."[3] Implicit in most general discussions of the Irish-Americans as an urban ethnic group is the notion that in the United States there was a two-fold deviation in their behaviour from certain norms. These were, first, that in becoming a city people in America they veered sharply from their rural background in the Old Country, and second, that they deviated from the norm set by contemporaneous immigrants to the United States from other countries in that the Irish had a much higher propensity to settle in cities than did other ethnic groups.

In explanation of this surprising urban orientation on the part of the American Irish, several related points are generally accepted by historians. Each of these points reinforces the other, and together they form a virtually seamless explanatory structure. For convenience, I am enumerating each fact as a distinct entity, but the reader should not lose sight of the fact that they dovetail, the one into the other, like a series of mortise and tenon joints. First, it is generally accepted that the Irish landed in America so broke that they could not immediately leave the Atlantic seaboard cities and take land in the interior. "Most of them had arrived penniless and had been 'immobilized' in the port where they landed,"[4] is a summation of the experience of the Boston Irish and it frequently is generalized to describe the situation throughout the New England and Middle Atlantic seaboard. The Irish immigrants were not permanently impoverished, however, and once they had accumulated cash they could have left the cities and moved to farms. Here a second explanatory tenet enters: "Lack of skills was far more important than a shortage of funds in determining the Irish-American decision to become city dwellers. Because manorialism and serfdom had not encouraged agrarian skills or knowledge, Irish Peasants were among the most inefficient farmers in Europe and were not equipped for rural life in America."[5] Thus, even when he had money in hand, the Irishman in America was too technologically backward to farm. Third, it is generally believed that even had he possessed the agricultural skills, the Irishman would not have chosen to farm, because the Famine had so seared him that he would not go on the land again. "The Irish rejected the land for the land rejected them," was William V. Shannon's epigramatic observation.[6]

Another popularizer has put it this way: "To the Irishman, the land had become a symbol of oppression; for him, farming did not connote the Jeffersonian image of the noble yeoman enjoying abundance, independence, and contentment. Rather, it meant poverty, long, arduous, unrewarding labor, dependence on an alien master and, possible starvation and eviction."[7]

But what about those migrants who came either before, or well after, the Great Famine? They, in common with the Famine migrants, shared a characteristic that is the fourth component of the agreed explanation of Irish behaviour in the new world. They were culturally unadapted to rural American social life: "The Irish temperament, unfitted for lonely life, shuddered at the prospect of a wilderness clearing without Irish fellowship."[8] Several general historians either quote or paraphrase a letter by an Irish immigrant who had done well in Missouri, but who looked back regretfully to the old days in Ireland, where after work:

> I could then go to a fair, or a wake, or a dance, and I could spend the winter nights in a neighbour's house cracking the jokes by the turf fire. If I had there but a sore head I would have a neighbour within every hundred yards of me that would run to see me. But here everyone can get so much land, and generally has so much, that they calls them neighbours that lives two or three miles off — och! the sorra take such neighbours, I would say. And then would sit down and cry and curse him that made me leave home.[9]

In practical terms this need for close and compatible neighbours meant that the Irish-Americans preferred cities. Even those who, by virtue of superior skills or financial acumen could live anywhere, chose to live in cities. And, "when the Irish finally did begin to move west, most of them preferred places like Chicago, St. Louis, St. Paul, and San Francisco to farms."[10]

These, then, are the four main components of the agreed explanation of why the Irish-Americans became a city-people. The components dovetail nicely one with another. Of course there are bits of scholarly filigree that cross-tie the main elements,[11] but in its four-square simplicity, the basic agreed explanation covers the main question in a fashion so clean, clear and simple as to be truly elegant.

Like any edifice, this structure requires certain invisible foundations, and there is nothing wrong with that, provided that the foundations are compatible with the structure which rests on them. In this instance, these, too, are four-fold. Implicitly, all recent synthesizers agree that the years from the Famine to roughly 1920 form the crucial period in Irish-American history. Second, it is assumed that after mid-nineteenth century, Irish-Protestant migration to the United States was virtually non-existent. Third, to the extent that Protestant migration is noteworthy, it is assumed that it was the Ulster-Scots (the "Scotch-Irish") who prevailed, rather than the Anglo-Irish and their major migration is believed to have been completed before the nineteenth century began. And, fourth, it is tacitly concluded from the three preceding assumptions, that one can justifiably limit the term "Irish-Americans" to persons of the Roman Catholic faith. Since these four assumptions are fully compatible with the agreed explanation of Irish-American behaviour, one is predisposed to accept them as being both reasonable and apposite.

(II)

What, then, is the problem: why should one be skeptical concerning the generally accepted view of the Irish in America? Let me approach that question in stages and, at first, indirectly. As an initial step, I suggest that American historians overcome their fear of the forty-ninth parallel and their inherent provincialism and briefly consider a case from Canadian history.

Until recently it was believed that the Irish in Canada had followed the same pattern of urbanization that is posited for the Irish in the United States and that the reasons for their becoming a city-people were similar, indeed nearly identical. Granted, there is much less scholarly work on the Irish in Canada than in the U.S. (which is hardly surprising, as

Canada has fewer historians), and also granted, it was conceded that there was a goodly number of Protestants amongst the Canadian Irish, but basically the pattern of urbanization and its accompanying explanations were the same as those which I have described for the United States.[12]

Then, recently, two separate studies looked at the primary data and suddenly the entire house of cards came tumbling down. The first, done by Professors A. Gordon Darroch and Michael D. Ornstein of York University, used the 1871 census to investigate occupational stratification and ethnicity. The 1871 census of Canada is an especially useful one, for it included, for the first time in Canadian official records, an indication for all persons, not only of their places of birth, but of their family backgrounds: that is, of their ethnicity. Darroch and Ornstein took a very large random sample from this census — 10,000 heads of households — and cross-tabulated ethnicity with several variables. The surprising discovery as far as the Irish were concerned is that as was the case for the members of every other major Canadian ethnic group, they were more likely to be farmers than anything else, and this held both for Catholics and Protestants. Nationally, 53.8 percent of the Canadian sample consisted of farmers. The farming figures for persons of Irish ethnicity was 58.3 percent for the Protestants and 44.3 percent for the Catholics. Thus, the belief that the Irish mostly settled into an urban proletariat was destroyed. Moreover, concerning those Irish Catholics who settled into urban occupations (the group most comparable to the "Irish Americans" as usually defined), their proportion of individuals in bourgeois occupations, in the professions and in artisanal work was virtually identical to that of the total labour force. Granted, there inevitably were lumps of disadvantaged Irish in several cities, but taking the national pattern into accounts, these people were no bigger a proportion of the Irish-ethnic group than they were of most other groups. The Irish in Canada, both Catholic and Protestant, were most apt to be farmers, and overall, were not occupationally disadvantaged.[13]

The second study, my own on the Irish in Ontario,

showed that whether one considers all individuals born in Ireland, all persons of Irish ethnicity, or separate Catholic and Protestant sub-groups, the picture is the same: that they settled in the countryside. For example, in 1851, 78.9 percent of the Irish-born persons living in Ontario (that is, Irish immigrants) lived in rural areas. In 1861 the percentage was 74.4 percent. Further, if one considers all persons of Irish ethnic background (something which becomes possible with the 1871 census), one finds that 66.3 percent of the Irish-descended Catholics and 83.2 percent of the Irish-descended Protestants were living in rural areas. Obviously, the difference between the Catholics and Protestants warrants investigation, but the key point is that *neither* group was an urban one. Both Protestants and Catholics were quite able to stand the loneliness and isolation of pioneering life and both were able to meet the technological requirements of frontier farming.[14]

Here I am not suggesting that the reader accept the Canadian and the American cases as being perfectly comparable. There are significant differences between the United States and Canada cohorts, but instead of throwing up roadblocks,[15] let me plead that American social historians consider the possibility that perhaps, just perhaps, the Canadian case is sufficiently relevant to raise at least two questions concerning their elegant edifice of explanation about Irish Americans. The first of these is: do not the Canadian data make one question the validity of the cultural assumptions that the Irish-Americans were technologically unable to adapt to frontier farming and incapable of bearing the loneliness of pioneering? And, second, and much more important: is the data-base concerning the Irish in America really trustworthy? Conceivably, the task of explaining why the Irish in America became a city people is not the right one at all.[16]

(III)

Let us look at the primary data and see what it does *not* reveal.

1. Initially, it is crucial to recognize the distinction between migrant groups and ethnic groups. The generation which was born in Ireland and which migrated to the United States is usually denominated "first generation American" by U.S. social scientists.[17] This group, distinguished by its foreign birth, is the foundation layer of the ethnic group. Their children, born in America, become the "second generation,"[18] their grandchildren the "third," and so on. Ultimately, the number of people with a sense of ethnic identity will be several times the original foreign-born cohort. Of course the sense of ethnicity diminishes as the Old Country recedes, generation by generation, but ethnicity is a perduring cultural characteristic and it has empirically demonstrable characteristics — in such things as religion, voting patterns, and family structures — and these characteristics often operate even after a person has consciously stopped feeling Irish, Italian, Swedish, or whatever.

With this as background, note this fact: there exists *no* body of basic demographic data on the Irish (or any other group) as an ethnic group in the United States. None. Until 1969–70 none of the decennial censuses of the United States asked a question concerning the ethnicity of the individuals whom they were enumerating, and the census is the only potential source of such data. Granted, in the late 1920s the American Council of Learned Societies tried to re-work the 1790 census data to give an indication of ethnicity at the end of the colonial period, but this effort failed miserably.[19] No further comprehensive attempt at dealing with ethnicity was made until 1969–70, when the Census Bureau asked an ethnicity question. Unhappily, the collection of the data was bungled and no firm conclusions came from it.[20] In 1980 the ethnicity question was again asked and one hopes that this time it will be processed competently.[21] But even if the Census Bureau is successful, we will have information on the Irish ethnic cohort only for 1980, a date somewhat too recent to help our understanding of a process of migration and adaptation to the New World that was primarily a nineteenth-century phenomenon.

2. *Never* have the United States census authorities

collected information on the religious affiliation of specific individuals. The Census Bureau once, in 1957, asked a religion question of a voluntary sample group, but this met with so much opposition that the attempt never was repeated.[22] This refusal to deal with religious persuasion except by querying the various denominations for their alleged total number of adherents, seems so perverse to non-American historians as to be almost pathological. But whatever the reasons for this refusal to enumerate individuals by religion,[23] it means that we cannot demonstrate that, as Lawrence McCaffrey has stated, Catholicism is "the banner of Irishness."[24] The equation of Irish-American with Irish-Catholic-American may indeed be accurate, but there are no comprehensive data that actually establish this point.

3. Given that there is no comprehensive data either on Irish ethnicity or upon the religious persuasion of individuals of Irish background in the U.S., it follows *mutatis mutandis,* that there are no cross-tabulations extant which relate either ethnicity or religious persuasion of persons of Irish background to such fundamental characteristics as their place of residence and occupation. Granted, there are several, indeed dozens, of valuable studies of the Irish in various cities of America, but in none of them is the matter of ethnicity and of religion defined for the entire population of the town or city with which the authors deal and for none of them is it established where in the total context of the Irish in America their study-group fits. This is not the authors' fault; the census data are lacking. But, unfortunately, because of the lack of data defining the entire Irish profile, ethnically and religiously, historians have studied the sub-groups on which data come most easily to hand — Catholics in large cities — and have given the impression that the characteristics of these easily-researched Irishmen were universal in America.

4. But, surely, there must be some pieces of comprehensive data about the Irish. There are. Beginning with the *1850* census of the United States, we know, at decennial intervals, the birth-place of everyone in the population.[25] This is useful indeed, as long as one remembers three points: first, that the

data on the foreign-born in general, and on the Irish in particular, is information only on immigrants, not on the bulk of the ethnic group; second, that the data on the Irish include both Catholics and Protestants, with no effort having been made to distinguish the respective proportions of each denomination; and, third, that the earliest data we have on the Irish reflect the situation *after* the extraordinary migration induced by the Great Famine had been several years in full spate. In other words, we have *no* demographic base line which allows us to determine what the character and extent of Irish migration to the United States were before the Famine. This is especially crippling, because, although it is quite clear that there was a heavy Irish migration to the United States before the Famine, the U.S. immigration statistics before 1855 are not trustworthy. (On this point see below, section IV–3).

Manifestly, the material available on the number of Irish-born persons amongst the American population from 1850 onwards is much better than no information at all, but it is not until 1860 that one finds even rudimentary printed cross tabulations of the data on Irish-born persons with residence in various cities and not until the 1870 census are data on occupation and on place of birth cross-tabulated. As will be discussed later (section IV-2) these data on the Irish born immigrants come so late in the collective history of the entire Irish ethnic group in the U.S., that their value is severely limited.

5. In 1870 the census authorities asked each individual whether or not he had foreign-born parents, but the information was elicited only in the form of a yes-or-no answer, not what country the parents were from. The next census, that of 1880, asked the specific origin of those natives of the U.S. who had foreign-born parents and cross-tabulated this material in a refreshingly useful fashion. This quasi-ethnicity item was as close as the Census Bureau ever came in the last century to dealing with ethnicity in the true sense. As one authoritative study conducted in the early 1920s lamented, "The foreign stock can be traced back only one generation. . . Beyond this the population must, in most

cases, be treated as an undifferentiated body of 'native stock.' "[26]

By now it should be apparent why the four assumptions that underly the agreed explanation of the Irish in America — that the really important migration began with the Great Famine, that the Protestants played no significant part in the flow after mid-century, that the only significant band of Irish Protestant migration to the U.S. were Ulster Presbyterians who crossed the Atlantic in the seventeenth and eighteenth centuries, and therefore, that Irish-American is a synonym for Irish-Catholic-American — have been kept discreetly implicit. There is an absence of systematic demographic data on each of these matters.

(IV)

The preceding points of necessity have been negative ones. Now let us take up a more positive outlook and thereby begin to escape from the evidentiary vacuum that underlies almost all general discussions of the Irish in the United States by adopting a set of new perspectives.

1. First, and easiest to do, historians would do well to agree that at whatever moment in time we are discussing the Irish, our ideal is to treat them as an ethnic group, not merely as a single generation of immigrants. This means that if our data are limited to only one or two generations, we will make it clear to the reader that there are other generations, third or fourth, which also are part of the Irish ethnic cohort. If we must acknowledge that we have reliable and conclusive data on, for example, only the immigrant generation in 1870 and that we know virtually nothing about the second, third and fourth generations who comprised the majority of the ethnic group, then so be it. Admitting what we do not know is the first step in getting the story right.

2. Second, one must define the time period that is most crucial in the history of the Irish in America and concentrate on that period as a first priority. Because demographic data became more and more extensive and accurate in the late nineteenth and early twentieth centuries, it is tempting to

concentrate on those years; but merely because research is easiest in that period, does not mean that those were the crucial years.

In point of fact, much of the Irish migration to the United States occurred well before the Great Famine. If one accepts for a moment the U.S. immigration records for the first half of the nineteenth century (as will be discussed later, they are, if anything, a serious underestimate of actual early Irish migration to the U.S.), then it is clear that the Irish migration has to be studied not, as in the usual case beginning with the Famine, but, at minimum, starting in the early 1830s:[27]

Irish Immigration, 1820–1900	
Decennial Period	Number
1820–30	54,338
1831–40	207,381
1841–50	780,719
1851–60	914,119
1861–70	435,778
1871–80	436,871
1881–90	655,482
1891–1900	388,416

Indeed, despite the absence of records before 1820, it may fairly be suggested that the end of the Napoleonic Wars is the proper time to begin focusing upon the Irish in the United States. That census data are absent for the period is irrelevant; the Irish were there, even if the census takers were not.

This pre-Famine group formed the foundation of the Irish ethnic cohort in the United States, and, if even a two-fold multiplier was in effect (a very conservative estimate), for each Irish migrant of, say, 1830, one can expect there to have been two second-generation off-spring in 1850–60 and four third-generation descendants in the last quarter of the nineteenth century. But, recall, that until 1880 no record was kept of the "Irishness" of the off-spring of Irish migrants and that the U.S. officials did not in the nineteenth century ever record the ethnicity of the grandchildren of immigrants.

Thus, from mid-century onward, there was a large, un-recorded, and demographically invisible Irish ethnic population which traced its roots in North America to the pre-Famine, not the post-Famine period.[28]

If the end of the Napoleonic Wars is the proper time to begin the history of the Irish in the United States, when does one stop? The history of the group is fascinating and well worth taking right up to the present day, but a first priority should be to deal with the group up to the point when its major components were set. There are several logical and practical possibilities. One is to stop at the period in which the total absolute number of Irish-born in the U.S. reached a plateau, 1870–90.[29]

Total Irish-Born in the United States	
1850	961,719
1860	1,611,304
1870	1,855,827
1880	1,854,571
1890	1,871,509
1900	1,615,459

After 1890 the number of the Irish-born in the U.S. fell rapidly, which is to say that the foreign-born component of the Irish ethnic population was dropping. From the time of the 1870–90 plateau onwards, one is dealing with an ethnic group whose characteristics are less and less influenced by infusions of the Irish culture from the homeland and increasingly determined by the group's experience within American society.

Another logical cut-off point would be 1860, for it was in

Year	Percentage Irish-Born
1850	4.15
1860	5.12
1870	4.81
1880	3.70
1890	2.80
1900	2.13

that year that the Irish-born proportion of the United States population reached its peak:[30]

This *terminus ad que'm* coincides with the onset of a decrease in the decennial increment in the Irish-born population.[31]

By stretching a point, one could argue that the end of the Famine migration marked the culmination of the crucial phase in Irish migration to the U.S., for after the 1850 census, each succeeding enumeration showed that the Irish-born were a declining proportion of the foreign-born population of the U.S.[32]

Year	Irish-born as Percentage of Foreign-born
1850	42.8
1860	38.9
1870	33.3
1880	27.8
1890	20.2
1900	15.6

And, considered as a proportion of the total immigration to the United States, the Famine generation was the end, not the beginning, of a trend:[33]

Year	Irish as Percentage of Total Arrivals
1820–30	35.8
1831–40	34.6
1841–50	45.6
1851–60	35.2
1861–70	18.8
1871–80	15.5
1881–90	12.5
1891–1900	10.5

The substantive point behind my mention of these various possible stopping points is that one must focus much earlier than usually is done if one is to capture the formative stages of the Irish-American polity. In practice, the two generations spanning the period from the end of the Napoleonic wars to roughly the beginning of the last quarter of the nineteenth century were the crucial ones for the Irish-Americans. In these years the immigrant and children formed the base population from which the multi-generational ethnic group later was formed. This several-generation group as it evolved in the late nineteenth and twentieth centuries deserves much more attention than it has received: but a first priority must be to focus on the pivotal years, roughly 1816–75, for unless the foundation group is accurately defined, the evolution of later generations cannot be measured.

A fortunate side effect of concentrating on the years before 1880 is that it helps scholars to define more precisely one aspect of the "two-fold deviation" of the Irish from the American norm, in this case the imputed tendency of the Irish immigrants to settle less often into rural life than did immigrants from other groups. There is no question whatsoever that in the twenty or thirty years after the Great Famine the Irish immigrants were different from the rest. For example, the 1870 census indicates that, considered as a percentage of foreign-born persons who held jobs, the proportions in agriculture was as follows:[34]

Immigrant Group	Percentage in Agricultural Employment
Entire foreign-born population	22.9
Irish	14.6
English and Welsh (combined)	25.6
Germans	26.8
Scandinavians	46.0
Italians	14.3

English immigrants and those from Germany, Scandinavia, and Great Britain (often lumped together in American ethnic history as the "old immigrants"), were different indeed from the Irish. But during the 1880s the source of immigrants to the U.S. began to shift towards Italy, Russia, and Austro-Hungary, a change which accelerated in the last decade of the nineteenth century until, finally, in the early twentieth century the "new immigrants" eclipsed in number the old.[35] Significantly, the Irish immigrants of the later period did not deviate much from the norms set by the "new immigrant" wave. In actual fact, save for the Bohemian-Moravian group with its high commitment to farming as an occupation, the Irish were more apt than most of the new immigrants to farm. A study of the foreign-born white male population who were ten years of age or above in 1920 (meaning that in the median case they had entered the U.S. in the year 1900), showed the following percentages as engaged in agriculture.[36]

Immigrant Group	Percentage in Agricultural Employment
Irish	13.5
Russian	4.1
Bohemian-Moravian	77.6
Italian	0.9
Polish	14.1
Slovak	2.5
Yiddish	0.6

Therefore, any discussion of the Irish as a unique band of immigrants should centre on the migrants who came before the 1880s. Thereafter, the Irish migrants behaved in occupation (and residency)[37] much like other immigrants, and their behaviour in matters of choice of occupation and choice of residence can be explained by factors common to all "new immigrant" groups. It is only in the era of the "old immigration" that one is justified in denominating the Irish as ethnic deviants and thus it is in that era wherein one should search for those cultural and economic determinants which made the Irish an unusual people in the New World.

    3. Third, parodically, one will break out of the evidentiary impasse concerning the Irish in the United States only by abandoning the U.S. as one's sole focus of attention and by adopting a North American perspective. There are several

reasons for this, each one compelling, but the most important is that Canadian government sources provide data relevant to the Irish in the U.S. that is not available from U.S. sources.[38] In particular, Canadian data are necessary if one is to escape from the vast dark area of Irish-American history, from the end of the Napoleonic Wars until the census of 1850.[39]

Part of the American problem is that, until 1855, U.S. immigration statistics are much less help than one would expect. The immigration act of 1819, effective in 1820, required that all ships bringing migrants to the U.S. should prepare passenger lists or manifests giving the sex, age, occupation and the "country to which they severally belong," of all of their passengers. The data thereby collected suffered by virtue of incomplete enforcement of the laws (and, thus, undercounting) and by an ambiguity in the definition of nativity: it was not made clear whether the country to which someone belonged meant their country of birth, of citizenship, or of last long-term residence. These matters were corrected by the immigration act of 1855, but that is too late to throw light on the crucial dark ages of the Irish migration into America.[40]

But even if the pre-1850 U.S. immigration data had been trustworthy, one still would need to adopt a wider, North American perspective. Why? Because before the mid 1840s when changes in the navigation laws removed the price advantage of sailing to St. John's, Newfoundland, St. John, New Brunswick, or to Quebec City, the cheapest way to get to the United States was by way of Canada. Hence, even had they been accurate, U.S. port-arrival data would seriously have underestimated the actual number of Irish-born persons who eventually fetched up in the States. One mid-nineteenth century authority estimated that in the 1820s (when most migrants from the British Isles to Canada were Irish), 67,993 immigrants therefrom came to the United States through Canada and that in the 1830s the number was 199,130 (again, at a time when most migrants from the British Isles to Canada were Irish).[41] This same authority estimated that U.S. immigration totals should have been increased by 50 percent to allow for arrivals from Canada. A rather more conservative estimate was made in the early 1870s and suggested that the number of foreign-born persons coming to the United States via Canada was as follows:[42]

1815–20	12,157
1820–30	26,524
1830–40	56,364
1840–50	90,718

Given that from 1825 onwards (when data become available) the Irish migrants comprised considerably more than half of the migrants from the British Isles to Canada,[43] it is highly likely that most of the persons in the above estimate were Irish-born.[44]

Were these individuals not recorded in U.S. immigation statistics? No. Efforts at recording land-border crossings into the United States began and then fitfully, only in 1853 and were completely abandoned during the American civil war. The practice was reintroduced in 1865, but abandoned as being unsatisfactory and without a legal basis in 1885. The counting of migrants from Canada and Mexico to the United States did not begin again until the fiscal year 1908.[45] An indication of the data thus lost is found in a study showing that for the years 1879–85, the very incompletely recorded immigration from Canada and Mexico together totalled more than one-seventh (almost 14.6 percent) of all recorded immigration into the United States (99.4 percent of this Canadian and Mexican total was Canadian). And since the Irish were a larger proportion of the immigrant population in Canada than they were in the U.S.,[46] then one can reasonably guess that more than one-seventh of the Irish immigrant flow was entering the U.S. unrecorded, and that at a very late date. Early in the process, before 1845, the proportion of flow from Canada must have been considerably higher, the Canadian flow comprising perhaps as much as one-quarter of the total Irish-born influx into the States.

Thus, if one is to make any headway in understanding the fundamental mysteries of pre-1850 Irish migration to the U.S., one must think in terms of a *North American* pool of migrants from Ireland, some of whom sailed to Canada and stayed, others of whom migrated directly to the U.S. and settled, but others of whom arrived in the U.S. and moved to Canada and many more of whom disembarked in Canada and subsequently moved on to the States.

There are two statistical series which try to define the primary dimensions of this North American pool of Irish migrants. Both of these series were put together during the late 1940s and early 1950s and they are far from being in agreement. Unfortunately, having been compiled roughly coterminously, each was published in isolation from the other with the result that neither addresses its disagreements with the other. The first of these appeared in 1953 and was done on behalf of the General Register Office of the United Kingdom by N.H. Carrier and J.R. Jeffrey. In its approach it was comprehensive, being a complete study of all of the available statistics on external migration from the British Isles from 1815 to 1950, the Irish data, which began in 1825, being one sub-set of the larger British Isles information base. The compilers were scrupulous in discussing the limits on the reliability of their data. In particular, however, it must be emphasized that the direct data on emigrants given below (ultimately based on ships' muster rolls, whatever the intermediate source), dealt only with migrants from Irish ports.[47]

But of course Irish emigration was not limited to Irish ports. Many Irishmen left for the New World from Liverpool and from Greenock and from a few other British ports. Until 1853, however, precise data on Irishmen on British-originating ships are not available, so some compensation has to be made. This is done in the second major emigration-series, that was published in 1954 by the Republic of Ireland's Commission on Emigration and other Population Problems. This body added to the Irish total two-thirds of the number of persons who sailed overseas from Liverpool in the period 1825–40 and for 1840 onwards made some

Table 1
United Kingdom Estimates of
Migration from Irish Ports to North America 1825–1850

Year	To United States	To Canada	Total
1825	4,387	6,841	11,228
1826	4,383	10,484	14,867
1827	4,014	9,134	13,148
1828	2,877	6,695	9,572
1829	4,133	7,710	11,843
1830	2,981	19,340	22,321
1825–1830	22,775	60,204	82,979
1831	3,583	40,977	44,560
1832	4,172	37,068	41,240
1833	4,764	17,431	22,195
1834	4,213	28,586	32,799
1835	2,684	9,458	12,142
1836	3,654	19,388	23,042
1837	3,871	22,463	26,334
1838	1,169	2,284	3,453
1839	2,843	8,989	11,832
1840	4,087	23,935	28,022
1831–1840	35,040	210,579	245,619
1841	3,893	24,089	27,982
1842	6,199	33,410	39,609
1843	1,617	10,898	12,515
1844	2,993	12,396	15,389
1845	3,708	19,947	23,655
1846	7,070	31,738	38,808
1847	24,502	71,253	95,755
1848	38,843	20,852	59,695
1849	43,673	26,568	70,241
1850	31,297	19,784	51,081
1841–1850	163,795	270,935	434,730
Grand Total 1825–1850	221,610	541,718	763,328

considerable augmentations in the Irish estimates but did not tell us on what basis these were done. ("The statistics based on the sources. [The Reports of the Colonial Land and Emigration Commissioners] . . . contain elements of estimation, the basis of which varied from time to time.") The resulting series purported to be a complete estimate of the Irish emigration to the New World.[48]

The main troubles with the Republic's series were, first, that unnecessarily large gaps were left in the estimate for the 1830s (the data, as the U.K. series indicated, were available), and, second, the procedures by which the compilers corrected the raw data for the 1840s were not recorded.

In any case, for the 1825–30 period, it is virtually certain that even the Republic's augmented estimates of migration to the New World were low, because the compilers only corrected for the probable Irish emigration from Liverpool. In fact, in addition to the Liverpool route (which was used almost exclusively for the U.S. trade from the south of Ireland) there was in many years a greater number of migrants from Greenock and Glasgow who went mostly but not exclusively to Canada. (That the Republic's commission ignored this trade from the north of Ireland is culturally diagnostic.) Second, children were undercounted, sometimes not being kept on ships' muster rolls, sometimes being counted as equal to one-third an adult, sometimes one-half. The under-enumeration varied from year to year, but in general was much greater for ships going to Canada than to the United States. Therefore, both the figures for the U.S. and for Canada need further augmentation, but those for Canada proportionally greater adjustment. Further, especially in the case of the Canadian trade, over-packed ships often off-loaded illegal passengers in Newfoundland or in the Maritimes before proceeding up the St. Lawrence River.

Here is not the place to try to resolve these problems, save to call attention to the work of William Forbes Adams which, despite its having been done half a century ago, still stands as the only somewhat successful attempt at grappling

Table 2
Number of Overseas Emigrants from Ireland (32 Counties),
Classified by Destination, 1825–1850

Year	United States	Canada	Total
1825	4,387	7,031	11,418
1826	5,447	10,669	16,116
1827	10,372	9,229	19,601
1828	7,573	6,816	14,389
1829	9,583	7,935	17,518
1830	12,467	19,877	32,344
1825–1830	49,829	61,557	111,386
1831	13,240	42,221	55,461
1832	14,675	39,184	53,859
1833			n/a
1834			n/a
1835	13,039	9,818	22,857
1836			n/a
1837	21,702	23,856	45,558
1838			n/a
1839			n/a
1840			n/a
1831–1840	62,656	115,079	n/a
1841	3,893	24,089	27,982
1842	6,199	33,410	39,609
1843	23,421	13,578	36,999
1844	37,269	16,485	53,754
1845	50,207	24,713	74,920
1846	68,023	37,889	105,916
1847	118,120	98,485	216,605
1848	151,003	23,543	174,546
1849	180,189	31,865	212,054
1850	184,351	25,264	209,615
1841–1850	822,675	329,321	1,151,996

directly with the fundamental problems concerning the data on the Irish migrants to North America. The field desperately requires someone with Adams' sense of proportion and skepticism concerning data and who is willing to work once again step by step through the primary sources.[49]

In arguing that one can discuss sensibly the size and nature of the Irish migration to the U.S. in the nineteenth century (and, most especially, in the years before the first census of the foreign-born in 1850), only by adopting a North American context, I am of course discussing only the migrants, the so-called first generation. There is more to the point than that, however. Recall that ultimately historians of the Irish in America would like to be able to deal not only with immigrants, but with the entire ethnic group. Hence, it is worth noting that in all probability, of these second- and third-generation Irish in America a significant component were the children and grandchildren of migrants who had settled not in the U.S., but in Canada. In the absence of direct studies on this matter, the point has to be drawn inferentially from the facts that (a) the Canadian-born were a large element in the U.S. population (for reference, comparative figures for the Irish are provided),[50]

| Year | Canadian-born | | |
	Number in U.S.	Percentage of U.S. Pop.	Percentage of Foreign-born
1850	147,711	0.64	6.6
1860	249,970	0.79	6.0
1870	493,464	1.28	8.9
1880	717,157	1.43	10.7
1890	980,938	1.56	10.6
1900	1,179,922	1.55	11.4
1910	1,204,637	1.31	8.9
1930	1,286,389	1.05	9.1

Year	Irish-born Percentage of U.S. Pop.	Percentage of Foreign-born
1850	4.15	42.8
1860	5.12	38.9
1870	4.81	33.3
1880	3.70	27.8
1890	2.80	20.2
1900	2.13	15.6
1910	1.47	10.0
1930	0.75	6.5

and (b) that persons of Irish ethnicity composed the largest non-French ethnic group in Canada until the late 1880s or 1890s.[51] Hence, unless one wishes to postulate a much lower propensity-to-migrate for Canadians of native Irish ethnicity than for other groups, one has to infer that a significant proportion of the Irish-American ethnic cohort actually came, most recently, from Canada, and was of Canadian nativity.

Obviously, what the U.S. census data say about the Canadian-born and what they mean in terms of the Irish in America are two different things. Although the Canadian-born were tallied as foreign-born (and thus, as first-generation Americans), the fact is that they were at least second, and sometimes third or fourth generation *North* Americans. Thus, they should be plugged into any explanation of the total ethnic pattern of the Irish in America, not in the immigrant generation, but in the second and subsequent generations. Just as the path of the Irish migrants to the U.S. can only be understood as a forked one, some coming directly, others via Canada, so that of the second, third, and fourth generations can only be understood if one accepts their duality of nativity, Canadian and U.S. Manifestly, once one recognizes these facts, the permutations of immigration patterns and of ethnic mobility multiply and

CAMROSE LUTHERAN COLLEGE LIBRARY

the accepted picture of the Irish in America as having stemmed from a simple, if cruelly uncomfortable, trans-atlantic passage to New York or Philadelphia, or Boston, disappears.

Finally, in arguing the absolute necessity of dealing with the Irish in the U.S. only within the context of all of North America, one should note that there are certain sources of data on the Irish in Canada that are not paralleled in the U.S. For instance, some Canadian provinces conducted censuses, well before the Famine. Those of the early 1840s are especially important, particularly that of Ontario wherein the bulk of the Irish in Canada settled.[52] These pre-Famine censuses are crucial, because they give us the only baseline we have for measuring the changes which took place amongst the Irish cohort as a result of the massive Famine migrations. Further, from the early 1840s onward, various Canadian censuses enquired not only into nativity but into religion. (That these items must be cross-tabulated by the researcher is vexing, but much less unfortunate than the U.S. case, wherein there is no religious data to tabulate.) And, as mentioned earlier, from 1871 onward, the Dominion of Canada census authorities enquired not only about each person's religion and place of birth, but about his ethnicity as well. (As in the case of the earlier data, the researcher must do his own cross-tabulation.) So, given that in some instances there well may be comparability between certain sub-populations of the Irish-Canadians and the Irish-Americans, and given then the high probability that large numbers of the children and grandchildren of Irish migrants to Canada eventually went to the United States, and given further the virtual certainty that large numbers of Irish migrants themselves settled in Canada only for a time before going to the States, there is only one conclusion: he who does not the Canadian data know, knows not the Irish in America.

4. Fourth, scholars must overcome an unfortunate piece of cultural blindness embedded in the historiography of the Irish in America, namely, that the Protestants from Ireland are not part of that history. This notion, seemingly shared by

Protestant and Catholic historians alike, has a long, if not entirely honourable, history, and one cannot pin its origin on modern historians. Prior to the massive migrations from Ireland to the U.S. during the middle decades of the nineteenth century, the Irish Protestants had been quite willing to be designated as Irish. The practical disadvantages of being associated with the influx of poor Roman Catholics, however, led to many Protestant affirmations of separate group-identity in the United States:[53] With this came the American neologism "Scotch-Irish" for the group who in Ireland were known simply as Scotch-Presbyterians, or in the twentieth century, as Ulster-Scots: "The term "Scotch-Irish" is an Americanism, generally unknown in Scotland and Ireland, and rarely used by British historians. In American usage, it refers to people of Scottish descent who, having lived for a time in the north of Ireland, migrated in considerable numbers to the American colonies in the eighteenth century."[54] Mark the last phrase, "in the eighteenth century," in the above definition provided by the most recent historian of the group, the sociologist James G. Leyburn, for it accurately summarizes the state of the historical literature, if not the historical reality. And, for historians of all stripes, it provides the basis for three massive (and misleading) simplifications:

1. that the Scotch-Irish and the Irish-American Catholics existed in different historical moments in U.S. history, the eighteenth and early nineteenth centuries for the Scotch-Irish and the second half of the nineteenth and the twentieth centuries for the Irish-American Catholics;[55]

2. that the Scotch-Irish and the Irish-American Catholics also were so distinct geographically and occupationally as to be virtually segregated: that is, the Scotch-Irish were frontiersmen, the Catholic, urbanites;[56]

3. that the meaning of "Protestant" amongst the Irish migrants to the U.S. is confined to persons who in the Old Country were Presbyterians of Scottish origin, and who, in the New World were Presbyterians, Methodists, or Baptists. Emigrating Protestants were not, it is believed, of English origin and not Anglican by denomination.

Actually, simplifications (1) and (3) almost certainly are not justified and number (2) is, at best, unproved and probably erroneous.

Why? Let us look at the available data. Again, the U.S. material is of no help, but data from Ireland and from Canada are germane. First, examine the Irish census material. Is it true that virtually all of the emigrants from Ireland from the Famine onwards were Catholics? If this is so, one should find some crude reflection in the census data. Specifically, one would expect (a) that the absolute number of Catholics in Ireland would have decreased considerably; (b) that the absolute numbers of Presbyterian and Anglicans would stay at least constant and (c) consequently, the Catholic proportion of the Irish population would have dropped dramatically and the Presbyterian and Anglican proportions would have risen with countervailing rapidity.[57]

If we take the first Irish religious census (that of 1834), and compare it to the next one (1861), something rather different seems to have happened:[58]

Year	Number of Catholics	Percentage of Population	Number of Anglicans	Percentage of Population
1834	6,427,712	80.9	852,064	10.7
1861	4,505,265	77.7	693,357	12.0

Year	Number of Presbyterians	Percentage of Population
1834	642,356	8.1
1861	523,291	9.0

That is, although the Anglican or Presbyterian proportions of the total Irish population rose, they too experienced a considerable decrease in their absolute numbers. Moreover, if one adds to the statistical series the data for the remainder of the nineteenth century, the results are striking:[59]

Year	Number of Catholics	Percentage of Population	Number of Anglicans	Percentage of Population
1871	4,150,867	76.7	667,998	12.3
1881	3,960,891	76.5	639,574	12.4
1891	3,547,307	75.4	600,103	12.8
1901	3,308,661	74.2	581,089	13.0

Year	Number of Presbyterians	Percentage of Population
1871	497,648	9.2
1881	470,734	9.1
1891	444,974	9.5
1861	443,276	9.9

Of course there is a myriad of possible hypotheses that would explain these trends in the census data,[60] but certainly there is a *prima facie* case for social historians investigating these two: that in the second half of the nineteenth century the Irish Protestants in general emigrated in large numbers and that this Protestant emigration was not solely from amongst the Ulster-Scots but even more from amongst the Anglican population (which, for convenience, if not with perfect accuracy, we may identify as the "Anglo-Irish").

Unlike the Anglicans, who were distributed, at least patchily, around the entire country, the Presbyterians were concentrated in Ulster. Thus, the data on post-Famine emigration from Ulster are illuminating, if somewhat sketchy.[61] These reveal that the historical province of Ulster (nine counties) was the second major provincial source of emigrants:[62]

1851–1900	Emigrants	Percentage
Munster	1,346,889	36.8
Ulster	1,015,737	27.7
Leinster	683,209	18.7
Connacht	616,439	16.8
Total on whom information Available	3,662,274	100.0

And, to take a mid-point in this period, 1871, the religious composition of Ulster was as follows:[63]

Religion	Percentage
Catholic	47.8
Anglican	21.8
Presbyterian	25.9
Other	4.5
	100.0

Granted, this does not prove that Protestants of whatever stripe migrated in large numbers, but note two facts: first, that 70.0 percent of the emigrants from Ulster in the 1851–1900 period came from the six counties, that is from the predominantly Protestant part of Ireland,[64] and, second, that within the historical nine counties of Ulster, the largest outflow in absolute terms came from the most Protestant counties, Antrim and Down.[65] No one would suggest that this proves that there was a major Protestant exodus from Ulster: a cynic might suggest that conceivably all the migrants were Catholics who were shrewd enough to leave at the first opportunity. But, cynicism aside, the hypothesis that large numbers of Ulster-Scots and of Anglo-Irish (both from Ulster and from the other provinces), left Ireland in the second half of the nineteenth century seems reasonable, given the available Irish data.

That, however, is as far as the Irish sources take us. From the Canadian sources, though, comes absolute proof that Irish Protestants in large numbers actually did emigrate. This is shown in my analysis of the Irish in Ontario, which indicated that roughly two-thirds of the ethnic group in 1871 was Protestant,[66] and, more important, in Darroch and Ornstein's Canadian national sample for the same year which showed that 38.0 percent of the Irish ethnic group was Catholic, 22.6 percent Anglican, and the remainder split amongst various Protestant denominations, the largest of which was Wesleyan Methodist (13.3 percent).[67]

At this point an Irish-American historian who is absolutely determined to keep the Protestants out of the history of the post-Famine Irish in America might argue that, yes, the Canadian data are fascinating, but they are also irrelevant because all of the Irish Protestants went to Canada and only Catholics entered the United States. Although inherently improbable, this idea cannot be directly disproved. However, remember that there was a massive influx of people born in Ireland into the U.S. via Canada and, further, there also were large numbers of individuals of Irish parentage who were born in Canada but who later entered the U.S. To keep the no-Protestants-need-apply barrier up, our zealous American historian also would have to posit that all the Protestants stayed in Canada and that only the Catholics left Canada for the United States. Manifestly, this kind of argument is silly. Much easier to contemplate is the suggestion of Maldwyn A. Jones that not only were the Ulster-Scots a considerable element in the pre-Famine nineteenth-century emigration to the U.S., but they also constituted a smaller, but considerable, element (perhaps 10 percent) of the total Famine exodus from Ireland, and that most of the post-Famine exodus from Ulster (90 percent of which went to the United States) consisted of Protestants of all denominations.[68]

This discussion of the probable continuing nature of Protestant migration to the United States in the second half of the nineteenth century deals only with the migrant generation. Realize here that one really should consider the probable character of the second, third, and fourth generation if one wants to deal with an ethnic group and then the necessity of including the Protestants becomes clearer. Given that, as Jones argues, Protestant immigrants were apt to be a higher proportion of the total flow in the years before the Famine than they were after it, Protestants would have formed a much higher proportion of the total ethnic group in the decades after the Famine than their numbers amongst more recent arrivals would suggest.

If one wants to get the story right, clearly one cannot segregate the Ulster-Scots from the Catholics in terms of chronology. Granted, the Ulster-Scots well may have been proportionately a larger part of the migrant flow to the U.S. before the Famine than after, but both groups, Presbyterians and Catholics, were intermingled in the formative years of Irish-American history, 1816-75.

Equally clearly, one cannot segregate the Anglo-Irish out of the migrant flow to the U.S. The Anglicans seem to have migrated out of Ireland in even greater numbers than did the Presbyterians — they certainly settled in substantial numbers in Canada — and one has the same compelling reasons for inferring that they moved to the United States in large numbers that one has concerning the Ulster-Scots.

And, finally, one should remain skeptical of the attempt to segregate Protestant and Catholic Irishmen in the States by occupation and residence: the Protestants as farmers and rural shopkeepers, the Catholics as an urban proletariat. There is as yet no direct demographic data that would validate this contention for any moment in the nineteenth century.

(V)

Adopting a set of new perspectives is a necessary pre-condition of breaking out of the evidentiary vacuum surrounding the Irish in America, but it is not enough. New data must be developed which provide at least some hint at what the characteristics of the over-all Irish group were in the crucial years between the end of the Napoleonic Wars and the beginning of the last quarter of the nineteenth century. The data must relate to the entire ethnic group, not just immigrants, not just Catholics, and not just city dwellers.

The task is dauntingly difficult and getting it done successfully will require several historians of the Irish in America to stop what at present they do well — writing local studies of the Catholic Irish in sharply delimited urban areas — and taking up doing what at present they do badly or not at all: defining where their particular local studies fit into the comprehensive picture of the Irish in the United States.

A simple, radical conceptual change is the first step.

Instead of taking as a focus, or set of foci, a specific geo-political unit (New York City, Boston, or whatever) and studying the Irish as a sub-set of that unit, one should *focus on the migrants themselves,* without preconceptions or discriminations concerning their occupation, religion, and eventual points of settlement. A migrant who settled in the Ozarks is just as important in determining the overall ethnic profile as one who set down in Philadelphia, and a member of the Plymouth Brethren is just as significant historically as a Catholic.

Given that simple conceptual breakthrough, there are five studies deserving high priority. The first of these is to do for the Irish in America what the Ontario census of 1841–42 did: establish a base-line concerning the size and religious affiliation of the Irish-born population in the New World prior to the Famine. The most promising source for beginning such a study is the National Immigration Archives in Philadelphia which contain over 30,000 names of pre-Famine Irish passengers to the United States. These data are not complete (they cover North America for some years, but only Boston and New York for others).[69] These immigration records must be combined with information for other ports. But, certainly there are enough data to draw an adequately-sized sample. The real problem, the daunting one, however, is that of *linkage.* Given the lack of U.S. data on religious affiliation, religious persuasion can most accurately be derived from sources in the homeland. This implies that to establish linkages, historians must employ the methods used by the too-often despised genealogists. A fortuitous side-effect of using these methods, however, is that when successful they provide information not only on religion but on place of origin in Ireland (an important and open question about the Irish in America is where they actually came from in the Old Country). Certainly, establishing such linkages is hideously hard work, but it can be done.[70]

A second, closely related study necessarily would be a duplication of the first, but for the Famine and post-Famine years, 1846 to roughly 1875.

Third and fourth, using the same data bases as in the first two efforts delineated above, we desperately need to know what happened to these immigrants in America. It is no use following them only to the American east-coast cities and saying that this means much (where else, after all, could they have gotten off the boat?). The record-linkage process must not only go backward to the Old Country, but must chart the immigrants' move forward into the New, establishing for the sample population the various individual migrations in America, and the occupations followed, and the dispersal patterns of their children. Once again, this is daunting, but successful prototype projects amongst migrant populations already have been done.[71]

Fifth, a large-sample study of the Irish migrants from Canada to the U.S. (both Irish-born and the children and grandchildren of Irish immigrants to Canada) is a high priority. Here too, prototype studies on Canadian migrants are being conducted.[72] In doing this study, the record linkages in Canada will be relatively easy to forge, as the Canadian manuscript censuses are in good order; the work south of the border will be very difficult, however.

Only when these studies are complete will historians have before them the basic demographic data concerning the Irish in the United States. We will know, then, within the limits of the sampling procedures employed, who the Irish in America actually were: their religion, geographic origin in the Old Country, their occupation in the New and their pattern of settlement throughout the country. Then, and only then, will it be appropriate for social historians to return to conducting studies of the Irish in specific areas. Then, and only then, will it be possible to deal with the vexed question of ethnicity, and with the several generations of persons of Irish background who, in the variety of their occupations, residence, and religion, were something far different from a simple immigrant "city people."

(VI)

Having been perhaps excessively prescriptive about what needs to be done if we are to escape from the elegant ignorance enshrined in the existing historical literature on the Irish in America, let me speculate about what the results of a set of serious studies such as are suggested above will show. These are merely informed guesses, but I am framing them in the form of hypotheses which can be tested empirically.

1. In the pivotal period of Irish-American history, 1816–75, it will be found that the Irish in America were not predominantly a city people, although the most visible lump of immigrants did indeed settle in cities. Precisely what constitutes a city, a small town, and a rural area is a difficult historical question and can become a methodological thicket. But for the sake of the present argument, let us assume that there were in mid-nineteenth century America, three sorts of places of settlement: (1) rural areas, defined — a definition used by the U.S. Bureau of Census through 1949 — as an empty land, agricultural land, and any hamlet, or village under 2,500 in population; (2) cities, which I am here defining as any concentration of population of 25,000 or more persons, certainly a very liberal lower limit; and (3) small towns, consisting of any municipality of 2,500-25,000 persons.[73]

Where did the Irish settle? If one considers only the Irish-born, not the entire ethnic group, and at quite a late date, 1870, one discovers that if one takes the fifty largest cities in the United States, the smallest of which had a population of 26,766, 44.5 percent of the Irish lived therein.[74] Or, to put it another way, well over half of the Irish immigrants did *not* live in cities.

This statement, though, actually *over*states the degree of urbanization of the Irish, because it deals only with the migrant generation and not the entire ethnic group. When earlier generations came to the States, they were more likely than those immigrants surveyed in the 1870 census to have settled eventually in rural areas or small towns because: first, the nation to which they came was much less urban than was that of 1870 (the United States was roughly 75 percent rural in 1870, but had been 85 percent in 1850, and 91 percent in 1830);[75] second, the pre-Famine migrants, a substantially sized group, came with greater resources in hand and not reeling from the trauma of the Famine. Presumably they were more apt and more able to move out quickly into the countryside and into rural and small town occupations.[76] And, third, the considerable number of Canadian-Irish who joined the Irish ethnic cohort in the United States were likely to be largely rural in distribution.[77]

Now, if it is true that the Irish in the U.S. up to 1870 were not a city people — and the census data are quite unequivocal on this point concerning the first generation — how does it come to be that in the twentieth century the Irish finally did indeed become a city people? This occurred for reasons that have little to do with their particular ethnicity, but with general causative factors affecting the entire U.S. population. Specifically, two major changes, both operative from roughly 1875 onwards, affected the composition of the Irish ethnic group. The first of these was discussed earlier: the "new immigration" of the latter two-and-a-half decades of the nineteenth century was much more heavily loaded towards settling in cities than was the earlier migration. This was a general phenomenon and presumably was determined by causative factors common to virtually all the migrant groups. Second, the children and grandchildren of earlier Irish immigrants who had settled in small towns and in the countryside, joined the urban drift that was common throughout the late nineteenth and early twentieth centuries in American society. David Ward, in *Cities and Immigrants* notes that, "the large proportion of 'new immigrants' from abroad with urban destinations was probably no greater than among native-born Americans who migrated after about 1875. In some areas, a large segment of the latter were the children of immigrants who had settled on the land earlier in the century. . . ."[78] There was nothing unusual or paradoxical in the Irish eventually becoming a city people: virtually every group did.

2. In the pivotal period of Irish-American history, 1816–75, it will be found that the process of settlement in the United States was not a simple matter of the Irish being

debouched at the ports and of their finding the way to the local Irish ghetto. Instead, it was a complex, multi-staged process that involved most immigrants in several moves during their life-time in the New World. Almost certainly, a pattern of "step-wise migration," as the historical geographers denominate it, will have been found to have prevailed.

And how can it have been otherwise? Given that most emigrant-boats docked at large port cities, but that most Irish immigrants did not live in cities, a complex intermediate process must have occurred. Individuals may have disembarked at New York or Philadelphia, but they found their way, in each case through an individual odyssey, to locales all over the United States. Granted, the atypical urban residual did plunk down, virtually where they got off the boat and did stay generation after generation (Oscar Handlin's Boston Irish are the best example), but these were a small minority. It is likely that the average Irish immigrant and his children and their children were just as restless, just as mobile, as were their counterparts amongst other ethnic groups.[79]

3. Whatever the details of the occupational-profile of the entire Irish ethnic group actually were, there will be no way of describing the Irish as an urban wage-proletariat. The pattern of residence makes this equation virtually impossible, but there is more to the argument than that. Recall here the earlier datum, that in 1870, 14.6 percent of the Irish immigrants over ten years of age who were employed and on whom there was occupational information, were directly engaged in agricultural work. This is a very significant minority. Additionally, however, farmers, agricultural labourers, ranchers and the like, were served by a wide variety of ancillary trades, most of them located in small towns, ranging from blacksmiths to coopers to millers to store keepers, occupations which, though not tallied as agricultural in the census, actually are part of the rural economic network. If one makes the very conservative assumption that for every Irishman in an agricultural job

there was another one in a related occupation in the rural economy,[80] then 29 to 30 percent of the Irish immigrants in 1870 actually were in the rural sector of the economy.[81]

The Irish-born immigrants of course were only part of the Irish ethnic group, and the crucial point is that the second and third generations who were living in the United States in 1870 were much more apt to be engaged in agricultural activities than were the immigrants: for the overall United States population, of those U.S.-born individuals who were ten years of age and above, were employed, and on whom we have data, 54.1 percent were engaged in agriculture in the direct, narrow sense, whereas the corresponding figure for the foreign-born was 22.9 percent.[82] So even if one assumes that the ratio of the percentage of U.S.-born persons of Irish ethnicity, as compared to the Irish immigrants' percentage, was only two to one, then nearly 30 percent of the American-born persons of Irish ethnic background were directly in the farm sector, and far more than half of them in the rural economic sector, broadly defined.[83]

Thus, a reasonable speculation is that when the entire Irish cohort is surveyed for the years 1816–75, the results will show that (1) a large body of Irish persons, both immigrants and American-born of Irish background, indeed was locked into the urban wage proletariat; but (2) that an even larger group was engaged in the rural economic sector, broadly defined, and (3) that the remainder found themselves in middling towns and in skilled trades and the professions. The really interesting point will be to see the relative size of the various sectors.[84]

4. Throughout the seminal period of Irish-American history, 1816–75, I believe that it will be found that Protestants comprised a significant continuous minority of the immigrant stream, and an equally significant proportion of the entire multi-generational ethnic cohort. How big? I think that if one wanted the most convenient crude indicator of what the likely Protestant proportion of the immigrant stream probably was in, say, any ten-year period or of what the Protestant proportion of the Irish ethnic group was, one

would simply determine what the Protestant proportion of the population was in Ireland at the census immediately at the beginning of the relevant decennial period. Which is to say, an estimate of roughly 20 percent (meaning approximately 18 to 22 percent) of the immigrant stream having been Protestants and 20 percent of the ethnic group having been Protestant would hold for the 1816–75 period.[85] This includes the years of the massive Famine exodus.[86]

5. It probably will be found that despite all the mythology concerning the Scotch-Irish, in the period 1816–75 a slight majority of the Protestant migrants to the U.S. were Anglican by faith and Anglo-Irish by descent. Anglicans out-numbered Presbyterians in Ireland throughout the nineteenth century, and, further, their absolute numbers declined more quickly than did the Presbyterians'. This suggests their having had a higher propensity to emigrate.[87]

6. In the two fundamental matters of choice-of-residence and in patterns-of-occupation, Protestants and Catholics will be found to have been very similar. Whatever differences there were as between the two major Protestant groups and the Catholics will be found to be primarily ascribable to differences in economic position in the home country, not to religion *per se* or to the cultural appendages that are attached to religious systems in Ireland.

To put this hypothesis in testable terms: a multi-variate analysis of the residence patterns and occupational distribution will show (a) that the best predictors of these matters in the New World will be the individual's occupation and social class in the Old World; (b) that the second-best predictors of an individual's residence and occupation will be the residence and occupation of his friends and relatives who migrated ahead of him.

This hypothesis flies in the face of a good deal of writing about Ireland and the Irish emigrants. Irish historiography, in contrast to that of most of the western world, by-and-large rejects social and economic class analysis as a basis of understanding the society (quite rightly, if it is presented as the sole basis) and substitutes for economic determinism a stringent form of cultural determinism, wherein virtually all matters of economic and social status are set by cultural factors. For example, one of the more attractive recent studies in this tradition suggests that in the

> age of migration, 1790–1922, many Catholic Irish were more communal, dependent, fatalistic and prone to accept conditions passively than were the Protestants they encountered in either Ireland or America, and less individualistic, independent, optimistic and given to initiative than were these Protestants. . . Indeed their perspectives were so pre-modern that to observers from modern business cultures, they often seemed "irresponsible," even "feckless" or adolescent.[88]

And so, the argument goes, they had a different, markedly less successful occupational profile than did the Protestants, and this for reasons inherent in their Catholic-Gaelic culture.

This I doubt. The only relevant study done with a substantial data base (10,000 cases), that of Darroch and Ornstein (discussed earlier) for Canada in 1871, showed that Catholic and Protestant Irish were remarkably similar in occupational patterns and achievement.[89] Culture undoubtedly is extremely important in the history of any people, not only the Irish; but to see culture as determining economic sub-structures is either perverse or wishful thinking. Protestants within the American immigrant stream will probably be found to have been slightly better off in terms of occupational status and slightly more rural in terms of residence, because they were more apt to have been raised on larger farms and in successful trades in the Old Country than were Irish Catholics. In other words, the slightly differing profiles in the United States will be seen to have been a function of the differing profiles in the homeland and to have nothing whatsoever to do with the two opposed Irish religious systems.[90] Put graphically, it would be a brave or naive scholar who would predict that the behaviour of an emigrant publican-cum-gombeen man from the Dingle peninsula would more closely resemble that of his fellow religionist, say, his parish priest, than it would that of another publican-cum-gombeen man, a black Presbyterian from Ballymena.

(VII)

Elegant?

No, the results of a serious restudy of the Irish-Americans will not be elegant. Instead of the Mondrian-like clarity of the presently-accepted description and explanation of the Irish in America, one will have a disorderly snarl of historical threads. In the right hands, these will be the makings of a Bayeux tapestry. The Irish ethnic group will be found to have been marvelously complex in its cultural roots, geographical origin in Ireland, and its settlement pattern in the United States; it will be found to be extraordinarily diverse in its migratory routes to the New World and in its step-wise migration through that world. In place of the artificial crystalline clarity of our present lens, we will come to see the Irish as amazingly variegated and, therefore, infinitely more fascinating.

Most important, the Irish Catholic migrant will be found to have been much quicker, more technologically adaptable, more economically alert, and less circumscribed by putative cultural limits from the Old Country than is usually believed; and, simultaneously, the Irish Protestants will be shown to have been a much more important part of the Irish-American experience than anyone — and especially they themselves — has wanted to admit.

Chapter Four.
The Irish in Canada:
Ontario, the Crucial
Case

(I)

The story of the Irish in Canada is not a strange history, but the history of their historiography is. It would seem that for anyone to propound a major misinterpretation of the Irish in Canada virtually would require an act of the will. Unlike the United States, Canada has excellent census records that, from 1871 onwards, give not only data on place of birth of the entire population, but information on ethnic background, religion, occupation, and place of residence. Even the enumerations of the early 1840s garnered data on place of birth, occupation, religion, and residence. Granted, the census officials did not cross-tabulate the various categories in the way an historian of the Irish would like, but this is an impediment, not a permanent roadblock.

As a prophylaxis against the misguided will of Canadian social historians, I should like to recite a decade of simple facts about the Irish in Canada, rather like a Dublin shawlie saying a decade of the rosary as protection against things wrong and inexplicable.[1]

1. Persons born in Ireland were the largest body of immigrants into Canada in the nation's formative years, that is, the period in which Canada was transformed from a refuge for displaced American loyalists into a viable federal state. During the pre-Confederation period, the British Isles

Table 1
Pre-Famine Irish Migration to British North America

Year	Unrevised Official Estimates of Total United Kingdom Migration of BNA	Migrants from Irish Ports	Migrants from Irish Ports as Percentage of all U.K. Migrants to BNA	Revised Estimates of Total Irish Migration to BNA from all U.K. Ports
1815	680	N/A		
1816	3,370	N/A		
1817	9,797	N/A		
1818	15,136	N/A		
1819	23,534	N/A		
1820	17,921	N/A		
1821	12,955	N/A		
1822	16,013	N/A		
1823	11,355	N/A		
1824	8,774	N/A		
1825	8,741	6,841	78.3	8,893
1826	12,818	10,484	81.8	13,629
1827	12,648	9,134	72.2	11,969
1828	12,084	6,695	55.4	8,824
1829	13,307	7,710	57.9	10,148

Year			%	
1830	30,574	19,340	63.3	25,679
1831	58,067	40,977	70.6	54,514
1832	66,339	37,068	55.9	50,305
1833	28,808	17,431	60.5	23,139
1834	40,060	28,586	71.4	32,315
1835	15,573	9,458	60.7	10,764
1836	34,226	19,388	56.6	22,528
1837	29,884	22,463	75.2	26,102
1838	4,577	2,284	49.9	2,908
1839	12,658	8,989	71.0	10,943
1840	32,293	23,935	74.1	28,756
1841	38,164	24,089	63.1	30,923
1842	54,123	33,410	61.7	42,884
1843	23,518	10,898	46.3	14,668
1844	22,924	12,396	54.1	17,725
1845	31,803	19,947	62.7	26,708

Table 2
Famine-Induced Migration of the Irish to British North America

Year	Unrevised Official Estimates of Total United Kingdom Migration to BNA	Migrants from Irish Ports	Migrants from Irish Ports as Percentage of all U.K. Migrants to BNA	Revised Estimates of Total Irish Migration to BNA from all U.K. Ports
1846	43,439	31,738	73.1	40,667
1847	109,680	71,253	65.0	104,518
1848	31,065	20,852	67.1	24,809
1849	41,367	26,568	64.2	33,392
1850	32,961	19,784	60.0	26,444
1851	42,605	23,930	56.2	31,709
1852	32,873	17,693	53.8	13,389

were the overwhelming source of migrants to Canada and of that flow the Irish were much the largest cohort. Table 1 indicates that the Irish influx began well before the Famine and that, even if one accepts the unrevised official government figures (which greatly undercounted Irish immigrants), the Irish outnumbered Scottish and English migrants *combined*.[2]

This flow of Irish migrants surged during the Great Famine and in the three years immediately thereafter, as is indicated in Table 2.[3]

From 1853 onwards, the number of Irish migrants fell (see Table 3). Even so, it was not until the late 1860s that migrants from England and Wales came to outnumber Irish

Table 3

Year	Total U.K. Migration to BNA	Total Irish Migration from all U.K. Ports to BNA	Irish as Percentage of Total U.K. Migration to BNA
1853	31,779	22,391	70.5
1854	35,679	22,900	64.2
1855	16,110	6,106	37.9
1856	11,299	4,354	38.5
1857	16,803	4,456	26.5
1858	6,504	2,158	33.2
1859	2,469	1,091	44.2
1860	2,765	1,215	43.9
1861	3,953	1,845	46.7
1862	8,328	3,107	37.3
1863	9,665	3,947	40.8
1864	11,371	5,610	49.3
1865	14,424	7,189	49.8
1866	9,988	3,921	39.3
1867	12,160	4,582	37.7
1868	12,332	3,692	29.9
1869	20,921	3,309	15.8
1870	27,168	2,877	10.6
1871	24,954	3,061	12.3

migrants in most years. During the 1870s and '80s, Scottish migration finally came to equal Irish, but it was not until the 1890s that the Scottish newcomers consistently outnumbered the Irish.[4]

2. As a result of the strength and duration of Irish migration to pre-Confederation British North America, the Irish comprised not only the largest immigrant cohort, but also the largest non-French ethnic group. Precisely when persons of Irish ethnicity became the largest ethnic group in Canada is impossible to state with precision, but a reasonable estimate is that they became ethnically prepotent in the early 1830s and stayed so until the late 1880s or early 1890s.

Unfortunately, the pre-Confederation censuses conducted by the individual jurisdictions in British North America tallied only foreign-born persons (that is, immigrants) and did not register ethnicity. Nevertheless, the pre-1871 data warrant attention, and they indicate that, even before the Great Famine, the Irish had become the largest foreign-born group in central Canada. (See Table 4)[5]

Of course, for every person born in Ireland who was tallied in these early censuses, there were several others of Irish ethnicity who had been born in British North America and were tallied by the enumerators as "native Canadians." It is risky to speculate on how large a "multiplier" one would need to translate the early figures on Irish-born persons into estimates of the size of the multi-generational ethnic population. The results of the first Dominion of Canada census of 1871 leave no doubt that at Confederation the Irish were the largest non-French ethnic group in the country. (See Figure 1)[6]

3. Nationally, it is certain that most persons of Irish ethnicity were Protestant, although the precise proportions are not known: the Dominion census collectors did not cross-tabulate items on religion and ethnicity. It will be shown below that, in Ontario,* both before and after the

_____

*"Ontario" is used in this chapter rather than "Upper Canada" or "Canada West."

Table 4
Pre-Confederation Estimates of the Irish-Born in Various Localities

Area	Year	Total population	Irish-born	Percentage	English-born	Percentage	Scottish-born	Percentage
Prince Edward Island	1841	47,042	5,160	11.0	2,650	5.6	5,681	12.1
Ontario	1842	487,053	78,255	16.1	40,684	8.4	39,781	8.2
Quebec	1844	697,084	43,982	6.3	11,895	1.7	13,393	1.9
Ontario	1848	725,879	57,604	7.9	64,560	8.9	140,673	19.4*
Prince Edward Island	1848	62,678	6,407	10.2	2,997	4.8	6,736	10.7
Ontario	1851–52	952,004	175,963	18.5	82,699	8.7	75,811	8.0
Quebec	1851–52	890,261	51,499	5.8	11,230	1.3	14,565	1.6
Newfoundland	1857	122,638	7,388	6.0	3,516	2.9	390	0.3
Ontario	1860–61	1,396,091	191,231	13.7	114,290	8.2	98,792	7.1
Quebec	1860–61	1,111,566	50,337	4.5	13,179	1.2	13,204	1.2
New Brunswick	1861	252,047	30,179	12.0	4,909	1.9	5,199	2.1
Nova Scotia	1861	330,857	9,313	2.8	3,090	0.9	16,395	5.0
Prince Edward Island	1861	80,857	4,971	6.1	2,500	3.1	5,653	7.0

*Note: This figure is manifestly in error

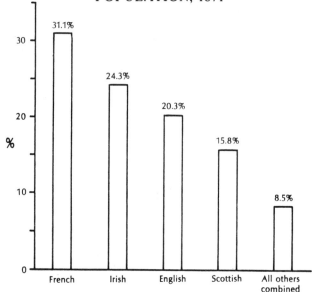

FIGURE 1: ETHNIC PERCENTAGES OF CANADIAN POPULATION, 1871

Famine migration, the ratio of Protestants to Catholics was roughly 2:1. A large-sample national re-study of the 1871 census by the sociologists Gordon Darroch and Michael Ornstein indicated that over 60 percent of the persons of Irish ethnicity were Protestant.[7]

4. Nevertheless, amongst persons of Irish ethnicity, the largest single religious affiliation has been Roman Catholic, because the Protestants are splintered between several denominations. In Darroch and Ornstein's 1871 sample, 38 percent of the Irish were Catholic. The next largest group of Irish-Canadians consisted of Anglicans, who represented somewhat under 23 percent of the Irish ethnic population.[8]

5. The prevailing perception is that the Irish have been a city people; yet, throughout most of their collective history in Canada — and especially in the era of their greatest influence upon the Canadian polity, the pre-Confederation era — they were overwhelmingly rural. Table 5 makes it clear that, nationally, the Irish did not become predominantly urban until after World War I.[9]

Table 5
Percentage of Persons of Irish Ethnicity
who Lived in Rural Areas

| Year | Four Original Provinces | | | |
	Ontario (Percentage)	Quebec (Percentage)	Nova Scotia (Percentage)	New Brunswick (Percentage)
1871	77.8	63.9	81.2	73.1
1881	70.4	58.6	73.2	72.6
1901	58.4	48.7	60.3	66.3
1911	51.2	43.6	49.4	63.1
1921	45.7	38.8	46.9	62.1
1931	42.8	29.9	45.0	59.6

Year	Entire Irish Population in Canada (Percentage)	Entire Canadian Population (Percentage)
1871	75.3	79.6
1881	69.7	74.3
1901	60.0	62.5
1911	52.8	54.6
1921	49.2	50.5
1931	45.3	46.3

6. Persons of Irish ethnicity did not merely inhabit rural areas: most commonly, the occupation of both Catholics and Protestants was farming. Despite the mythology that the Irish Catholics were incapable of farming, it was by far the most common occupation for Catholics of Irish ethnicity in Ontario (which held the largest concentration of Irish Catholics), Quebec, and New Brunswick at the time of Confederation. Only in Nova Scotia in 1871 did semi-skilled workers outnumber farmers amongst the Irish Catholics.[10]

7. There are only two satisfactory studies on the economic position of the Irish in the years of their greatest national importance (the pre-Confederation period). These indicate

that as an ethnic group they were reasonably successful. Professor R. Marvin McInnis's two-tier random study of the farmers in Ontario in 1861 has shown that the Irish immigrants were slightly less prosperous as a group in the farming sector than was the general population, but not disastrously so.[11] This is just what one would expect of any immigrant group, as most began a step behind native Canadians in terms of money in hand and experience in Canadian farming techniques, and the Irish were not markedly worse off than any comparable group of immigrants that chose to farm in Ontario. The other study, that of Professors Darroch and Ornstein, has shown that in 1871 Catholics of Irish ethnicity were represented in the "bourgeois occupations" (merchant, manufacturers, etc.), in white collar work and in artisan work in virtually the same proportions as the Canadian population as a whole. This also held true for the Protestants of Irish ethnicity.[12] Granted, there were exceptional cases where the Irish-born lumped together as lower social strata (Hamilton, London, Kingston, and, perhaps, Halifax), but these were deviations from the national pattern and were transitory phenomena, characterizing, not the entire ethnic group, but only a minority.

In other words, there is no conceivable way that the Irish as an ethnic group can be equated with an urban proletariat.

8. Since Confederation (and, probably, since the early 1830s), between one-half and two-thirds of persons of Irish ethnicity have lived in Ontario. In most post-Confederation years, Quebec contained the second largest group, though more recently both Alberta and British Columbia have surpassed it. (See Table 6)[13]

9. Considered as a proportion of their entire provincial populations, the Irish have been most important in Ontario, New Brunswick, Prince Edward Island, and, probably, equally important in Newfoundland. Table 7 provides both the absolute numbers of persons of Irish ethnicity in each province since Confederation and the percentage which they formed of each provincial population.[14]

Table 6
Proportional Distribution of Persons of Irish Ethnicity in Canada
(Percentage)

Province	1871	1881	1901	1911	1921	1931	1941	1951	1961
Ontario	66.1	65.5	63.2	57.2	53.3	52.6	52.5	50.3	49.8
Quebec	14.6	12.9	11.6	9.6	8.6	8.8	8.7	7.7	7.4
Nova Scotia	7.4	6.9	5.6	5.1	5.0	4.6	5.1	5.3	5.4
New Brunswick	11.9	10.6	8.4	7.2	6.2	5.4	5.4	5.0	4.7
Prince Edward Island		2.7	2.2	1.9	1.7	1.4	1.5	1.4	1.0
Manitoba		1.0	4.8	5.6	6.4	6.3	6.0	5.4	4.8
British Columbia		0.3	2.1	4.1	4.9	5.8	6.6	8.6	9.5
Northwest Territories		0.1	0.1	0.0	0.0	0.0	0.0	0.0	0.1
Saskatchewan			1.1	5.4	7.7	8.5	7.6	5.9	5.3
Alberta			0.8	3.8	6.2	6.6	6.6	6.7	7.6
Yukon			0.1	0.1	0.0	0.0	0.0	0.0	0.1
Newfoundland								3.7	4.3
Total Percentage	100	100	100	100	100	100	100	100	100

Table 7
Persons of Irish Ethnicity of Total Provincial Populations

Year	Ontario		Quebec		Nova Scotia		New Brunswick		Prince Edward Island		Manitoba		Canadian Total*	
	Number	Percentage	Number	Percentage	Number	Percentage	Number	Percentage	Number	Percentage	Number	Percentage	Number	Percentage
1871	559,442	34.5	123,478	10.4	62,851	16.2	100,643	35.2	N/A	N/A	N/A	N/A	846,414	24.3
1881	627,550	32.6	123,749	9.1	66,067	15.0	101,284	31.5	25,415	23.3	9,885	15.9	957,403	22.1
1891	Ethnicity Data not Collected in Compatible Form in this Census													
1901	624,332	28.6	114,842	7.0	54,710	11.9	83,384	25.2	21,993	21.3	47,418	18.6	988,721	18.4
1911	614,502	24.3	103,720	5.2	54,612	11.1	77,839	22.1	19,987	21.3	60,583	13.1	1,074,738	14.9
1921	590,493	20.1	94,933	4.0	55,712	10.6	68,670	17.7	18,743	21.2	71,414	11.7	1,107,803	12.6
1931	647,831	18.9	108,312	3.8	56,453	11.0	66,873	16.4	17,698	20.1	77,559	11.1	1,230,808	11.9
1941	665,339	17.6	109,894	3.3	65,300	11.3	68,801	15.0	18,459	19.4	76,156	10.4	1,267,702	11.0
1951	723,888	15.7	110,189	2.7	76,479	11.9	71,750	13.9	19,019	19.3	77,802	10.0	1,439,635	10.3
1961	873,647	14.0	129,326	2.5	93,998	12.8	82,485	13.8	19,786	18.9	84,726	9.2	1,753,351	9.6

1971 and 1981 "Irish" no longer permitted as an ethnic category by federal census officials: Irish lumped with English, Scottish, and Welsh

Year	British Columbia		Northwest Territories		Saskatchewan		Alberta		Yukon		Newfoundland	
	Number	Percentage	Number	Percentage	Number	Percentage	Number	Percentage	Number	Percentage	Number	Percentage
1871	N/A	N/A										
1881	3,172	6.4	1,374	2.4	N/A	N/A	N/A	N/A	N/A	N/A	N/A	N/A
1901	20,658	11.6	41	0.2	10,644	11.7	8,161	11.8	2,559	9.4	N/A	N/A
1911	43,831	11.2	135	2.1	58,069	11.8	40,668	10.9	897	10.5	N/A	N/A
1921	54,298	10.4	234	2.9	84,786	11.2	68,246	11.6	369	8.9	N/A	N/A
1931	71,612	10.3	296	3.0	104,096	11.3	79,978	10.9	198	4.7	N/A	N/A
1941	83,460	10.2	230	1.9	95,852	10.7	83,876	10.5	335	6.8	N/A	N/A
1951	124,098	10.7	619	3.9	84,811	10.2	96,549	10.3	1,097	12.1	53,334	14.8
1961	165,631	10.2	1,056	4.6	92,133	10.0	134,102	10.1	1,670	11.4	74,791	16.3

*For certain years small anomalies in the census processing resulted in the national total being slightly different from the column sums.

Table 8
Post-Confederation Irish Migration to Canada
1870–1978

Years	Total Immigration into Canada	Irish Immigration* into Canada	Irish Immigration as Percentage of Total Canadian Immigration
1870–79	328,876	24,520	7.5
1880–89	849,615	46,941	5.5
1890–99	372,474	11,390	3.1
1900–09	1,398,989	21,341	1.5
1910–19	1,860,269	43,249	2.3
1920–29**	1,264,220	88,500	7.0
1930–39	252,044	19,814	7.9
1940–49	428,733	24,185	5.6
1950–59	1,555,966	65,619	4.2
1960–69	1,366,025	27,645	2.0
1970–78, inclusive***	1,332,821	23,064	1.7
Grand Total, 1870–1978, inclusive	9,677,211	396,898	4.1

*Irish immigration includes that from both Northern and Southern Ireland. Since 1920, Ireland has been partitioned, the south being politically independent, the north continuing to be a part of the United Kingdom.

**Figures for 1926–59 include persons of Irish birth who came to Canada from the United States.

***Irish figures not available after 1978.

10. Ever since Confederation, the importance of the Irish as a constituent element in the national social fabric has been declining, a fact amply illustrated in Table 7 above. The decline occurred because the Irish formed a smaller percentage of the post-Confederation immigrant-stream than persons of Irish ethnicity had done in the total Canadian population at Confederation. (See Table 8 for post-Confederation immigration data.)[15] That is, the Irish proportion of the population was diluted by later, non-Irish immigration.

(II)

Manifestly, if one wishes to get to the heart of the history of the Irish in Canada, one should look first at the area where they most frequently settled — Ontario — and at the years in which they were the largest ethnic group in the society — mostly before Confederation.

This brings us face to face with the first unusual characteristic of the historiography of the Irish in Ontario: the paucity of historical literature on the subject is noteworthy and, indeed, strange. Once one has referred to Nicholas Flood Davin's fine old exercise in name-dropping, *The Irishman in Canada* (1878), and to John L. Mannion's illuminating study of rural material culture, *Irish Settlements in Eastern Canada. A Study of Cultural Transfer and Adaptation* (1974), one has mentioned all of the books and monographs which deal directly with the Irish in Ontario as an ethnic group. Fortunately, there are several monographs available which deal with the Irish as a political group and others that deal with institutional matters, but these skirt the central issue of ethnicity. The dearth of studies on Irish ethnicity in the region that is now Ontario is underscored when one makes the natural comparison to the Irish-Americans. In the nineteenth century, they wrote massive volumes memorializing the Irish contribution to the rise of urban America and to their part in the creation of American democracy and, sometimes, put forth a modest claim for the Hibernian basis of all western civilization. This contrast becomes all the more striking when one realizes that the Irish in Ontario (and indeed in all of the four original provinces) were a much larger proportion of the population than the American Irish were of that of the United States.[16] Why is so little known about the Irish in Ontario, where, before Confederation, they settled in the largest numbers?

Part — but only part — of the problem is that, although post-Confederation data are available in abundance, before the 1871 definitive census, information is scarce. Although it is possible to make reasonably accurate revised estimates of the number of persons who came from Ireland to Canada before 1871 (as was done in Tables 1-3), what one really wants to know is the answer to two additional questions: what was the proportion of migrants to Canada who actually settled in Ontario, and what was the breakdown of those settlers as to the proportions that were Catholic and Protestant?

One can begin to answer these two questions only in the early 1840s, when adequate Ontario census data become available. The 1842 enumeration inquired into place of birth of the province's residents. In that year, Upper Canada had 78,255 Irish-born inhabitants, making the Irish by far the largest non-indigenous group.[17]

In interpreting Table 9, the crucial point to note is that, large though the immigrant numbers were, the enumeration procedures radically underrepresented the extent of new additions to Ontario society. This occurred because the census authorities recorded only the birth place, not the ethnic background, of each individual. Thus, although the mother and father in a family of recent arrival were enumerated as being of European birth, their children, so long as they were born in Canada, were recorded as native Canadians, with no distinctions in the records between them and the children of, say, third-generation loyalists. At minimum, one should define as members of an identifiable ethnic group not only those born abroad, but at least the first generation born in Canada; indeed, in most groups the sense of identifiably ethnic identity has run considerably longer.

Table 9
Birthplaces of Ontario Population, 1842

Country of Birth	Numbers	Proportion of Ontario Population
		(percent)
Canadian-born		
English Canadian	247,665	50.8
French Canadian	13,969	2.9
Sub-total Canadian-born	261,634	53.7
Foreign-born		
British Isles		
Ireland	78,255	16.1
England and Wales	40,684	8.4
Scotland	39,781	8.1
Sub-total British Isles	158,720	32.6
United States	32,809	6.7
Continental Europe	6,581	1.4
Sub-total Foreign-born	198,110	40.7
Not Known	27,309	5.6
Total population	487,053	100.0

Source: Derived from 1842 census, as found in *Census of Canada,* 1871, vol. IV, p. 136.

Ideally, the 1842 census should be reprocessed in its entirety. Failing that, there are three methods of redacting the 1842 data, each helpful in part, but none totally satisfactory. First — Revision A — one can begin with the base population of Ontario before heavy emigration started and define this group, plus the numbers accruing to it by natural increase, as the "native Canadian" population. This figure will be less than the native-born category, as defined in the 1842 census. The difference between the two numbers, presumably, will consist of the first generation of offspring of foreign-born parents, and their grown children, in cases of early migrants. Then, one adds this ethnic figure to foreign-born populations as shown in the 1842 census, to obtain an aggregate total of the foreign-born and their offspring. Next, one adds a portion of this corrected ethnic figure to each ethnic group in proportion to its existence in the population in 1842, and, in theory, obtains a more accurate indication of the relative numerical importance of each group than is provided in the original census data. Specifically, *if* one takes the base population of Ontario to have been 100,000[18] in 1812 and the rate of natural increase to have been 30 percent per decade,[19] *then* the "true" native indigenous population in Ontario in 1842 would have been approximately 219,700. One could then estimate the ethnic derivation as follows:

Revision A

	(percent)
Indigenous Canadian	45
Irish	18
English and Welsh	10
Scottish	10
United States	8
Continental Europe	2
Unknown	7

For many reasons (in particular, the shakiness of the estimate of the base population: in 1812 it may well have been closer to 70,000 than to 100,000 — and the arbitrary nature of the percentage of rate of natural increase) these estimates are highly questionable.

Thus, we abandon Revision A and attempt Revision B. Fundamentally, this is an attempt to estimate the first-generation ethnic population and to add this number to the figures for the foreign-born and thus to provide an indication of ethnicity over two generations. Here we (1) "correct" the raw population data for 1842 by distributing the "unknown" category amongst the various ethnic categories in proportion to the relative size of each group. This is not unreasonable — they were, indeed, born somewhere, and a proportional distribution makes more sense than any alternative allocation.[20] (2) We now determine the hypothetical number of families in Ontario (an actual number was not enumerated). We do this by dividing the number of married people — 155,304 — by two and then multiplying by 1.028 to take into account single-parent families (this multiple is derived from the 1848 census, as comparable information was not available for 1842).[21] This yields us an estimate of 79,826 family units in Ontario in 1842. (3) We assume that both the propensity to marry and family size does not vary by ethnic group. Actually, this assumption is conservative, because in most societies immigrant groups have larger families than do long-established residents. The conservative procedure guarantees that our revision will, if anything, err on the side of caution. (4) To obtain the average number of children in each family, we divide the number of children fourteen years of age and under — 224,023 — by the estimated number of families and obtain 2.8 children per family. The reader will recognize that this too is a highly conservative procedure as far as estimating ethnicity is concerned, both because many children stayed *en famille* beyond age fourteen, and because the *completed* family size (the total number of children born in the lifetime of a marriage) is greater than the actual number in the family at any given time. (5) Finally, we subtract the imputed number of first-generation born in Canada from the "Canadian" total and add it to the appropriate ethnic total. These procedures yield the following estimate of the ethnicity of Ontario's population in 1842:

Ethnicity	Revision B Estimate	Percentage
Born in Ireland or born in Canada of Irish-born parentage	120,949	24.9
Born in England or Wales or born in Canada of English- or Welsh-born parentage	62,884	12.9
Born in Scotland or born in Canada of Scottish-born parentage	61,480	12.6
Sub-total for British Isles	245,313	50.4
Born in the United States or born in Canada of American-born parentage	50,720	10.4
Born in Continental Europe or born in Canada of European-born parentage	10,169	2.1

Canadian-defined as the second and succeeding generations born in British North America	180,851	37.1
Grand total	487,053	100.0

The revisions suggested above are conservative in part because they were based on an assumption of average family size — 2.8 children per family — that is very small indeed. This figure comes from a statistical definition of family size as including only children fourteen years of age or younger.

Let us turn to Revision C. In making it, we will follow the same procedures and make the same assumptions as for Revision B, with one exception: instead of taking 2.8 as the average number of children in each family, we will take 5.76 as the average family size (including parents). This figure comes from the census of 1851 which enumerates as family members all those living in the family unit, regardless of their age. (The 1851 census was the first to collect data permitting this kind of calculation.)[22]

Revision C		
Ethnicity	Estimate	Percentage
Born in Ireland or born in Canada of Irish-born parentage	134,363	27.6
Born in England or Wales or born in Canada of English- or Welsh-born parentage	69,859	14.3
Born in Scotland or born in Canada of Scottish-born parentage	68,298	14.0
Sub-total for British Isles	272,520	55.9
Born in the United States or born in Canada of American-born parentage	56,348	11.6
Born in Continental Europe or born in Canada of European-born parentage	11,296	2.3
Canadian-defined as the second and succeeding generations born in British North America	146,889	30.2
Grand total	487,053	100.0

Whereas Revision B was a conservative recension of the ethnicity data, Revision C probably goes too far: when transposed to the 1842 data, the average family size calculable from the 1851 census leaves too few single people in the society. Taking Revision B and Revision C together, however, we have a set of bracketing figures. These can be considered the boundaries of probability and somewhere between them will be found the truth of the matter.

The long chase through the extant statistical sources leads to one clear conclusion: that even if ethnic identity is defined very narrowly (as lasting through the first generation born in Canada, and no longer) only a moiety, or less, of the Ontario population in the early 1840s can be considered native Canadian. The constellation of ethnic groups from the British Isles constituted, as minimum, half of the population, and, amongst all ethnic groups, the largest was the Irish: a quarter of the population, at the least, and probably more. This was *before* the massive Irish migrations of the Famine years.

(III)

Here it would be comforting to introduce a simplification — to claim that the main reason that the historical literature on the Irish in Ontario is so thin is that the Irish who migrated there were predominantly of the "wrong sort," in the sense that they were not from the Catholic majority of the Irish population. From that Catholic majority arose Irish nationalism and it was this nationalism that not only triumphed in the home country but was celebrated by the predominantly Catholic Irish who settled in the United States. Historians love winners, but the Protestant Irish who predominated in Ontario were not part of the romantic, victorious, and memorable tradition of Irish nationalism, and are hence easily (although wrongly) consigned the role of reactionary, uninteresting, and, in the context of Irish historiography, forgettable losers.

This explanation actually is more plausible than stating it in so bald a fashion may imply, as it is based on some sensible observations about the general nature of large migrations. That the major causes of human migrations are economic was of course the observation that underlay Ravenstein's classic Laws of Migration, formulated in the 1870s and '80s.[23] This is not merely a truism, but an important operational point in analyzing Irish migration, for economically-induced or motivated migration — as distinct from compelled migrations, such as, for example, the expulsion of almost the entire Acadian population — is selective.[24] And, crucially, this selectivity, taking all migrants together, almost always tends to be bimodal. Specifically, in most societies from which migrants issue, there is a sharp distinction between those who leave because of "plus factors" (such as, say, a young shopkeeper who — leaves to seek better commercial opportunities in another city) and those who respond chiefly to negative factors (as, — say, the herdsmen of Eretrea, forced to move by dearth of vegetation). The one group is positively selected, the other negatively, and if one plots the characteristics of migrants using almost any index, whether education, class, or financial position, one can expect to get a J-shaped or U-shaped curve.[25]

It is possible to argue that this bimodality would be interesting in any population, but that, concerning the Irish, it is absolutely pivotal, for Irish society in the first half of the nineteenth century was itself rent by a series of social dichotomies: the Catholics and Protestants were virtually endogamous tribal groups; economically, the distinction between the agricultural subsistence sector and the rest of the economy was severe; and the north-eastern quarter of the country (roughly eqivalent to present-day Northern Ireland) was geographically, socially, and economically distinct from the rest of Ireland. These various Irish dualities were not coterminous, but they did overlap. As related to Irish migration to Upper Canada, the Irish dichotomies might be taken to imply that not merely was there a radical change in the character of Irish migration consequent upon the Famine, but the pre-Famine migration to Canada was overwhelmingly Protestant and that occurring thereafter, mostly Catholic.

But reality intervenes. Neither the pre- nor post-Famine emigration fits neatly into this pattern. Granted, it is well known that the Irish port from which, in most pre-Famine years, the largest number emigrated to British North America was Belfast;[26] and it is undeniable that the Protestants were predominant in Ulster. But it is a long way from these two points to conclude solidly that the bulk of the pre-Famine emigrants were Protestants or, indeed, that most migrants actually hailed from Ulster — as distinct from embarking there — whatever their religion.

S.H. Cousens has made a remarkable series of studies of the pre-Famine Irish demographic data, for our purposes the most important being a discussion of regional variations in emigration from 1821–41. In the absence of trustworthy direct emigration figures, he has calculated reliable indirect indicators of emigration before the Famine, region by region, through analysis of population change in each census district. His research reveals that migration came mostly from the northern half of Ireland (from Ulster and the neighbouring parts of Leinster and Connaught) and least from the south. Specifically, counties Longford, Westmeath, Londonderry, and Donegal had the highest pre-Famine rates of outward migration. Cousens notes that emigration was especially strong in areas in which there was a domestic textile industry: this domestic industry was severely hurt by the post-Napoleonic slump, combined with the spread of textile mechanization. (That the fringe areas of the domestic textile industry were hurt more than the central Lagan valley industry is a reasonable assumption; the rise of mechanical production in Belfast and environs absorbed thousands of otherwise displaced textile workers). In the southern half of Ireland, emigration was especially strong in small pockets (in particular, parts of counties Limerick, King's, Queen's, Wicklow, and Cork), from which small Protestant minorities engaged in weaving had a high emigration rate. In contrast, the subsistence agricultural areas of Connaught and Munster produced relatively few emigrants. (Counties Clare, Kerry, and Galway had the lowest emigration rates, 1821–41). Thus, it is fair to assess the pre-Famine emigration as comprised largely of migrants who were in reduced circumstances, but well above the poverty line.[27]

Thus, from Irish data we know that (1) in most pre-Famine years, Belfast was the most common port of out-migration; (2) that most migrants came from the northern half of Ireland; (3) that most came from the relatively prosperous areas of the country, not from the subsistence regions; and (4) that Protestants had a higher propensity to emigrate than did Catholics.

Yet, in the absence of direct data on out-migration, we can *not* conclude (1) that most migrants came from Ulster. The northern half of Ireland and the province of Ulster are not at all the same thing, and it was the Leinster and Connaught counties which border on Ulster that had the highest out-migration rates. And parts of Ulster (in particular, County Antrim) had very low emigration rates; (2) *nor* can we conclude that the bulk of pre-Famine migrants necessarily were Protestants. Although Protestants certainly had a higher propensity to emigrate than did the Catholics, there were fewer of them in the general population. As far as Irish sources are concerned, we can go no further.

Moreover, there is an absence of Ontario data bearing directly on the issue of ethnicity and religious affiliation (the 1842 census tallied both country of origin and religious affiliation, but did not cross-tabulate these categories). What can one do? The answer is: quite a bit, provided one proceeds with a large degree of humility and sedulously avoids the "fallacy of false precision." Ideally, one would like to see a complete retabulation of the 1842 census for the entire province, but that would be so expensive a proceeding as to be chimerical. Failing that, a random sampling, comprising several thousand cases, would be desirable, and perhaps some day that will be done. For the present, however, one must be satisfied with employing accounting procedures which permit a reformulation of the aggregate data. The reformulation detailed below, which gives an estimate of the Protestant-Catholic breakdown amongst the

Irish, should be read as being the most likely division within a possible range of two to three percentage points either way. Given the assumptions which one must make in the reformulation process and given the shaky nature of the 1842 census, to claim any greater degree of precision would be to invite hubris.

The Right Reverend Alexander Macdonnell, the Catholic bishop of Kingston and one of the best-informed observers of the Ontario religious situation, stated in 1838 that "the Catholics, who compose a great proportion of the population of Upper Canada, are either Irish emigrants, Scots highlanders, or French Canadians."[28] This can be employed as the basis for a formula for estimating the religious composition of the Irish, as follows: (1) begin with the Catholic population as reported in 1842, 65,203; (2) from this, subtract the total of French Canadians;[29] (3) doubtless there were some French-Canadian Protestants, but assume that their numbers equal those of Catholics born in Continental Europe, England, Wales, and the United States, or those of the first generation of such parentage; (4) assume that 3 percent of the Scots-born and of the first generation born in Canada of Scots parentage and 3 percent of the second generation Canadian-born inhabitants of non-French origin were Catholics and subtract these figures from the preceding sub-total. (Actually, this probably under-estimates somewhat the Catholic proportion of the Scots-born and first generation Scots populations, and overstates that of the non-French, second-generation Canadian-born group;[30] (5) the remaining number of Catholics can be taken to equal the number of Irish inhabitants (either Irish-born, or of the first generation born in Canada) who were Catholics. This number is slightly under 44,000; (6) finally, by comparing this figure for the inferred total for Irish ethnicity,[31] one has a figure for the Catholics amongst the Irish-born and first-generation Irish born in Ontario in 1842 of 34.5 percent.

Forget now all the procedures and the individual numbers. Instead, focus on the two key points that have emerged; (1) that before the Famine, the Irish population in

Upper Canada was mostly Protestant, but (2) that the Irish-Catholic minority was formidable, indeed, much larger than was supposed by contemporaries and by later historians. The Protestant-Catholic split is best described as roughly 2:1. One can accept this with considerable confidence. Changes in detail of our calculations would budge the results a percentage point or, at most, two or three, either way, but the historian who is content to deal in words can be confident in accepting that there were about twice as many Protestants as Catholics amongst the Irish in Ontario.

(IV)

Remember that this was *before* the Famine. And then recognize how complicated the picture has now become. Instead of a simple dichotomy between early-arriving Protestants and later Famine-starving Catholics, one must deal amongst the Irish with two groups of early emigrants, Protestant and Catholic, each of whom had emigrated with resources in hand and with aspirations intact, and each of whom would have relationships with the later arrivals. Implicit in this observation is the point that most pre-Famine Catholics were not pauper peasants, although, undeniably, there were pauper emigrants amongst both Catholics and Protestants.

Indirectly, by establishing that the Catholics comprised such a large proportion of the pre-Famine population, one opens the door to another level of understanding — and of complication. If one compares the probable religious persuasion of those of Irish derivation in 1871 with that calculated for 1842, one discovers that the Catholic proportion of the Irish in Upper Canada has stayed virtually constant — *not* risen as one might expect following the Famine: it was approximately 34.5 percent in 1842 and 33.8 percent in 1871.[32] Either there was a high degree of apostasy amongst Irish Catholics (a suggestion that cannot be considered even remotely possible) or, *despite* the Famine in Ireland generally having affected the Irish Catholics more severely, the stream of migrants was still a dual stream and the bulk of the emigrants to Upper Canada continued to be Protestant.

(V)

If the paucity of studies of the Irish as an ethnic group in nineteenth-century central Canada is one strange characteristic of the extant historiography, the second is this: that what, until recently, has been the accepted viewpoint has been wrong, and not just in minor details, but fundamentally, completely, and, seemingly, inexplicably. One says "inexplicably" because, even though it is quite hard to obtain direct data on the Irish in Ontario before Confederation, anyone with even a nodding acquaintance with the copious and easily-available demographic evidence concerning the entire Ontario population in the immediate post-Confederation years, would have recognized that the standard version of Irish ethnic history prior to Confederation could not have been accurate. (That standard version is discussed below; the easily-accessible post-Confederation evidence is included in my decade-of-simple-facts in Section I of this chapter.)

In practical terms, the accepted statements of who and what the Irish in Ontario were were defined in articles and in an unpublished thesis, by H. Clare Pentland and, in a single pivotal article, by Kenneth Duncan, respectively a political economist and a sociologist. Pentland's work was presented chiefly in his unpublished thesis ("Labour and the Development of Industrial Capitalism in Canada,")[33] and in two articles: "The Development of a Capitalistic Labour Market in Canada" *(Canadian Journal of Economics and Political Science)*[34] and "The Lachine Strike of 1843" *(Canadian Historical Review).*[35] So important has Pentland's work been in forming the "new Canadian social history" that I am devoting an entire essay (chapter five) to examining the evidentiary basis for his view-point. Here, suffice it to say that Pentland took the picture of the Boston Irish and applied it to Ontario: "Oscar Handlin's *Boston Immigrants, 1790–1815* (Cambridge, Mass., 1941) provides an excellent discussion of the character of Irish immigration into America. Most of the findings for Boston apply equally to Irish immigration into Canada."[36]

Kenneth Duncan was rather more acute an observer of social phenomena than was Pentland, and in his "Irish Famine Immigration and the Social Structure of Canada West," he rejected the Boston model of Irish social disorientation and instead presented a broader interpretation which, while still based on U.S. models, was more widely applicable, or so he contended. This article of Duncan's, originally published in the *Canadian Review of Sociology and Anthropology*,[37] was twice reprinted in general books of social studies[38] and, according to Michael Cross, the former editor of the *Canadian Historical Review*:

> The sociological stream in Canadian social history is typified by "Irish Immigration and the Social Structure of Canada West" by Kenneth Duncan who generalizes on the peasant nature of the Irish of the 1840s and on the attitudes of the receiving society. Historians generally have been uneasy with models and preconceived theories; Duncan, however, demonstrates how valuable they can be if filtered through an open and sensitive mind.[39]

Duncan's argument concerning the Irish in nineteenth-century Canada had the following primary components. (1) The key question was "Why did the Irish peasant become a city man? Why did he prefer an urban slum to an independent farmstead . . .?"[40] (2) "The famine immigrants were not merely Irish but largely southern Irish Roman Catholics."[41] (3) These Irish Catholics were too technologically backward to farm in Canada. "A number of contemporary jokes make it evident that the Irishman often did not know how to yoke oxen or hitch horses, plow a furrow, or use an axe."[42] (4) Also, they were unable to save enough money to get into farming, for "the immigrants did not show any tendency to save money from urban employment and enter farming. . . ."[43] (5) And, living in large urban ghettos allowed the Irish to maintain their close communal social structure. In sum, "if the immigrants rejected rural life in Canada they did so in order to retain their peasant values."[44]

This putative pattern has nothing whatsoever to do with Ontario's history. If the reader will compare it to chapter three's analysis of the historiography of the Irish-Americans (especially Section I), its provenance becomes clear: Duncan's analysis is simply the standard Irish-American story, transferred to the canvas of Ontario. The most effective way of demonstrating how totally inapplicable to Ontario this pattern is, is to compare his fundamental assertion — the one on which his entire analysis depends — with the available demographic evidence:

> To sum up, disease, ignorance, and poverty made the entry into agriculture exceedingly difficult for the famine migrants and they became, it would appear, urban by compulsion.
> *Later, however, when circumstances altered, the Irish remained urban.*[45] (Italics mine.)

Urban? let us see.

The censuses of 1851 and 1861 tallied the birthplace of all inhabitants of Ontario and also indicated whether the populace lived in cities, towns, or villages, or in the countryside. These enumerations had their flaws, but are quite serviceable for defining the fundamental characteristics of the population. Irritatingly, however, the census authorities did not cross-tabulate place of birth and place of residence, so one must do this task oneself. The job is clerical and tiresome, but not methodologically controversial. The results: in 1851, 14.0 percent of the inhabitants of Ontario who had been born in Ireland lived in cities (the average size of which was 14,253 inhabitants); in 1861, 13.6 percent of the Irish-born lived in cities (the average size of which had risen to 20,777).[46] A group urban by compulsion? Hardly.

But let us be generous and include as urbanites all those who lived in incorporated towns and villages, irrespective of how small those settlements were. We find then that an additional 7.1 percent of the Irish-born are included as of the 1851 census (living in towns and villages, the average size of which was 2,111). And, in 1861, 12.0 percent of the Irish-born in Ontario resided in towns and villages (whose average size was 1,957).[47] Now, it is hard to see how living in a town of 2,000 in the typical case, can be viewed as an urban experience, but if one wishes to accept it as such and to add these town and village residents to the inhabitants of the cities, one still finds that in 1851 only 21.1 percent of the Irish-born in Ontario lived in cities, towns, and villages (averaging 4,030 residents in size) and in 1861 the proportion was 25.6 percent (living in towns, villages, and cities whose average size was 3,077).

The unavoidable fact is that, even employing the broadest possible definition of "urban," one has to conclude that the overwhelming majority of the Irish migrants to Ontario settled in the countryside. In 1851, 78.9 percent of the Irish-born lived in rural areas, and in 1861, the percentage was 74.4 percent, and that by the most narrow of definitions of rural.

Those figures deal with the Irish-born. Perhaps their children drifted to the cities and perhaps the real urban disposition of the Irish only came out in the first and second generations born in North America. The 1871 census provided a self-definition question in which each individual's national descent was to be recorded "as given by the person questioned."[48] In modern terms, this is a subjective ethnicity item, one which is dependent wholly upon the self-perception of the individual tallied. Of the individuals in Ontario who reckoned themselves as being of Irish descent (whether Irish-born, second generation, third, or subsequent), their place of residence was as follows:[49]

Cities (average size: 26,517)	9.5 percent
Towns and Villages (average size: 2,148)	13.0 percent
Total Urban (including all cities, towns, and villages (average size: 3,266)	22.5 percent
Total Rural	77.5 percent

Clearly, actually to describe the experience of the Irish migrants and their descendents in Ontario as having been an urban one requires an act of faith sufficient to move mountains.

There may be a plausible explanation. Possibly, just possibly, the Roman Catholics amongst the Irish-born or Irish-descended lived in urban areas, and thus underwent the trauma of being a religious minority and an impoverished immigrant group in an urban society — or so one could argue.

Here, the available data present us with a double difficulty: not only was there no cross-tabulation relating to the urban-rural breakdown to ethnicity in the 1871 census, but no attempt was made to cross-tabulate religious persuasion and ethnic origin. (And, of course, before 1871, ethnicity was not dealt with at all.) However, a reasonably simple two-stage redaction of the 1871 data permits us to view the Irish-descended Catholics as a distinct group: first, one does a simple piece of bookkeeping, tallying the residence pattern of each of the major ethnic groups; second, one then employs the equation developed earlier to distinguish the imputed number of Roman Catholics amongst the Irish in each major type of residential area.[50] The results for 1871 are as follows:

Catholics of Irish descent, living in cities (average size 26,517)	14.7 percent
Catholics of Irish descent, living in towns and villages (average size: 2,148)	19.0 percent
Total Urban Catholics of Irish descent (including all cities, towns, and villages) (average size: 3,266)	33.7 percent
Total Catholics of Irish descent living in rural areas	66.3 percent

Given that only one in three Irish Catholics in Ontario settled in areas that can even remotely be considered urban — and given the fact that only one in seven settled in cities — it is impossible to apply the usual "American model" to the Ontario situation, either as it involves Catholics or Protestants.[51] We must deal with the Canadian Irish on their own, not American, terms. This is all the more important because, as demonstrated in chapter three, the "American model" does not even fit the evidence concerning the immigrants from Ireland and their descendants in the United States.

Chapter Five.
H. Clare Pentland, the Irish, and the New Canadian Social History

"Racism has never been very far
below the surface in the white societies
of Western Europe and North America."
Paul Phillips[1]

(I)

As an act of intellectual self-mortification, historians should read *Mein Kampf,* or at least a fair slug of it, every ten years or so. It reminds one forcibly just how demented an ideology or set of ideas can be and still have general acceptability in a society. Ultimately, the responsibility of a scholar, whatever his discipline, is to examine accepted views of how the world works and to try to bring these views into line with reality: hysterical fears must be deflated by cool, rational examination, dogmatic statements of "facts" must be given the test of empirical verification. Most important, scholars can help turn society away from *ways* of thinking, from fallacies that, if left unexamined, become the very marrow of a twisted ideology.

I was undergoing this decennial mortification, trying to make it through one chapter of *Mein Kampf* a day,[2] when I came across a review in the *Canadian Historical Review*[3] by my friend Bryan Palmer of the posthumous publication of the revised version of H. Clare Pentland's 1960 University of Toronto Ph.D. thesis, "Labour and the Development of Industrial Capitalism in Canada." This work appeared, edited by Paul Phillips, as *Labour and Capital in Canada, 1650–1860*.[4] Palmer's review, a ringing endorsement of Pentland's work, was based on a recognition of the fundamental fact that the Canadian historical profession believes in a scholarly counterpart of the doctrine of Apostolic Succession: that is, the claim to legitimacy on behalf of any new school of history is greater if the proponents of that school can point to a venerable Canadian founding father. This situation is somewhat inconvenient for the more radical of the "new Canadian social historians," for their best work harkens, not to Canadian roots, but to the English social historian, E.P. Thompson, who, arguably, is the only historian of our time in the English-speaking world who merits the appellation "seminal."[5] Canadian social historians who follow Thompson's example have been subjected to a certain amount of cultural prejudice, in that their work sometimes has been dismissed, or at least down-graded, for being based on a foreign inspiration. Thus, Palmer provides an alternative indigenous founding father of the new Canadian social history: "For those who deplore creeping Thompsonian culturalism and the importation of foreign models, then, a dose of Pentland may be just what these doctors should order up as a cure for their apoplectic reaction to what has been rather incorrectly dubbed the 'new' labour history."[6] Of course Pentland's volume is not perfect, and Palmer mentions many relatively minor flaws, but, at heart, he believes that it is a major work, the touchstone of modern Canadian social history:

> Pentland's book has endured, however, in spite of his own reservations and its long gestation. It has survived because of its interpretative boldness and synthetic sweep. Like all truly great works of historical analysis, *Labour and Capital in Canada* probed a wide range of sources, marshalled empirical evidence in an innovative argument, and provided a generalized and theoretically poised account that retains much of its

analytic force in spite of an outpouring of recent books and articles that expand upon points raised by Pentland, prove him wrong in specific particulars, or establish that certain events or developments demanded more research than Pentland could devote to them.[7]

Now, Bryan Palmer in my opinion is one of the two or three best historians in Canada (*not* one of the two or three best young historians — a condescending phrase, that — one of the best, period). An indication of his stature is that when he gets something wrong, he gets it *really* wrong, and, even then, he is still worth one's attention. Reading his assessment of Pentland's work is like watching Reggie Jackson take batting practice on a day when his timing is a bit off; even though the ball keeps arching foul, he hits it a long way and with style.

What has this to do with *Mein Kampf?* Palmer's review set me to re-reading Pentland's book, and, fresh from Hitler's volume, it struck me that Pentland's analysis of nineteenth-century Canadian history and Hitler's of early twentieth-century German history work the same way. Of course, I am not comparing the character of the humane Pentland and the ghastly Hitler, but I am comparing the character of their historical analyses. If my observations are correct, then perhaps H.C. Pentland is not the ideal founding father for the new Canadian social history.

(II)

Mein Kampf, published in two volumes in 1925, is many things, prophecy, billingsgate, and vituperation, and, among them, an attempt to provide an historical explanation for the immediate past of Germany. Chapters ten and eleven, "Causes of the Collapse" and "Nation and Race," contain the heart of Hitler's work as an historian. His argument can be systemized as follows:

1. Hitler defined an historical phenomenon that must be explained, the fall of an advanced industrial capitalist state, namely the German Second Reich. By this he does not mean the loss of World War I: "Certainly the loss of the war was of

terrible importance for the future of our fatherland; however, its loss is not cause, but itself only a consequence of causes."[8] The collapse to which he referred was multidimensional and involved social, economic, cultural, and moral dimensions (as he defined them). Hitler was trying to explain the collapse of an entire economic-social system.

2. Hitler charted certain intermediate variables that acted as mechanisms leading to the ultimate decline of the Reich. These were not "factors" that were added up in a single-minded fashion. Hitler's intervening explanatory variables were simultaneously recognized as symptoms of the Reich's decline and as the proximate, but not the ultimate or penultimate, cause of that decline. These intermediate variables were:

A. Most visible, highly consequential, but not all-important, were economic forces. In the peace that preceded the war, the German economic system became an advanced industrial state. This had the social effect of reducing the proportion of the peasantry in the population and increasing the big city proletariat. The concentration of the new proletariat in the cities made highly visible the contrast between rich and poor. "Abundance and poverty lived so close together that the saddest consequences could and inevitably did arise. Poverty and frequent unemployment began to play havoc with people, leaving behind them a memory of discontent and embitterment. The consequence of all this seemed to be political class division."[9]

B. The influence of capital permeated the state. "Economic life grew to be the dominant mistress of the state. . .,"[10] was Hitler's formulation. This hegemony of capital extended to the highest level of government: "Unfortunately, the domination of money was sanctioned even by that authority which should have opposed it. His Majesty the Kaiser acted most unfortunately by drawing the aristocracy into the orbit of the new finance capital."[11]

C. The rise of finance capital had an aspect that was simultaneously economic and social in its consequences: property was being alienated from the individual and transferred to the agencies of finance capital. *"A grave economic symptom of decay was the slow disappearance of the right of private property, and the gradual transference of the entire economy to the ownership of stock companies."*[12] (Italics Hitler's.)

D. Simultaneously, a cultural breakdown was occurring, one which Hitler formulated colloquially as *"the steadily increasing habit of doing things by halves,"*[13] and as *"the increasing cowardice in the face of responsibility, as well as the resultant half-heartedness in all things."*[14] (Italics Hitler's.) The evidentiary referents of this cultural breakdown were:

i. educational system that produced not independent persons but "compliant 'walking encyclopedias.'"[15]

ii. an information infra-structure that was at odds with the German people's true national interest. In particular, the liberal press "was actively engaged in digging the grave of the German people and the German Reich," as were the "lying Marxist sheets."[16]

iii. the family structure was undercut and this reduced the cultural and physical integrity of the German people. Hitler identified a pre-war phenomenon that continued into the Weimar era: "Our whole public life today is like a hothouse for sexual ideas and stimulations. Just look at the bill of fare served up in our movies, vaudeville and theatres, and you will hardly to be able to deny that this is not the right kind of food, particularly for youth."[17] He spent several hundred words on the dangers of prostitutes and of syphilis, a concern that may not be entirely without autobiographical reference.

D. The war did have an impact, Hitler said, in that it speeded things up. "For the German people, it must almost be considered a great good fortune that its period of creeping sickness was suddenly cut short by so terrible a catastrophe, for otherwise the nation would have gone to the dogs more slowly perhaps, but all the more certainly."[18]

3. All of those intermediate variables, at once both symptoms and mechanisms of the decline, were related,

each to the others, in a complex causal web, and a professional historian could easily have filled a book discussing the permutations of these interrelationships. Hitler, however, proceeded quickly to adumbrate the ultimate and the penultimate causes for which these intermediate factors were the visible mechanisms:

A. His ultimate primary variable (unlike the rest of his argument, which refers, with varying degrees of implausibility, to historical events and thus can be examined by the evidentiary standards of an historian), is completely exogenous to the situation that he is trying to explain and must be accepted either upon faith or upon evidence garnered from outside of the specific context that Hitler is dealing with, if his explanatory network is to work. (This sort of an approach is not uncommon in historical work; historians long have applied to historical situations concepts from economics, sociology, or psychology whose validity is taken as a given, rather than proven, in a specific historical context.) For Hitler, this ultimate primary variable is the theory of racial purity. *"Blood, sin and desecration of the human race are the original sin in this world and the end of a humanity which surrenders to it."*[19] (Italics Hitler's.) He expounds this point at great length, specifying the physical, cultural, and economic results of all racial crossing.

B. To tie his primary variable to the intermediate variables detailed earlier, Hitler's system required a component that would relate to racial purity and, simultaneously, could be shown (or at least alleged) to relate to each of the intermediate variables. Conceivably, he could have used not a simple penultimate variable, but a complex matrix. Instead he chose to insert an ethnic mastercog into his system — the Jews. He then showed how, in his view, the "original sin" of racial impurity, through the Jews, affected each of the economic, social, governmental, and cultural factors that he had used as intervening variables.

Thus was Hitler's historical analysis of the fall of the Second Reich complete. Whatever its vices, and they are many, these should not obscure the fact that this was indeed an historical explanation, not mere political rhetoric, and that it can be judged by the same techniques through which one adjudges any historical explanation: its definition of the phenomenon-to-be-explained, the precision of its intervening variables, the accuracy of the description of their relationship to available evidence, the appropriateness of its exogenous assumptions, and the adequacy with which these assumptions are related to the intervening variables and, finally, to the phenomenon-to-be-explained. This is essentially a matter of judging whether Hitler was a good or bad historian. The matter of his accuracy or inaccuracy in factual statements has been treated at length by German historians and need not be drawn out here: although on some matters — such as the interplay of finance capital and the old aristocratic-monarchic hegemony he was acute — by and large he either used irrelevant intervening variables (syphilis was not a significant direct cause of the fall of the Second Reich) or tied his variables together outlandishly (the lunatic use of the Jews as the warp of his explanatory system is too well known to require comment). Thus, in a technical sense, Hitler was a bad historian.

But to talk in terms of his adequacy as an historian is to keep the temperature of one's assessment artificially low, for at some point history that is bad in the technical sense can become bad, even evil, in the moral sense. Hitler was not the first writer of history to cross the line between the technically bad and the morally opprobrious — nor will he be the last — but the particular manner in which he crossed the line bears notice. He did so when in his explanatory machinery he introduced the ethnic mastercog. He ascribed to an ethno-religious group ("race" in his terminology) characteristics which they did not have and for which he could produce very little evidence, and against the existence of which putative characteristics an unbiased observer would have found ample evidence.

The employment of an undocumented ethnic mastercog — that is, the stereotyping of racial, religious, and ethnic groups — is something that must continually be guarded against, as it is not merely bad history in the technical sense. As historians we must be particularly wary of racist thinking, as the people we are dealing with usually are long dead. If one traduces, say, any present-day Canadian ethnic group, its members are apt to correct the record with a heartening vigour, but such corrections do not spring forward when dealing with ethnic groups of three or four generations back. Once an historian manages to insert into the accepted national literature a theory that involves the "ethnic mastercog," then racial (or religious) prejudice becomes built into the standard accepted history of the nation in question. And if racism is an accepted attitude in any nation's explanation of its own past, then inevitably racism will be part of its future.[20]

(III)

Many, perhaps most, Canadian social historians know H. Clare Pentland's major work on labour and capital in Canada as an unpublished thesis, a product of his studies in the years 1948–61. Pentland, however, revised and improved the work and, although revision apparently was not completed when he died in 1978, the posthumous published version (1981) can be taken as representing the most considered statement of his views.

Although the title of the published version refers both to labour and to capital, its claim to originality lies in its discussion of the creation of the industrial labour market and of the changes in the nature of the labour process in an industrializing central Canada. Only chapter V deals with the rise of capital and this is simply a Canadian version of the then-standard description of the English industrial revolution that dominated English economic history between the two world wars. The explanation of the industrial revolution consisted of assembling numerous "factors," the supply of which was soon to produce industrial development. Pentland followed this English pattern:

> Good land, canals, and railways, an adequate supply of labour in the market, and protection: all did their work of changing Canada into an integrated economy at the stage of manu-

factures after 1850. But they could not do it alone. One more important ingredient was required for this transition: a transformation of values and attitudes to provide the "Moral conditions of Economic Growth."[21]

Pentland's real interest, however, was not in capital itself, but in the way in which labour became part of the emerging new industrial matrix.[22] Therefore, to be true to his interests and competence, one must focus on the labour question which commands most of his attention. On this topic, Pentland's analysis can be systemized as follows:

1. He defined an historical phenomenon that must be explained, namely, how it came to be that in the second half of the nineteenth century central Canada: "approached the classical (abundant) labour market of industrial capitalism."[23]

To make such a monumental question more susceptible to close analysis, Pentland detailed three stages of development:

A. A pre-industrial, but capitalistic, form of labour organization that he denominated "personal labour relations."[24] This was a relationship of mutual dependence between employer and labourer. "The employee, tied to one employer, usually made himself submissive and agreeable. The employer, deprived of the sanction of dismissal, substituted positive incentives to induce conscientious work."[25]

B. These arrangements were succeeded by various transitional forms, which:

C. eventually produced the labour organization of true industrial capitalism. In this phase, the labour market was characterized by "the creation and continuance of a large enough labour force that employers could always hire the number of workers wanted, whenever they wanted." Under these circumstances, workers had to bear their own "overhead costs" (that is, they had to maintain themselves on their own resources in slack seasons), "and yet to be available for use, even for very short periods."[26]

2. Pentland employed certain intermediate variables as mechanisms that led to the third stage, mentioned above,

the labour market of industrial capitalism. Some of these he discussed directly, others he presented for the reader to garner from heuristic case histories. (The firms of Calvin, Cook and Co., the St. Maurice Forges, the Marmora iron works were his chief examples.)

Variables included:

A. The development of technology and of the communications infrastructure were taken virtually for granted. Though he chose not to emphasize these items, Pentland certainly was well aware of their importance.

B. Cultural changes amidst the middle class that Pentland denominates "the pushing puritanical attitudes appropriate to industrial capitalism."[27] These included a wide range of phenomena, ranging from the middle classes' gaining control over most political institutions, to their interest in technology and their belief in the "spreading gospel of efficiency."[28]

C. The power of the industrial capitalists, which was directed, among other things, towards creating "such obstacles to the acquisition of property that the labour market could not be unduly depleted by the escape of wage earners to remunerative self-employment."[29]

D. The hegemony of the middle class in certain cultural matters — most notably the temperance movement — which resulted in a more disciplined, more obedient working class. The spread of mass educational institutions presumably had the same result.

3. These intermediate variables, of course, are interrelated in a variety of ways and each has a direct causal connection in Pentland's argument to the historical phenomenon which he wishes to explain — the emergence of the abundant labour market of industrial capitalism in central Canada. Necessarily, these same intermediate variables also are related to a set of logically antecedent primary variables:

A. The fundamental, ultimate, causal agent for Pentland was taken directly from elementary classical economics, namely, that the relative bargaining power of labour and capital depended upon the amount of labour available in any given situation. This theoretical assumption is completely exogenous to the situation and has to be accepted on faith.[30] (There is, of course, a great deal of corroborative evidence in other studies, ranging virtually all the way back to David Ricardo and, indeed, to Adam Smith.) Although Pentland does not make the position clear, it seems fairly certain that he believed an abundant labour market:

i. is a necessary precondition to the development of the industrial capital labour market, and;[31]
ii. that an abundance of labour has as its inevitable consequence a dissolving of traditional arrangements and a movement towards the labour market of industrial capitalism.[32]

Therefore, under his scheme, Pentland either had:
i. to prove that in most Canadian labour markets there was indeed a surplus pool of labour, or
ii. show that there was a source of labour so large that it was safe to infer (without proving directly) that an abundant pool of labour existed.

B. Pentland chose the second alternative (and thereby was freed from the necessity of giving any operational specifications of a labour surplus). Therefore the penultimate variable, the one on which his whole structure rested, was the massive population increases in central Canada of 1815–60. Here, again, Pentland had two possible points of concentration:

i. the natural increase in the indigenous population, or
ii. immigration from outside of Canada. The first of these, however, was inadequate causally (although not without a minor impact), as the rate of natural increase was small, relative to in-migration.[33] Equally important as the immigrants' numbers were certain important qualities in their culture. "The overseas immigrants are of the greatest importance, not only because of their substantial contribution to the numbers of Canada's population, but also because their character and technical equipment played a

great part in changing Canada's industrial structure."[34] Thanks chiefly to the in-flows, "from about 1840, the Canadian market was well-stocked and possessed the reserves of a developed capitalist market,"[35] and, presumably, further immigration only increased the supply of labour reserves.

Pentland further sharpened the definition of his penultimate variable. For analytic purposes he divided this putative labour reserve along the ethnic axis. According to his way of thinking, the potential labour reserves came from:

i. the French-Canadians, who did have a rapid rate of natural increase. "But, except for the small force of traditional wage earners, like the shipyard workers, French-Canadians were not really in the labour market. They were not really out of it either; they occupied a residual position, for labour could be obtained with some effort. However, the peasant's attitude to the market was negative. He scarcely offered any competition to immigrants for jobs . . . ."[36]

ii. The aboriginal inhabitants, a group that had long been at least on the margin of the commercial economy. However, "it seems proper to conclude that French and Indians exhibited some child-like qualities that encouraged their organization into paternalistic labour systems,"[37] and thus kept them from being a factor of significance in the emerging labour market of industrial capitalism.

iii. The Americans, who, according to Pentland, set the tone of Canada's English-speaking regions until about 1840. He states that most Americans became farmers. "The character of the American influx ensured the rapid economic development of Canada, but it ensured also that Americans would not have a large place in the labour market. This was so, not because the Americans had any inhibitions in respect to the market as the French had, but because the bulk of them became small farmers who were neither employees nor employers."[38]

iv. The English immigrants, Pentland claims, were promoters of the industrial revolution. According to him, they "were distinguished from other immigrant groups by their possession, in their hands and heads, of the most advanced industrial technology of the age . . . . The consequence of this preference of the English industrial workers for their accustomed employments was that most of them who came to Canada before 1850 found no adequate use for their skills and went on to the cities of the United States."[39] Those who stayed were artisans, clerks, managers and professionals, and, although important in providing the modern skills needed for industrialization, did not contribute significantly to creating the abundant labour reserve of industrial capitalism.

v. The Scots, who consisted of two sub-groups, the highlanders and the lowlanders. The highlander was "a peasant, he was untutored and undisciplined in the ways of capitalistic communities . . . . The Highlander did not compete in the Canadian labour market any more than he could help. Rather, he settled on a farm. His success as a farmer was good by his own standards, bad by other people's."[40] As for his compatriot, the lowlander, "all the Lowland emigrants possessed in a high degree the skills and attitudes suited to a capitalist economy, and they were generally successful by capitalist standards."[41] Therefore, "it may be said of both sets of Scots together that most, as small proprietors, were withdrawn from and neutral to the labour market."[42]

Who was left? Given that immigration from continental Europe was of only tertiary importance numerically, there was only one logical alternative: the Irish. It is the Irish who, in the structure of Pentland's argument, became the pivotal and simple ethnic mastercog. His entire historical structure stands or falls on whether or not his view of the Irish is correct. In particular, his claim that there was indeed a surplus labour force — which, remember, was not proved directly by examination of specific markets but only

intuited from population and immigration aggregates —
will vanish in an instant if he is wrong about the Irish.

It is well known that the Irish were not a single group and
that their divisions were religio-national: as between persons
of English origin (mostly Established Church adherents),
those of Scots background (for the larger part Presbyterians), and "native" or "Celtic" Irish (usually taken to
mean the Roman Catholics). Pentland understood this, and
proceeded to fashion his ethnic mastercog with precision:

> i. He dismissed those Irish persons of English back-
> ground from the Canadian migration flow. "English
> Protestant settlers in Ireland preferred the role of land-
> lord and, except for the Quakers, they contributed only
> modestly to emigration."[43]
> ii. Ulster Presbyterians, Pentland noted, were a signifi-
> cant part of the immigration stream in the two and a half
> decades after the end of the Napoleonic Wars. "Ulster-
> men made up the majority of workmen available for hire
> in the 1820s and 1830s and therefore were important for
> the labour market of that time. However, they passed
> quickly into the society of small independent farmers."[44]

Thus, by a process of elimination, Pentland had defined
sharply his ethnic mastercog, the Irish Catholics.

These immigrants had two alleged characteristics that,
according to Pentland, made them the effective causal agent
in central Canada in the latter half of the nineteenth century
of the classical (abundant) labour market of industrial
capitalism:

> i. They came to Canada in large numbers. Pentland
> estimates that in 1861 there were 280,000 "effectively
> Irish" in Ontario and Quebec.[45]
> ii. Equally important, the Irish Catholics had "peculiar
> behaviour patterns. . . ."[46] "They showed almost no
> interest in farms. . . . Irish Catholics chose the city because
> of their preference in employment, as British artisans did.
> But the Irish did not aspire to be merchants or artisans.

Their enterprise was confined, in the first generation to the operation of fourth-rate taverns and boarding-houses that catered, primarily to succeeding Irish immigrants. Few were craftsmen, and these few were of indifferent quality. What the great majority of Irishmen sought was wage employment at labouring jobs in the company of their fellows."[47] Pentland considered and rejected several sociological explanations of this alleged pattern (such as the suggestion that the Irish stayed in cities to be near their priests: "the Irishman was superstitious rather than religious")[48] and boiled it all down to one statement: "Irish love of company was not simply an extreme manifestation of the compulsion that drives even isolates to seek companions sometimes. Rather, *the Irishman was a primitive man, half a tribesman still.*" (Italics mine)[49]

Thus, Pentland's logical structure was complete. "Until the Irish Catholics came, the market, though fairly well supplied with workmen for permanent and semi-permanent jobs, lacked labour reserves."[50] This primitive man, half a tribesman still, holds the same place in Pentland's argument that another "tribesman" served in a not entirely dissimilar argument published in Germany in the mid 1920s.

(IV)

What I have just done is outrageous. H. Clare Pentland is the one accepted saint of the new Canadian social history and Adolf Hitler was a monster. That, in part, is the point, however. Within most mankind, not least of all within professional scholars — in each of us — lies the potential for doing the worst, while convincing ourselves that we are serving the best.

Pentland's analysis is so important to Canadian history as presently practised that it would be a disservice to the profession (and, I think, unfair to him) to stop with the analogic presentation given above. Conceivably, his argument could have taken the shape that it did for reasons dictated by historical reality. So, for the moment let us forget the apparent racism in his work and examine the less volatile question of where he rated on the spectrum of historical competence, from very good all the way down to very bad. If Pentland was a good historian, then his argument will have conformed to historical reality and the racism in his work will have been apparent, not real.

The fairest test of Pentland's historical competence lies in the statements he made concerning immigrants in general and especially the Irish Catholics, for demonstrably these were the most important parts of his argument concerning the existence of a labour surplus and the parts, therefore, on which he can be expected to have exhibited his historical expertise at its best. Herein a basic ground-rule in evaluating his competence will be that it will be judged *only* in terms of his using — or having failed to use — evidence that was available during the time he was working on the original thesis, 1948–61, and on the revisions of the thesis made off-and-on from 1961 into the 1970s. No newly discovered sources will be employed, although one may properly refer to recent studies of materials that were available to Pentland had he wished to use them.

Within those ground-rules, one of the things that strikes anyone familiar with the literature on immigration from the British Isles is that Pentland was unfamiliar with the two most definitive statistical studies that were extant at the time he was writing. His basic statistical series for data on migration from the British Isles to North America,[51] the fundamental data-line for his whole argument about surplus population, was derived from S.C. Johnson's *A History of Emigration from the United Kingdom to North America 1763–1912* and from W.A. Carrothers, *Emigration from the British Isles with Special Reference to Development of the Overseas Dominions*. The first was published in 1913, the second in 1929. Pentland was unaware of two major, indeed monumental, studies published during the very period he was researching and writing the thesis: *External Migration. A Study of the Available Statistics, 1815–1950* by N.H. Carrier and J.R. Jeffery[52] and the Republic of Ireland's *Commission on Migration and Other Population Pro-*

blems.[53] These were not obscure documents. They were widely disseminated by the governments involved and, at the time of Pentland's writing, were the definitive statements of Irish migration patterns in the nineteenth century and of the overall migration patterns from the entire British Isles. For Pentland not to have known of them is similar to a political historian's being unaware of *Hansard.*

This reflects badly on his competence, but not, it is important to note, on his actual argument. Had Pentland encountered these studies, he actually would have strengthened his case. The statistical series that he took from Johnson's and Carrothers' books lumped together all migrants from the British Isles to British North America, but the studies published in 1950 allowed a break-down by nationality, thus providing data that Pentland needed on individual ethnic groups. In particular, the data printed in the two major investigations of the 1950s would have allowed Pentland to correct his factually-inaccurate statement that "in the 1850s English immigration seems to have become as predominant as the Irish had been earlier."[54] Actually, although the number of Irish migrants fell from 1853 onwards, it was not until the late 1860s that migrants from England and Wales came to outnumber Irish migrants in most years.[55] Since Pentland's entire case hinged on there having been a surfeit of Irish immigrants, that case would have been at least indirectly bolstered by his having read the major immigration studies of the 1950s.

Considerably more disconcerting was Pentland's predilection for the "whole cloth" method of historical argument: that is, he simply made up major bodies of data. This was not the small-time forgery of someone who writes bogus footnotes, but something far grander, an ability to present an entirely fictional conclusion, one presumably based on a body of research data which, in actual fact, turns out to be non-existent. In their way, his powers were awesome.

Let us take as examples of his fictive powers four instances. These are relatively mild in that, although they reflect badly on his competence as an historian, they are not instances of his cheating in argument. In each of these cases, the data that he makes up either are irrelevant to his chain of argument or probably reflect what the historical truth will be found to be — when someone eventually does the research. First, a minor example to show his mind-set. Pentland was interested in Ulstermen as part of his Irish contingent, and he states flatly, without citation, that "immigrants at Quebec after 1815 were about 60 per cent Irish, and these overwhelmingly from Ulster."[56] The reason there is no citation for this "fact" is that, although records were kept concerning the point-of-sailing for each ship — and many sailed from Ulster — there are no systematic records on the place of origin of the people on these ships available until 1853, and even those are far from perfect.

In this instance, Pentland's creation of an historical "fact" has little to do with his main argument, but in a second instance it does: he stated as an absolute matter of historical fact that most Americans who came to central Canada became farmers.[57] I suspect that he is right, but no citation of this "fact" is given because, in the present state of knowledge, there can be none. Pentland defined Americans as everyone from the early loyalists onwards, a multi-generational cohort. But the census records of the pre-Confederation period ask only for place-of-birth (that is, they denominate only the immigrant generation among Pentland's "Americans") — and the first Dominion censuses did not include Americans as a separate ethnic group. Perhaps in the future some very expensive multi-generational study of American immigrants will be made, but none was available to Pentland and none is available now. Clearly Pentland's source of this "fact" was H. Clare Pentland.

Similarly, in a third instance of his creativity, Pentland stated categorically and without citation that the Ulstermen in central Canada passed quickly into the ranks of small independent farmers.[58] Again, I suspect that Pentland was right, but there is no way that, writing in the 1950s, he could have established the point: the manuscript censuses of his period — the only comprehensive data-base on occupation — asked only what country a person was born in and not what province within that country. Thus, this lacuna in the data occasioned another act of creativity.

Indeed, Pentland's use of census data is fascinating. Aside from citing, presumably inadvertently, a census which does not exist ("the 1861 census of British-born in Canada")[59] Pentland established a category for several censuses which never existed in fact and for which he gave no adequate derivation: the "effectively Irish," by which he meant Irish-Catholic immigrants and their Canadian-born offspring.[60] This phrase indicated "those Irish Catholics in culture and behaviour, including those born outside Ireland."[61] Now this undeniably is an interesting attempt to escape from the sad fact that until 1871 census data gave only place of birth and no indication of the ethnicity of those English-speaking persons born in Canada. The trouble is that for the years 1825–61 Pentland does not tell us how he performed the calculation, but instead only gives anecdotally-based speculation,[62] and then, for his 1871 figure, his entire explanation is as follows:

> The number of persons in Ontario and Quebec who confessed to Irish origin in 1871 was 683,000. This total is estimated to consist of 260,000 Irish Catholics and 425,000 Irish Protestants. *The estimates, which can only be approximate, are reached by balancing origins, religious denominations and places of birth.*[63]

The italics are mine and are meant to emphasize that his explanation is no explanation at all. The authority for the conclusion is not the data, but the author. Again, I suspect that Pentland is roughly correct,[64] but in historical writing, unlike fiction, we do not permit the author to be the primary source of the story.

The examples presented up to this point establish Pentland's fictive proclivities, but consist only of relatively harmless instances of shoddy scholarship.[65] His creativity on these matters either was irrelevant to the force of his argument or, while presently undocumented, is (in my own subjective judgment) apt eventually to be confirmed when the subjects of his *dicta* finally are examined by historians. Pentland's creative propensities, however, shaded into matters on which he *may* have been cheating in his main argument. For example, Pentland had a particularly difficult problem in conceptualizing what the nearness of the United States did to his allegedly abundant labour reserves. The problem was that the United States presented a latent torpedo to his argument, for higher U.S. wages always potentially could draw off enough Canadian workers to destroy any chance of there being an abundance of labour in central Canada. Thus, he admitted in a footnote that it was "true that Canada had the easy way of getting rid of surplus labourers by letting them go south — the province had been cleared of its surplus in 1838."[66] Why, then, did not the Canadian labour reserves evaporate, not only in 1838, but in every year? The closest he came to answering was in another note, stating that there was a "floor placed under Canadian wage rates by the nearness of the United States market."[67] This conceptual confusion — which seemed to imply that the creation of an industrial-capitalist labour market in Canada was dependent as much upon prior developments in the United States as upon immigration to Canada from the British Isles — was not resolved.

Instead, Pentland simply used the United States as a siphon, which drew off ethnic groups whose existence was inconvenient for the purposes of his argument. In particular, in order to make the Irish Catholics his mastercog, Pentland had to get the English out of the picture. (The Scots were too small numerically to function by themselves as an alternative labour reserve.) He dealt with the English in three operations. In one of these, he declared that "the most numerous and important group of English emigrants were industrial workers," who were "distinguished from other immigrant groups by their possession, in their hands and heads, of the most advanced technology of the age."[68] Second, he declared that "the evidence indicates that the majority of the Englishmen who arrived in Canada before 1850 proceeded on to the United States."[69] The reason for this was that Canada had not yet industrialized, so "that most of them who came to Canada before 1850 found no adequate use for their skills and went on to the cities of the United States."[70] Thus, he asserted that only after 1850, when Canada experienced its own industrial revolution, did most of these immigrants stay. Hence, Pentland neatly removed the English as a potential labour reserve: they were skilled and, before 1850, most of them just passed through anyway.

These assertions are literally incredible. Pentland's claim that the evidence indicates that the majority of Englishmen who arrived in Canada before 1850 proceeded on to the U.S. cannot be credited. This is not merely because he did not cite any evidence, but because there is no adequate source of such data on which the assertion could possibly be based. Records of border-crossings into the United States were not kept by Canadian authorities. United States authorities did not begin to make any efforts at recording border-crossings from Canada into the United States until 1853, and then these records were very incomplete and were abandoned completely during the American civil war.[71] Here, Pentland's "fact" is pure fiction.

So, too, is his assertion — again without reference to any body of data — that most English immigrants to Canada were skilled workmen. The only way to substantiate such a claim would be to analyze the census data which Pentland had available to him, a tedious procedure, but one which he could have assayed. Obviously, he had to overcome the *a priori* argument that since farming was the leading occupation in the country it probably was the predominant occupation of any large sub-group. He had to prove not merely the existence of differentials as between various sub-groups, but very large differentials indeed. A modern, large-sample study, which has used the census data which Pentland ignored, has shown that in 1871 (the first census for which ethnicity data are available and certainly not too late to be suggestive for Pentland's period), for persons of English ethnicity, farming was far-and-away the most common occupation (46.9 percent of the male heads of households of the ethnic cohort in Ontario and 43.9 percent in Quebec) and that artisans were only a secondary minority (23.1 percent in Ontario and 17.0 percent in Quebec).[72]

Interestingly, Pentland was nearly silent concerning the possible flow from Canada to the American republic of the one group known to be particularly attracted to that nation: the Irish Catholics. He asserted (again with no reference to evidence) that it is likely that, between 1816 and 1835 (the period of alleged Ulster-Scot dominance), half or more of the Irish immigrants to Canada went to the United States.[73] But then he dropped the notion, for the post-1835 period, when, allegedly, Catholics dominated. The reason for this is obvious. If one allows for the possibility of a considerable drain from Canada to the United States of Irish immigrants — people who Pentland believed were overwhelmingly Roman Catholics — it undermines his notion that great bodies of Irish Catholic workers were trapped in Canada and formed the critical mass in the establishment of the abundant labour reserve of Canadian industrial capitalism. So, to help his argument, Pentland made up fictions about the English workers being largely skilled and having migrated on to the U.S. before 1850, and ignored any possible evidence that the Irish Catholics could have been mobile.

If the "facts" that Pentland created relating to secondary migration to the United States are very much a grey area, they lead us to topics on which his cheating was gross — areas in which his fictional statements demonstrably were both central to his main argument and had such a low probability of being true as to be virtually certainly false. Specifically, four matters will be discussed, in ascending order of importance. Each of these is central to his argument that the Irish Catholics were the ethnic mastercog in creating an alleged abundant labour pool in central Canada.

First, Pentland completely falsified the situation concerning the Irish Protestants of English ancestry. In a breathtakingly dogmatic statement, Pentland asserted that "English Protestant settlers in Ireland preferred the role of landlord and, except for the Quakers, they contributed only modestly to emigration."[74] This claim is important to his argument, because if a significant number of English-background Protestants (the "Anglo-Irish" group which, in practical terms, can be identified with adherents of the Anglican church) left Ireland, then his equation of the great Irish migration of mid-century with an Irish-Catholic migration becomes difficult to maintain. His statement, quoted above (again, he cited no evidence whatsoever to back it up) is almost certainly wrong, on two counts, one empirical, the other theoretical. The first is the more important, and stems from Irish census data. Note what happened to the Irish Anglican population between the first Irish religious census and the next one:

Year	Number of Anglicans
1834	852,064
1861	693,357[75]

The Anglican population, which, because of its superior social position, did not experience a crisis of mortality during the Famine, nevertheless declined sharply. The most likely — but not the only — explanation of this decline in numbers is that many of the Anglicans emigrated. This suggestion ties in with a second, theoretical reason for Pentland's view being so very wrong: immigration studies, from the great Ravenstein onwards, have shown that migrants tend to be a selected group, and this is particularly true of long distance migrants. Put simply, in a bad situation, it is only the better off who can afford to get out. Although Pentland is wholly in error in equating the Anglo-Irish with landlords — the largest groups were farmers, not landlords, and the next largest group were engaged in trade and manufacture, as even a cursory look at the Irish census would have shown him[76] — it is true that they were above average socio-economically. Which is to say that one would expect them to have a high relative propensity to emigrate. One can argue about what proportion they actually comprise of the Irish emigrant stream. The one thing one cannot do, however, is dismiss their existence as part of that stream.[77]

Second, in order to mould the Irish Catholics into his ethnic mastercog, a source of abundant labour, Pentland traduced them with a contempt for the data available to him that is truly magisterial. "The native Irish, a primitive people, were subjected to social and economic conditions that prevented their developing industrial skill or discipline [true enough, they lived mostly in the countryside] and robbed them of morale and enterprise"[78] [certainly untrue]. These primitives, Pentland implied, came mostly from Munster and, later, from Connacht, the most over-populated and economically backward parts of the country.[79] "Proprietorship, in town or country, no doubt struck the Irishman as a different and desirable status, but he hardly aspired to it himself. It was beyond both his ambitions and his wants. It required a capacity for management and a capital, which he had no way to acquire. . . . Above all, it implied a calculating individualist outlook, a divorce from group life, which was difficult for the Irishman to assume."[80] "It is understandable that he should bring his standards to [North] America with him, but it is understandable also that he should earn contempt and dislike by his primitiveness."[81] Now, leaving aside the economic question of whether or not the typical Irish Catholic was capable of accumulating capital, the key point in Pentland's argument is cultural: that the Irish Catholic lacked "capacity for management" and the "calculating individualist outlook:" he was a primitive, tribal man. Given the strength of these assertions, it is a pity that Pentland was unaware of the existence of the published Irish censuses or that, if he was, he did not choose to analyze them, for they contain data which reflect on his beliefs. Failing to look at the Irish censuses directly, he could have conveniently picked up the published works of S.H. Cousens, who, in the early 1960s, published a series of articles in major scholarly journals indicating what the Irish censuses implied about emigration from that country. In particular, Cousens' analysis reveals that Irish migration in the relevant period came not, as one might expect, from the poorest sections of Munster and western Connacht. In fact, the concentration of outward movement came from "north central" Ireland, that is from southern Ulster, especially, and the counties of Leinster and eastern Connacht that border thereon — relatively prosperous parts of the country. More important, from whatever region they came, the emigrants were not in general the nation's "primitives." The truly poor and truly unlucky starved to death; of those who survived, the landless labourer was least likely to be able to provide himself with passage money to the New World; nor could the subsistence farmer. Who, then, made it out? Individuals who had been small tenant farmers, who operated, not subsistence farms, but small commercial operations, who knew how money worked, how to accumulate savings, and had, in many cases, the good sense to sell their last cash crop, pocket the money and, instead of paying the landlord, make a midnight flit to the seacoast and thence to North America. The areas from which the rate of Famine exodus was greatest, north-central Ireland, were areas in which the increase in poor rates (consequent upon local destitution caused by potato failure) fell most heavily upon the tenant farmers. It was these farmers who, making prudent economic calculation, cleared off rather than be ruined. Primitive? Incapable of individualist calculation? If anyone in the western world was capable of making and acting upon calculations of their (and their own immediate family's) advantage, it was the Irish Catholic small tenant farmers who, seeing economic ruin as inevitable if they stayed in Ireland, hied across the sea.[82]

Third, crucial confirmation that Pentland was wildly fantasizing in his assessment of the limited abilities and cultural propensities of the Irish Catholics is found in his categorical statements about their residential and occupational pattern in Canada: "Irish Catholics congregated in cities and on canals, whereas other groups disappeared into the back country. . . ."[83] "In fact, they showed almost no interest in farms."[84] Why did they avoid agriculture specifically and live in the country generally? Because, Pentland says, the Irishman had had a bad experience with farming in the Old Country and, further, because proprietorship, whether in the town or in the country, was beyond his capacity for management and his capital.[85] These reasons are fascinating, particularly because they are used to explain a fictional situation, one that Pentland created out of whole cloth and, as is the case with his other sorties into pure fiction, necessarily without historical documentation. Had Pentland spent any time examining the published census data for central Canada, he would have found that the overwhelming majority of Irish Catholics lived outside of the major cities and mostly in the countryside. My study of the Ontario census data in 1871, based on primary information easily accessible to Pentland, revealed the following profile:[86]

Persons of Irish Catholic Ethnicity	Percentage
Living in cities (average size 26,517)	14.7
Living in towns and villages (average size 2,148)	19.0
Living in rural areas	66.3

Admittedly, the 1871 data can only be crudely suggestive of the situation at mid-century, but the line of Pentland's argument (a chronology of increasing industrialization from mid-century onwards), means that by his own lights there should have been an even higher proportion of Irish Catholics in rural areas earlier in the century. And, had he done any analysis based on the manuscript census data (available to him during the period in which he was revising the thesis for publication), he would have found that far and away the most common occupation for persons of Irish Catholic ethnicity was farming: 44.3 percent of persons of Irish Catholic background were farmers in the Dominion of Canada in 1871, well over twice the combined number of labourers and servants.[87] The reason why Pentland had to fabricate his facts about the Irish Catholics being over-whelmingly urban and non-agricultural is simply that: if the huge majority of them were not found in his putative industrial (urban) reserve army of labour, his whole theory was discredited.

Finally, Pentland also fabricated a description of the occupational behaviour of those Irish Catholics who did indeed settle in the cities and, as was his practice, cited no direct data, even census data, for this fictional maundering. "Irish Catholics chose the city [already demonstrated to be false] because of their preference in employment, as British artisans did. But the Irish did not aspire to be merchants or artisans. . . . What the great majority of Irishmen sought was employment at labouring jobs in the company of their fellows."[88] In many cases even had the Irish Catholic aspired to proprietorship "it required a capacity for management and a capital, which he had no way to acquire."[89] Here again, one has a statement of a fictional and false "fact," coupled with a racist explanation for the "fact." If the Irish Catholics had neither the desire nor the ability to rise above labouring jobs held in the company of their fellows, then it is very hard to understand how, considering the Dominion of Canada as a whole, in 1871, males of Irish Catholic ethnicity had a slightly higher proportion of merchants than did the Irish Protestant, or the Scottish or the German cohorts, had a somewhat higher proportion of white collar workers than did the Irish Protestants, and had a proportion of artisans equal to that of the Scottish and markedly higher than that of the Germans and somewhat above the Irish Protestants. And, in the rural areas (where, according to Pentland, they could not cope) the Irish Catholics had a slightly greater proportion in the bourgeois occupations than did either the Scots or the Germans.[90]

Yet, for such arcane mental operations is H. Clare Pentland said to be the father of the new Canadian social history.

(V)

No, my presentation of the parallel structures of the historical sections of *Mein Kampf* and of *Labour and Capital in Canada 1650–1860* was not outrageous after all.

Initially, I showed that Pentland's mode of historial explication was structurally congruent with an archetypically racist historical argument. Then, I examined the possibility that it was the contours of the historical data, not racism, that determined the shape of Pentland's argument. Historical data, however, were found to have had little to do with most parts of Pentland's argument and demonstrably Pentland had not performed as a competent historian. Indeed, he had made up most of his most important "facts" and then used his racist concepts to "explain" them. (Of course, as the Hitlerian template reminds us, the racist prejudices almost certainly were antecedent and the "facts" fabricated to fit them.) What we have in Pentland's book is not history but social pathology.

Can the analysis be tidied up, the racism taken out and the rest (whatever that might mean) accepted as valid? Is it possible to be embarrassed at the racism in Pentland's work, but to shrug it off as regrettable, but as not affecting his fundamental analysis?[91]

This will not do. The racism cannot be tidied up; the racism cannot be cauterized. As I have shown in detail, racism determined both Pentland's alleged data and his explication of those data. *Racism was his structure* and, once that racism is removed from his book, the whole argument collapses, a tatty rag dummy without a skeleton.

Will Canadian social historians face up to this point? Some few perhaps, but the "new" social historians are apt to fight hard, and like disappointed millenarians waiting overlong on a mountain-top for a bent prophecy to come true, they are more likely to expend great ingenuity in proving that the problem is not with the Scriptures but with the Word having been misread by the unworthy. In this regard, there is great wisdom in John Le Carré's observation that, if you have been sold a fake painting, "the more you pay for it, the less inclined you are to doubt it."[92] The investment in Pentland's credibility has been great on the part of many Canadian social historians and no one likes to be confronted with his own gullibility. Still, it must be faced. Until the influence of *Labour and Capital in Canada 1650–*

1860 is expunged, racism will lurk in the inner core of the new Canadian social history, like cancer cells deep within bone marrow.[93]

(VI)

That judgement, true to the record though it be, is too final. History as a discipline has great recuperative powers and even our profession's worst failures can be put to positive use as lessons that will help us to do a better job in our collective enterprise in the future. H. Clare Pentland's book can be employed as a pedagogical tool and as a source of evidence of cultural attitudes of a clarity we rarely find.

As a teaching device, the volume can, and should, be assigned to undergraduate and graduate students alike, as the basis for teaching them to recognize the hall-marks and devices of racist thinking and thus how to avoid being gulled. Obviously, we would like our students to have continually poised on their lips the phrase, "what is the evidence?" concerning any statement of fact, but in practical terms they cannot be expected to check everything. In racist writing, however, there are certain code phrases, inevitably highly value-loaded, that should set them immediately to checking footnotes and watching closely for solecisms. These racist phrases sometimes are hard to catch. Two practical suggestions might help. One of these is for the student to substitute another term, a neutral one, for the ethnic or racial group about which some statement is made. For instance, if one substitutes "women" for Celtic peasants in Pentland's section of Celtic inherences, one would have something like the following: "The tone of such societies is antagonistic to change and to capitalistic rationality. [Women] are incapable of saving themselves — though they might postpone catastrophe by war, or by serving in the British Army, or by finding more land under seigneurial tenure."[94] Perhaps the original statement is true, but certainly it deserves checking. Second, the student can identify potentially racist thinking by substituting a derogatory racist epithet for whatever the original reference group is; and if the epithet fits nicely into the sentence, then the student should start digging into the footnotes, and doing so sceptically. The following sentences from Pentland involve substitution. "Some of the [niggers'] misery could have been relieved, it is true if he had been less inept, indolent and improvident." "Thus, [the wops] would do anything to get land except save for it." "It may be wondered whether physical weakness was not an important reason why the [Jewboys] did not seek the heavy work or canal construction, and why employers did not want them. . . ."[95]

Undeniably, differences do exist as between ethnic groups and these are important objects of historical investigation. Once students start checking value-loaded statements, they can be taught — using Pentland as a case study — how to notice the lateral shifts in meaning which can twist potentially useful statements of ethnic diversity into racist stereotypes. Every statement concerning the behaviour of an ethnic group necessarily must be a statistical statement, either implicitly or explicitly, and, once that statistical base is obscured, a racist stereotype replaces it. Thus, it is useful (providing the evidence is cited) to say that "Most Swedes are blonde," or, better, that "Fifty-one per cent of all Swedes surveyed in a large sample were blonde." But it is a massive distortion in meaning, suddenly to start talking about "the blonde Swedes" as if the being Swedish and being blonde are necessarily synonymous. Sometimes it is necessary for an historian to write *as if* an ethnic group were a single phenomenon, but every time that is done there is a danger of sliding into stereotyping. In practical terms, three simple rules can guide students. First, every time a racial or ethnic group is personalized into a single figure, closely examine the data ("The Irishman was superstitious rather than religious").[96] Second, unless the data base is extremely good, generalities that are presented as absolutes should be viewed as possible racist stereotypes ("In the cities, too, the Irish remained peasants").[97] Third, beware of any statement concerning what "most," "the majority," or even "many" of any large body of people did, especially if that body is a racial or ethnic group, when such statements are based on anecdotal rather than statistical evidence. Pentland, for example, strung together skeins of quotations about the various inadequacies of the French Canadians and the Irish.[98] These were merely nineteenth-century stereotyped comments which happened to fit his twentieth-century racism. Anecdotal evidence can be useful as illustrative material, but the only way to establish a fact about a large body of people is to have a large body of data that deals directly with the behaviour of the people involved. And, in large populations, these data can best be described statistically. As Pentland's book illustrates, no amount of anecdotal material (such as contemporaries stating that "the Irish" in central Canada were urban slum rats) can overcome the myriad census data which established the opposite (that, on the contrary, most of them lived in the rural areas).

One further lesson can be taught, using Pentland as a case study. This is to pay special heed, to be particularly sceptical, when a writer uses "plantation vocabulary." By this, I mean the kind of smarmy, patronizing "understanding" that permitted a pious ante-bellum slave owner to note that it was a shame that his "boys" were so backward, but it was not their fault, and no surprise, considering what they came from. This plantation vocabulary permits a writer to propagate stereotypes and racist ways of thinking and simultaneously to make it appear as if he, a person of wide sympathies, has nothing to do with this regrettable racism. Pentland played this trick again and again, as when he explained that "the Irishman [singly personified once again] . . . was far below the European standard both in living and working. It is understandable [note that word] that he should bring his standards to America with him, but it is understandable also that he should earn contempt and dislike by his primitiveness" [an endorsement of a racist stereotype].[99]

These pedagogical uses aside, Pentland's book has potential value to our profession as a rare form of historical document in Canadian ethnic history. One of the hardest things for social historians to trace is what happens to the certain attitudes of members of an ethnic group in their second, third, and subsequent generations. Immigrants bring with them attitudes, prejudices, and beliefs about the nature of the world, and these undoubtedly are modified by their experience in Canada, but something is passed on to their children, and, in further modified form, to their children's children. These attitudes, modified through the generations, persist like an underground stream, influencing the outlook and behaviour of the immigrants' Canadian-born descendants long after the later generation have ceased to think of themselves as anything but primarily "Canadian." The valuable thing about H.C. Pentland's book is that it potentially is a case study of actual behaviour on the nature of which we have precise empirical evidence (he wrote a book), that well may relate to the perdurance of certain ethnic attitudes. Pentland was a fifth generation Canadian (that is, the fourth generation born in Canada), a descendant of an Ulster-Scots weaver from County Down who came to Upper Canada in 1821.[100] The amazing point is that H. Clare Pentland, writing in the 1950s, 60s, and 70s, highly educated, influenced by at least two major schools of European economic history, evidenced the same ethnic cosmology, the same prejudices, that were common amongst the Ulster-Scots of the cottier-weaver class in the three or four decades after the abortive 1798 Rising: an affinity for the lowland Scots, a contempt for the highland Catholics (one sub-group of which was perched on the north Antrim plateau), a dislike of the French (who had continually made alliances with the treasonous Irish natives), a mixed admiration-dislike of the "real" English (founded on their being perceived as simultaneously successful and arrogant), an equally uneasy feeling about the people of English descent who lived in Ireland (fellow Protestants, but too often anti-Presbyterian), and, most of all, an abiding hatred and contempt for the Irish Catholics, a group seen as scheming, dishonest, feckless, priest-ridden, superstitious, and, in sum, a body of backward pagans.[101] Pentland's book seems to be an important piece of evidence concerning the perdurance of a specific ethnic cosmology, running strong, just below the surface, for a century and a half in the New World, and one awaits a biographical study of Pentland that will indicate in detail the precise mechanisms in his family by which these Ulster-Scots cultural values were preserved.

Pentland's book provides a second, almost equally rare opportunity to document something about the unstated, but fundamental, attitudes of English-Canadian historians. Just as Pentland's behaviour (writing a book) apparently yielded empirical evidence of certain enduring ethnic attitudes, so the way in which the book has been reviewed, footnoted as authoritative, and assimilated into other books (the writing of which is a form of behaviour that leaves empirical evidence about the respective writers) tells us a great deal about the underlying attitudes of those members of the historical profession who have dealt with Pentland's study. Here the salient points are that, despite Pentland's virulent racism and his fabricating many points of evidence to fit that racism, many Canadian scholars have assimilated Pentland's world view. Only a few have quibbled around the edges concerning that racism, and no one has pointed out directly and in detail the outrageous nature of his racist case. Here, one thinks of Sherlock Holmes' famous case in which the key evidence was the dog-that-didn't-bark. Why did no dog bark? Manifestly, a thorough study of the usage and assimilation of Pentland's work by Canadian historians is in order, and to that future investigator I would suggest two hypotheses that, amongst others, will deserve investigation. The first of these is simply that, alas, a quiet and pervasive racism remains within segments of the English-Canadian historical profession. Second, that one historical determinant of that racism seems to have been the nineteenth-century Ulster-Scots ethnic cohort. If it is noteworthy that H. Clare Pentland seems to have carried over the ethnic cosmology of his early nineteenth-century Ulster-Scots forebears, it is truly astounding that the hegemony of those values was tacitly accepted in the 1980s by English-Canadian social historians, not all of whom, I fancy, have strong Ulster-Scots roots. Ironically, in his very racism, H. Clare

Pentland may have provided us with a valuable indicator of the saliency of the Ulster-Scots tradition in the making up of modern English-Canadian culture.

Finally, the sanctification of Pentland as the putative founding father of the new Canadian social history reminds one that nationalism is merely the more respectable cousin of racism and, almost inevitably, the two are tied together. One does not find the one without the other being close by. Remember that, in part, Bryan Palmer was goaded into his encomium for Pentland by critics of the new Canadian social history who felt that, if the new social historians had learned their trade at the feet of a foreigner, their work was somehow suspect. Thus did the demands of Canadian nationalism lead to an affirmation of a particularly opprobrious form of English-Canadian racism.

Who, then, is the seminal figure to whom one may trace most of that which is good, humane, and competent in the new Canadian social history? Of course it is E.P. Thompson, and that is a heritage for which no one need apologize. If, after reading Thompson's writings, one wants to understand more about them, one should read Bryan Palmer's *The Making of E.P. Thompson: Marxism, Humanism, and History*.[102] Now *that* is a good book.

Chapter Six.
Mass Schooling in Ontario: the Irish and "English Canadian" Popular Culture

Introduction

Slightly more than fifty years ago, William Sherwood Fox suggested, in an undeservedly neglected article, that one could find at least partial explanation of the character of the people of Ontario and of those western provinces most influenced by Ontario, by examining the school books used by the mass of children from the late 1840s to the late 1870s.[1] The Ontario school books, in their way quintessentially and paradoxically Upper Canadian, were the "Irish National Readers," a sequential series of texts that were widely used in the English-speaking world, except for the United States of America. In pointing to the use of these books in the common schools of Ontario, William Fox implicitly raised two extremely difficult historical matters. The first of these is the extent and nature of cultural transfer from the Old World to the New. Most historians pay passing lip-service to the undeniable fact that much of Canada's nineteenth-century culture was directly derivative from transatlantic roots, but then quickly turn to indigenous Canadian developments. This is sensible, if misleading historically, for it is notoriously difficult to document the precise extent of the cultural transfer and the precise mechanisms of its having occurred. The second problem tacitly recognized by Fox is that it is very difficult to ascertain the extent to which the "official" version of the popular culture (as represented by such things as school curricula, preambles to legal statutes, and civic proclamations) actually was assimilated into the everyday popular culture of the common people.

In reflecting on these matters, it is helpful to keep in mind an appropriate visual image: the patterns produced by the extraordinary snakes, dragons, and mythic beasts, twisted and elongated, which spiral through Celtic art work, and are familiar in such artifacts as the Tara Brooch and the Book of Kells. Which is to say: the linear rhetorical mode so beloved in political historiography (wherein, for example, one cabinet member jawbones another into supporting a given measure and thus tips the balance so that a bill eventually becomes a statute) does not pertain in matters of this sort. Instead, one has a series of intertwining motifs, each comprising part of a pattern that is convincing only in its totality.

In the present study, one of these almost circular motifs stems from the fact that, undeniably, the popular culture of nineteenth-century Ontario was influenced by several hundred thousand children having been forced to read Irish school books. Simultaneously, however, it is also true to say that the choice, use, and acceptance of these books in themselves were determined to a considerable degree by the pre-existent character of the popular culture of the people of Ontario. Although the Irish national school books are at the heart of any discussion of cultural transfer from Ireland to Ontario, other related matters follow the same perpetually intertwining pattern. For instance, it will be shown that not only did the Ontario educational network depend upon Irish school books, but, also, that the fundamental structural lineaments were imported from Ireland. Again, when one tries to determine to what extent the importation was the reflection of indigenous Canadian values or to what degree it changed these values, one encounters an infinite regression. It is particularly striking that the evolution of the administrative structure of the schools of Ontario followed a set of paradigms previously set down in Ireland. On one level, this occurred as the school system, which was intended to be non-denominational, actually evolved into a dual-confessional network, exactly as had happened in Ireland. Was this because denominationalism was inherent in the Irish prototype, because of specifically Upper Canadian conditions, or both, the one cause reinforcing the other? Again, one has a Celtic conundrum, the snake swallowing its own tail. And, amongst all these conditions, it will be shown that the most surprising pattern, the one which is virtually uncanny, is the way in which individual Canadian actors in the drama took up positions that had very specific, but earlier, counterparts in transactions overseas.[2]

Part I
(I)

Adolphus Egerton Ryerson was the key to the whole situation, and he surmounted the scene like the inaugural majuscule on an illuminated carpet page. Ryerson's career is too well known to require recapitulation:[3] suffice it to say that from 1844 to 1876 he was the animator, controller, and guardian of a system of mass elementary schooling that was formed in his own image, although not entirely of his own devise.[4] To understand Ryerson's role, it is important that one adopt not the narrow perspective of personal biography (interesting though his life is) but recognize that he was the active agent in one of the major transatlantic cultural transplantations of the nineteenth century.

As a person of national prominence long before his appointment to the education department, Ryerson had a great deal of bargaining power and was able to stipulate that his term of office should begin with his making a perambulation of various spots of interest to an educationalist, in the

United States, and, more important, across the Atlantic. Ryerson left for his European tour at the end of October 1844, returned in December 1845, and thereupon issued a set of lucubrations that clearly were intended to be monumental — the famous 1846 *Report on a System of Public Elementary Instruction for Upper Canada* — and simultaneously he began his career as a provincial educational administrator, one marked by extraordinary devotion to duty, an administrative style that was at times teeth-rattlingly vigorous and outspokenly tactless, and by undeniable successes and equally undeniable failures.

The jurisdiction which Ryerson left in the fall of 1844 (for convenience, "Ontario" rather than the little-used "Canada West" is here adopted) possessed a signal characteristic that was a crucial aspect of the context for Ryerson's investigations and later administration: the largest ethnic group was the Irish. This had probably been true as early as the 1830s and in all probability continued to be the case into the late 1880s.[5] In 1871, to take the first Dominion Census, persons of Irish ethnicity comprised 34.5 percent of the Ontario population, Scots 20.3 percent, and English and Welsh 27.1 percent.[6]

Although Ryerson's tour undoubtedly helped him to make up his mind concerning how to structure Ontario's educational system, it is important to realize that his mind was not a *tabula rasa*. He was well informed about various nations' educational systems and showed a leaning towards the Irish and the English examples. Even before leaving Canada, he had suggested to the government that, in addition to a superintendent of education, "there should be a board of education appointed for Canada West, similar to the Educational Commissioners for Ireland, or the Educational Commission of the Privy Council in England."[7]

Ryerson's tour included most western European countries, but his investigations began and ended with the United Kingdom. Significantly, Ryerson's *entrée* into the educational establishments of the British Isles and of Europe was provided by Lord Stanley, the United Kingdom's Colonial Secretary.[8] Stanley had an informed interest in education and, as Chief Secretary for Ireland under Earl Grey from 1830–33, had been responsible for forming the Irish national system of education. Stanley's famous "Letter" of October 1831 to the Duke of Leinster, which set out the ground rules for the establishment of the Irish educational system, was such an important public document that into the 1870s it frequently was reprinted in United Kingdom parliamentary papers.[9] Thus, Stanley's cordiality to Ryerson was more than simply the *noblesse oblige* of the Colonial Secretary to one of the functionaries of the Empire; in Ryerson's fulsome letter-of-thanks to Stanley for his having granted an interview, Ryerson mentioned several detailed educational matters, obviously as addenda to what had been a discussion of educational systems.[10]

Upon his return to Ontario, Ryerson began producing a document which he fully intended would have the same place in Canadian history as Lord Stanley's "Letter" had had in Irish history: it would serve as the *magna carta* of an entire educational system. Ryerson's *Report* of 1846[11] is an impressive document, stylistically pleasing, and approaching 200 pages in length. The document mixes a certain worldliness, as in Ryerson's knowledgeable references to transatlantic men and systems, with an earnest, palpably sincere, concern for the moral and intellectual uplifting of his fellow Upper Canadians. To modern academic readers, the *Report* seems in part to be an example of a now generally unfamiliar genre, the extended pastoral homily, and at points one can easily imagine Ryerson delivering it as a three-day sermon. Much more familiar, however, is the other genre to which the *Report* conforms: the padded undergraduate term paper.

That is not said flippantly. Ryerson had spent more than a year travelling while being paid a government salary and had taken up the time of hundreds of educational officials in a score of countries. Thus, of necessity, he dropped names and appeared to take seriously the myriad examples of his former hosts. This served the dual purpose of courteously indicating to foreign officials and governments that their time with him had not been wasted, and of showing Canadian officials that he had not been in Europe as an Upper Canadian Gil Blas. All this rodomontade, however, disguised the fact that his central ideas, like the points made in the term paper of a lazy undergraduate, came almost entirely from one source. Ryerson was importing, not just the school books, but the entire Irish national system of education into Upper Canada.

If one goes behind Ryerson's *Report* (which, in places, was masterful in its ambiguity) and looks at the 1846 Common Schools Act that he drafted and, more important, at the day-to-day administrative system he created, one finds that two structural principles underlay his system. These were the centralization of a great deal of authority in the person of the superintendent of education for the province, and, paradoxically, a high degree of autonomy at the local level. At the top, along with Ryerson and his ever-growing staff, was a Board of Education — later renamed the Council of Public Instruction — for Ontario. It will be recalled that, even before going abroad on his tour, Ryerson had favoured having such a board of distinguished advisors on either the English or the Irish model. In Dublin he conversed with several of the Irish commissioners of national education[12] and manifestly came to prefer the Irish to the English model. This was only sensible, for the English body, being a sub-committee of the Privy Council of the United Kingdom, was not entirely appropriate to British North America. In his *Report* of 1846, Ryerson made reference to the Irish board[13] and, much later in the document, he recommended the creation of such a body for Ontario. Indeed, because the printing of the *Report* had been overtaken by events, he was able to add a footnote to this recommendation to the effect that such a board already had been created.[14] This was possible because the 1846 Education Act, drafted by Ryerson, included provisions for a seven-member board (one of whom would be the superintendent of education) with various duties relating to setting school texts, establishing normal schools, and advising the superintendent on policy matters.[15] Despite this official mandate, the board was little more than a front for

Ryerson, useful for reducing religious tensions and conciliating politicians, and for giving some of his more arbitrary decisions an aura of collective reason. In 1849, when proposed revisions in the school laws threatened to make the superintendent of education the agent of the board, rather than vice versa, Ryerson complained vigorously to Robert Baldwin of the prospect of seeing himself "deprived of the protection and advantage of the application of the principle of responsible government as applied to every other head of Department, and made the subordinate agent of a Board which I have originated, and the members of which I have had the honour to recommend for appointment."[16] In this instance, Ryerson won. At the centre of the system, power remained concentrated, wonderfully.[17]

Ryerson, who had spent so many years in the peripatetic Methodist cause, knew the province well. It was not Prussia or France; its population was highly dispersed and overwhelmingly rural, and the civic infrastructure was weak as compared to that of the continental countries. Ryerson had to rely on hundreds and hundreds of local bodies, created for the express purpose of forming schools in myriad individual localities — 2,500, rising to 4,400 by 1870. Trustees of each "school section" held legal title to the schools as pieces of real property, and they chose the teachers.[18] Local control of the schools was no mere theoretical construct. An impressive body of research by Professor R.D. Gidney has shown that, in day-to-day management, the schools were under close local supervision. Although there was a mass of bureaucratic paper circulated from Ryerson's headquarters in Toronto, especially after 1850, Gidney's work clearly establishes that central policies had to be consonant with the wishes of the local management or those policies came to nought.[19] From the very beginning, Ryerson recognized that the local powers had to be conciliated and cajoled, and he made five tours of the province — in 1847, 1853, 1860, 1866, and 1869 — conducting one- or two-day meetings with school trustees, explaining his policies, and encouraging their compliance with his wishes.[20]

The seemingly paradoxical mixture of centralization and localism did not involve mere similarity to the Irish national system of education; it came as close as was realistically possible to being its reincarnation in the New World. The Irish system, formed in 1831,[21] involved a centralized structure, consisting of a "resident commissioner" and an unpaid board, "the commissioners of national education," who collectively served as the central control agency in Ireland, just as Ryerson and his board did in Ontario.[22] And, at the local level in Ireland, a great deal of power — most importantly, the ownership of school property and the appointment of teachers — was in the hands of local trustees who were very jealous of their prerogatives.[23]

Because, from earliest days, one of the hallowed myths of the New World has been that it was, and is, radically different from the Old, Ryerson's importation of the Irish administrative structure might at first seem to have been quixotic or unrealistic. Quite the contrary: the importation was extremely shrewd, for, from the viewpoint of someone creating a school network, Ireland and Ontario in the middle of the nineteenth century were remarkably similar. In the first place, each was under colonial rule, albeit for quite different reasons. Ireland, despite formally being a part of the United Kingdom, actually was governed in the nineteenth century as a colony, meaning, among other things, that there was a high degree of central government authority. Moreover, in Ontario, as in Ireland (but for very different reasons), there was a relatively weak tradition of local government, at least by the comparative standards of Scotland, England, or the United States. The Irish population was overwhelmingly rural, as was the case in Ontario. Thus, in Ireland, and later in Ontario, the natural solution was to combine centralized authority with new civic agencies to manage schools in each local, usually rural, area. With considerable prescience, Egerton Ryerson had recognized that the Irish pattern fit.

Having introduced the basic structure of the Irish educational pattern, Ryerson had also imported its chief problem, a notoriously weak system of "middle management." Obviously, given the potentially incompatible principles of administrative centralization and of extreme localism, one needed a flexible and efficient intermediate means of reconciling the two levels of management, the central and the local. One alternative, employed in England and Wales (in a rather dissimilar situation), was for the central authorities to give money to various nationally organized voluntary societies which would then meter out the funds and, perforce, strongly influence the actions of local school managers. The religious heterogeneity of Ontario, and particularly the general sensitivity concerning anything that looked like an endowment of a religious establishment, precluded the adoption of this approach by Ryerson.

Another method of establishing a middle level management was to do as the Irish commissioners of national education had done and create an "inspectorate," whose members moved about the countryside, visited schools, checked to see that major regulations were obeyed, and reported back directly to the commissioners in Dublin. The employment of inspectors (which certainly was not unique to Ireland) was something of an afterthought by the educational planners and was added as a functional arm of the Irish system six months after the system itself was created, and then only by copying the procedures of a Protestant educational society, the Kildare Place Society. The Irish inspectorate grew from eight men in 1832 to 32 in 1844 and, by 1847, involved four "head inspectors" as supervisors over the ordinary inspectors. The Irish system of inspection was only moderately successful. The inspectorate was not strong enough organizationally to serve as efficient middle managers, and, instead of facilitating communication between the upper and lower levels of administration, actually came to impede it. In the mid 1850s, it was found that the Irish inspectors were a full year behind in transacting business in their central office: this included 11,000 reports that had been filed but not dealt with and involved whole rooms filled with unread reports.[24]

Nevertheless, when Ryerson surveyed the Irish system in

the mid-1840s, these failings were not yet apparent. In his 1846 *Report,* Ryerson asserted that "there is no class of officers in the whole machinery of elementary instruction on whom so much depends for its efficient and successful working, as upon the local Superintendents or Inspectors."[25] Ryerson's perception of the superintendents as middle managers is clear in an analogy he presented: "What the Government is to the system, and what the Teacher is to the School, the local Inspector or Superintendent should be within the limits of his District."[26] The 1846 Common Schools Act and the amending act of 1847 both provided for the positions of superintendents, but with a provision that sharply undercut their value as middle managers: superintendents in the rural districts were to be appointed by the district councils and the board of school trustees in the towns and cities.[27] Ryerson accepted these provisions against his will, for in effect they meant that, lacking as he did the power to appoint and dismiss the superintendents, he had less influence over them than did the local politicians.[28] To make matters worse, even after 1850, when the schools act of that year permitted the county councils (which had replaced the district councils) to appoint a single school superintendent for each county instead of numerous township-based superintendents, as previously had been the practice, most civic authorities chose to multiply jobs, by appointing several part-time township superintendents. Instead of having a cadre of two or three score full-time inspectors dependent on his administrative will, Ryerson had to work through more than 300 part-time locals, each of whom owed his job to the local county council.[29]

Thus, Egerton Ryerson found that in trying to employ the same solution to his "middle management" problems that the Irish had tried — the employment of school inspectors — the result was similar: at best, moderate success.

(3)

Of course, there are other ways for a central educational authority to overcome the lack of a truly effective set of intermediate managers, and one of these is to control the myriad authorities from inside. For example, the Irish commissioners of national education had shown that they could strongly influence what went on in thousands of individual classrooms, by influencing the way in which young teachers were taught to do their job. In 1834 they had established a training department which, by the time of Ryerson's visit, was operating a normal school in Dublin with several full-time staff and suitable facilities. In addition, they had obtained in 1837 government approval for a network of model schools to cover all of Ireland. These plans did not move forward until mid-1845, just the time of Ryerson's visit. The Irish commissioners planned, and in the late 1840s introduced, rudimentary certification requirements, in the form of special examinations for those model school pupils who planned to enter teaching.[30] A single normal school, a set of model schools, and basic teacher certification — this was the Irish formula.

On his grand tour, Ryerson visited normal schools in the United States and on the Continent, but in his judgement none came up to the standard of those in the British Isles. "I have visited Dublin, Glasgow and Edinburgh," he wrote, "where I had an opportunity of inspecting by far the best normal and model schools I have anywhere seen, either in England or the United States."[31] The Scottish normal schools impressed Ryerson, but the recent schism in the Church of Scotland made the Scottish situation an inappropriate model. The English normal schools were impressive. "The three normal schools with their accompanying model schools which I had visited in London are excellent ... but they are by no means so complete in their organization, or so advanced in their operations as is the establishment of the Irish national board in Dublin which has, I think, the pre-eminence over all similar establishments in the British Dominions."[32] In his *Report,* Ryerson put a normal school at the top of his list of requirements.[33]

In fact, Ryerson had assimilated not only the Irish model for a normal school, but all three aspects of the Irish formula. His 1846 act provided not only for a central normal school under his own control, but made it permissible for school districts to establish model schools and gave district school superintendents the power to certify as fit or unfit all teaching candidates, a first step in what eventually was planned to be a full system of teacher certification, one tied to a teacher training network.[34]

Significantly, not only did Ryerson import the Irish formula for training teachers, but he hired their personnel. In 1846, when searching for an appropriate headmaster for his projected normal school in Toronto, Ryerson wrote to the Irish commissioners of national education for a suggestion and gladly accepted their nominee: John Rintoul, a Scot, who was the deputy head of the Dublin normal school. Rintoul's wife took ill, however, and he hesitated for the better part of a year, before turning down the proferred Toronto headmastership in June 1847.[35] This set Ryerson back, and explains why the Toronto normal school did not open until later in 1847.[36] Ryerson wrote to the Irish commissioners again asking for help, and they responded with the gracious promptitude of a mission board answering a desperate appeal for help from the darkest foreign lands. This time they sent Thomas Jaffray Robertson, an M.A. of Trinity College, Dublin, and an able man: he had been created the first "head inspector" of the Irish national educational system, as well as having served in the Dublin training college. This ended Ryerson's search for a headmaster, and he was able to open his training college in early November 1847.[37]

An arresting confirmation of the importance of the Irish mode of teacher training in Ryerson's Ontario system involved John George Hodgins, who for long years served as Ryerson's Number Two in the system. Hodgins, born in Dublin, had come to Canada while young. He studied under Ryerson at Victoria College, and, as early as the spring of 1843, Ryerson seems to have been grooming him as a potential assistant for the time when, as then seemed probable, he would take over the Ontario school system. In the spring of 1845, Ryerson sought permission to appoint Hodgins "clerk" of the new educational establishment.[38] As training for work as Ryerson's assistant, Hodgins was sent to the Dublin normal school for six months, and there he not only learned the Irish methods of teaching and administration and became familiar with their unique series of school texts, but made some valuable personal contacts. Hodgins daily visited the central administration offices of the Irish education commissioners and formed "a most agreeable acquaintance with the Right Honorable Alexander Macdonnell."[39] Macdonnell, at one time chief clerk in the Office of the Chief Secretary for Ireland (the key administrative agents of the Irish government), had become in 1838 the "resident commissioner" of Irish education, which meant that he held the most important civil service appointment in the educational system.[40] Alexander Macdonnell was an Anglican, but, crucially, he was a relative of Bishop Macdonnell, the senior Roman Catholic prelate in Ontario,[41] and, as will be discussed later, amiable relations with the Catholic church were all-important to the success of Ryerson's educational designs.[42]

(4)

By now, some of the reasons why the Irish National Readers became one of the components of the official culture of English-Canadians in Ontario should be clear. Ryerson had imported an educational structure very similar (albeit not quite identical) to the Irish one, and with it he had introduced the Irish problem of an attenuated and weak level of middle management. As a means of solving this Irish problem he had tried two answers employed in Ireland — a school inspectorate and influencing of school teachers by training and certification procedures. But at the heart of the Irish system in the Old Country was another set of mechanisms: a set of school books which, while not compulsory, were so educationally attractive and so cheap that they were almost universally employed. In Ontario, uniform school books were a way for a central administration to overcome the fissiparous tendencies of the 2,500 odd school boards with whom Ryerson had to deal (a number that had risen to

4,400 by 1870). This does *not* explain why Ryerson chose the Irish books, but it does indicate why he would have strong motives to adopt some set of uniform text books.

In point of fact, there were two further compelling reasons that made the Irish books the only real possibility. First, educationally, they probably were the best set of basic texts in the English language and, almost certainly, were the most attractive in the British Empire. Second, the content of the books was particularly appropriate to the ethnic configurations of mid-nineteenth-century Ontario.

Consider the matter of quality.[43] The Irish National Readers provided a sequential, graded system of instruction from infant classes to what now would be considered secondary schooling. These characteristics are easily stated, but the rarity of these virtues in books of the first half of the nineteenth century must be under-scored. Most sets of school books of the time were hit-and-miss affairs, not uniform in approach or presentation, and often there were gaps between one book and the next. The Irish books, virtually alone in their time, provided a ladder of learning through which a working-class child not only could acquire literacy, but could move smoothly into literary and scientific topics previously reserved solely for the middle classes. The merit of these books became especially well-known in England. One witness before the 1837 select committee on Irish education, a man familiar with the books used by the voluntary societies in England, testified: "I think they are far superior to any books I ever saw, and I have sent down some specimens of them to the towns with which I am connected in the north; and it has been so generally the persuasion of everyone, that I know one schoolmaster of an extensive national school who at his own expense has sent up and bought a set of them."[44] A conservative estimate indicates that nearly one million Irish school books were being used in England in 1859.[45] In 1861, the members of the Royal Commission on Popular Education in England were forced to admit that the Irish national school texts were the most popular and widely used set of books in English schools.[46]

Ryerson became convinced of the superiority of the Irish books when on his educational grand tour:

> While in Scotland, conversing with one of the ablest teachers there — if not the ablest I have ever met in any country — Mr. Oliphant, Master of the Free Church Normal School in Edinburgh, I asked him what series of Elementary School Books he preferred: He promptly replied, the Books published by the Irish National Board; that, although from early use and association, he was attached to Thompson's, yet he had used the Irish National School Books for two years and preferred them to all others that he had ever seen. The school books of the Irish National Board are coming into extensive use, both in England and Scotland, as well as in Ireland, published under such auspices, and thus tested and recommended, they may be safely and advantageously introduced into our Canadian Schools.[47]

Whether or not the Irish National Readers were as educationally superior to the dominant American primers, the McGuffey's Readers, as they were to their English and Scottish rivals is not clear, but the point is moot: the political conservatism of Ontario generally, and Ryerson's own loyalty to the British Empire, meant that, although American books might be tolerated for a time in individual schools, they could not be made a part of a centrally-imposed province-wide curriculum.[48]

In his 1846 *Report,* Ryerson mentioned approvingly the text-book policies of France, Prussia, and England, but reserved his strongest accolades for the Irish books. The context of that praise is salient: he viewed the Irish books not only as educationally desirable but, equally, as helping to solve the administration problem of dealing with hundreds of local educational satrapies. He used the United States — in particular Connecticut, where no fewer than 204 different sorts of school books were in use — as his case-to-be-avoided. In contrast to their centrifugal tendencies, he recommended that "the responsible and delicate and difficult task of selecting and recommending books for Schools can, I think, be more judiciously and satisfactorily performed by a provincial Board or Council than by any individual Superintendent."[49] And Ryerson, as stated earlier, planned to control the provincial board that performed this delicate and difficult task. The 1846 Common Schools Act gave Ryerson and his board exactly the powers which he desired.[50]

Although Ryerson seems to have decided to adopt the Irish books primarily because of their intrinsic merit and because of their extrinsic relationship to the administrative structure that he was creating, this predisposition was confirmed by the books being very cheap.[51] The Irish commissioners of national education, being the publishers of the most popular school books in the British Isles, achieved major economies of scale in the production and distribution processes and, moreover, they sold their books at, or near, cost price outside of Ireland.[52] Ryerson directly imported books from Dublin, but also was permitted by the Irish authorities to have them printed in Canada. Ryerson left the printing of the Irish school books in Canada open to all publishers and printers who wished to enter the business.[53] This was a skilful, if slightly cynical, use of Free Trade. In effect, he was letting the printers of Canada compete amongst themselves in reaching the price level set by the Irish publishers who had massive economies of scale. If the Ontario prices rose significantly, school trustees would buy the books which the education department imported from Ireland, and thus drive prices amongst Canadian printers down to the Irish level.[54]

As of 1 January 1847, all foreign (read: American) books were officially excluded from the schools of Ontario.[55] Ryerson allowed school trustees gradually to phase-in the Irish Readers as their existing school books wore out and required replacement. Finally, in 1859 he enforced a complete ban on American books, by warning the school trustees that a failure to comply with the no-American regulation would mean a forfeiture of the provincial school grant.[56] In 1866, when there were more than 4,000 common schools in operation, only 54 were not using the Irish Readers.[57] The Irish Readers continued to be used until 1877,[58] although in 1868 Ryerson reluctantly permitted a set of "Canadian Readers" (often known as the "Ryerson Books") to be introduced.[59] This series, while containing much original and indigenous content, owed much of its material to the Irish National Readers, although the arrangement of the items was different from the Irish originals.[60] In 1883 the Department of Education authorized two new sets of readers (the "Canadian Series" adapted by Gage from a series published in Scotland and the "Royal Readers," first published in Scotland by Nelson and Sons), and the next year an indigenous set of books (the "Ontario Readers") was compiled by the department. Ryerson's Readers, with their strong Irish roots, finally were removed from the official list in 1887.[61] The boundaries of the Irish period of prepotence in the curriculum of the schools of Ontario (as distinct from influence upon the structure) was from roughly 1850 to 1880, a not-unimportant period in Ontario's history.

(5)

At this point, language threatens to betray historical reality. By establishing the "influence" of the Irish Readers, one is in danger of pre-judging an issue that should be left open. Specifically, one can easily assume that the hegemony of some alien culture was being established in the province, and this is an especially easy assumption to make, as Egerton Ryerson was a notoriously strong personality with very pronounced political and moral views. Moreover, his adoption of the Irish books and of many of the other components of the Irish school system seems to have been done without deep consideration of the opinions of the "consumers" of education, that is, the parents and the school children. Yet, one should at least consider the possibility that the reason the people of Ontario so readily took to the Irish-based school system in general and to the books in particular is that they fitted their desired values and needs quite well. Even if Ryerson's motives for what he did and the populace's reasons for accepting his actions have no direct link whatsoever, that does not matter: an autocrat with good sense or good luck can come to the same conclusion as a responsible democrat.

As far as the Irish national school books were concerned, the crucial point is that their content was *not* Irish in any narrow sense. Indeed, later Irish nationalists resented the books strongly, because they contained no element of indigenous Irish culture, and no Irish history. The books later were described by Irish nationalists as "West British," and, shorn of its derogatory overtones, the description is accurate. The books dealt with Ireland chiefly as a geographic entity. Politically, they inculcated a loyalty to the Crown and to the United Kingdom's system of representative government. There was little, if anything, in the books that was not just as relevant (and perhaps more so) to the life of an English, Welsh, or Scottish child as to an Irish youth.

This generalized "West British" content was nearly as appropriate to the population of Ontario as it was to that of the British Isles themselves. As mentioned earlier, over four-fifths of the population of Ontario in 1871 was of British and Irish ethnicity, many of them foreign-born. Amongst the foreign-born, the wide-spread popularity of the Irish books in the British Isles meant that they were themselves most apt to have learned to read in the Old Country from the very same books which their children used in Ontario, a point of cultural continuity that can only have been comforting to parent and child alike.

Central to the Irish Readers' acceptance both in the British Isles and in Ontario was their strong infusion of Christian religious teaching and moralizing. Emphatically, these books were not secular. Morally, they pressed for the practising of the minor Christian virtues: not lying, not boasting, being kind to parents, and, also, keeping one's hands clean and being careful when on the road or street. On a narrower religious note, the series had a gradual expanding treatment of religion. The *First Book* taught the children simple lessons, such as: "God loves us, and sent his Son to save us. The word of God tells us to love him. If we are bad, God will not love us, and we will not go to him, when we go from this world."[62] The *Second Book* included a good deal of biblical history, such as the story of Adam and Eve, the Flood, and so on, and the *Third Book* had even more. In the *Fourth Book,* New Testament theology was assayed and the doctrine of Christian Salvation was articulated.[63] This religiosity is hardly surprising. On both sides of the Atlantic, in the mid-Victorian era the consumers of education demanded that religion be integral to the educational product.

Not just any religious belief would do, however. If each sect could not have its own set of doctrinally-tailored school books (it was agreed that in a common schools system this was impossible), each wanted the books to be dogmatically neutral as between Christian denominations. In practical terms, this meant that the books must satisfy both the Roman Catholics and the various Protestant sects. The Irish National Readers were originally modelled on the texts of the Catholic Book Society of Ireland[64] and had been vetted by the Roman Catholic Archbishop of Dublin to be sure that they did not offend Catholic sensibilities. British Catholic authorities also found the books satisfactory. Indeed, the secretary of the Roman Catholic Poor School Committee in Great Britain wrote in 1851 that "they regard [the Irish books], after much examination and experimental use, both as being *per se* the best elementary series in the language, and also the most suitable for adoption in any possible scheme of national education."[65] In Ontario, even in the worst days of Catholic dissatisfaction with Ryerson's system, on the issue of "separate schools," the texts were tacitly accepted.

As for the susceptibilities of the various Protestant denominations, the books also had undergone the scrutiny of the Anglican Archbishop of Dublin and of an important Presbyterian clergyman. The texts were neutral as between Protestant denominations. (Although some Irish Presbyterians at first objected to the "mutilation" of the scripture in certain scriptural extracts,[66] their complaints soon ceased.) This neutrality as between Protestant denominations was an absolutely necessary prerequisite for the Irish books' acceptance in England, as that nation's schools were split during the middle decades of the nineteenth century between two warring educational societies, that of the Established Church and that of the non-conformist denominations. Similarly, in Scotland, after the Great Disruption of 1843, acceptance of a set of texts was predicated upon their doctrinal neutrality. And so too in Ontario, where it was common to find children of up to half a dozen Protestant denominations in the same common school.

In suggesting that the moralizing, the religiosity, the political conservatism, and the British loyalism of the Irish Readers were not incompatible with the ethnic background and cultural values of the Ontario populace, am I not ignoring the considerable body of literature on the relationship of education and social control? No, but much of that literature is both naive and ideologically loaded. During the 1960s, educational historians increasingly became aware that education involved social control of one person or group by another, and this observation began appearing in educational histories with the same frequency as the statement that education involves the passing on of values from one generation to another was found in the preceding generation's educational histories. Of course, education is a form of social control, but so to state is no more an increment to knowledge than to note that the purpose of a light bulb is illumination: Socrates, after all, was dispatched because his views of social control in the educational process differed from those of his fellow citizens. What one needs to know is by what educational mechanisms social control was affected and who was influencing whom.

This leads one to the second general drawback in the literature of social control as related to education: an implied, but rarely proved dialectic, usually is tacitly accepted, one which makes it seem as if social control always works from the top downwards. Education, therefore, comes to be viewed as a means for the ruling class to control the lower orders. Indeed, it can be, but, equally, it is possible that educational institutions can be a form of social control whereby a community, whatever its class structure, imposes upon its children a commonly shared set of values and beliefs. Undoubtedly, Egerton Ryerson had strong views, and he wished the people of Ontario to accept them. But note this: under the 1850 Education Act it was optional for a local school board to levy property taxes to provide free schools (as distinct from the old method of raising voluntary subscriptions or charging each parent on the rates), and yet, by 1870, 4,244 of the 4,400 school sections had voluntarily adopted such a levy.[67] Manifestly, Ryerson's cultural prescription was not something forced on the people; they wanted it, and they showed this by voting with their pocketbooks, that most democratic means of cultural affirmation.

(6)

Having said that the British loyalism, the religiosity, and the moral tone of the Irish Readers fit well with the background of the Ontario populace, and, therefore, that the books can be seen as merely articulating a set of values which the people themselves wished enforced, there is one aspect of the Irish Readers which is so striking — and so lacking in immediate cultural resonance — as to be noteworthy. This is their manifesting a massive dose of classical political economy. Economics was a new academic field. The first professorship of political economy at Oxford was not founded until 1825 and that at Trinity College, Dublin, in 1832. Even granting that, with the conversion of Sir Robert Peel, Free Trade became the official creed of the British Empire in 1846, economics was a science of the élite and certainly was not part of the popular culture of Ireland, Great Britain, or Ontario. Thus, if there was any cultural component of the Irish school system that was imposed from the top downwards, it was the view of the character of the economic system.

The causal chain which eventually resulted in classical political economy becoming part of the official culture that was fed to most Ontario school children is sinuous and illustrates once again the complex pattern of transatlantic cultural transfer. The effective historical lever was that extraordinary liberal Anglican divine, Richard Whately, and the starting point of the story for our purposes was Whately's first meeting with the future political economist, Nassau Senior.[68] During the years 1812 to 1820 Whately was a resident fellow of Oriel College, then the most intellectually prestigious of Oxford colleges, and, as was the custom, he took private pupils for coaching for final examinations. One of his early private pupils was Nassau Senior, who had just taken his B.A. examination. Senior had been asked a question on the divinity examination in the very words of the catechism, but had failed to answer. When the examiner sarcastically remarked, "Why, sir, a child of ten years old could answer that!" Senior had replied, "So could I, sir, when I was ten years old." Not surprisingly, Senior was "plucked." He sought out Whately, and, when asked by his intended coach what class of a degree he intended to take, Senior answered coolly, "a first,"[69] and under Whately's tutelage he indeed did so. Now, the point about Whately as a tutor is that he kept very close ties with his best pupils and was willing to learn from them as well as teach them, and as Senior in his later years grew to be an adept in the emerging field of political economy, Whately learned a great deal. This relationship is symbolized in the fact that in 1825 Nassau Senior became the first holder of the Drummond Chair of Political Economy at Oxford; the second incumbent, from 1829–31, was Richard Whately.

Although Whately did not make a significant contribution to economics as a technical discipline, his *Introductory Lectures on Political Economy,* delivered in 1831 and published a year later, were a virtually-evangelical defence of the new science against charges of its being incompatible with Christianity. His keenness touched a responsive chord in the book-buying public, and by 1855 the lectures were in their fourth edition. Whately's enthusiasm for political economy could never have affected the outlook of Ontario school children had he not been appointed (to the surprise of virtually every knowledgeable political and ecclesiastical observer of the time) as Archbishop of Dublin in 1831, the very year that the Irish national system of education was founded. Whately, along with the Roman Catholic Archbishop of Dublin and a ranking Presbyterian divine, was appointed among the commissioners of national education in Ireland. Whately took a keen interest in the school system, most particularly in the school books.

In 1833 Whately proposed to the Society for Promoting Christian Knowledge, a major Anglican association in England, that a tract of his authorship on political economy be published for the schools. As an experiment, their publisher, Parkers, privately put out a booklet by Whately entitled *Easy Lessons on Money Matters for the Use of Young People* which was designed to teach basic political economy to children aged eight and above. Several editions were published, but the readership apparently was mostly middle class. Whately, however, wanted to reach the poor with this new secular gospel, and his attachment to the new national educational system in Ireland provided that opportunity. Thus, the first four sections of *Easy Lessons on Money Matters* were inserted into the *Third Book* of the Irish reading series and the remaining six sections into the *Fourth Book*.[70] This material was augmented in later editions by items from Adam Smith and some economic fairy tales by a Mrs. Marcet, and, under Whately's influence, economic precepts were interlarded into the remaining Irish readers as well.

In 1840 the British and Foreign School Society, seeing the success of the Irish books, published its own series of readers, which were modelled closely on the Irish books and contained numerous lessons on political economy, some taken directly from Whately and others modelled on his style. Similarly, in 1848, the Society for Promoting Christian Knowledge reprinted, with Whately's permission, the *Fourth Book* of the Irish series — the one which contained so much of his *Easy Lessons* — and in the same year the Society began to publish on their own the full edition of *Easy Lessons*. And in 1868, when the National Society (an Anglican body) began to publish a full line of texts of their own, they included several Whately extracts, as did the series of readers begun in 1860 by the Catholic School Society. "In short," according to the most informed student of the subject, "virtually every advanced reader published by religious bodies from the late 1830s to 1880 had its quota of Whately, or imitations or adaptations of his articles."[71] This was in addition to the direct inclusion of Whately material into the Irish Readers which, one should recall, were themselves the most widely used set of school books in the British Isles. It is no exaggeration to say that several generations of school children in Ireland, England and Wales, and, to a lesser extent, in Scotland, learned the official version of how the economic system worked through the words of Archbishop Richard Whately. And so, too, did the children of Ontario.

Whately's political economy was politically radical, in the sense that it was associated with a removal of civil disabilities against minority groups (he had favoured Catholic emancipation) and with approval of an extension of the franchise to groups lower on the social scale, but his radicalism does not come through in the Irish Readers. Instead, the economic system is presented as a piece of Newtonian machinery that one interferes with only at peril. At its simplest, this meant that the poor should not wish to take the property of the rich, for that would upset the economic mechanism. According to the *Supplement* to the *Fourth Book*:

> Can it be supposed that the poor would be better off if all the property of the rich were taken away and divided among them, and no one allowed to become rich for the future? The poor would then be much worse off than they are now . . . They would not work near so profitably as they do now, because no one would be able to keep up a large manufactory or farm well stocked, and to advance wages to workmen, as is done now, for work that does not bring in any return for, perhaps, a year or two.[72]

Similarly, it was thought that the economic machinery could only be made less efficient if wage levels were not allowed to rise and fall freely. The common eighteenth-century practice of legislating wage levels was condemned:

In former times, laws used to be often made to fix the wages of labour. It was forbidden under penalty, that higher or lower wages should be asked or offered for each kind of labour than what the law fixed. But laws of this kind were found never to do any good; for when the rate fixed by law for farm-labourers, for instance, happened to be higher than it was worth a farmer's while to give for ordinary labourers, he turned off all his workmen, except a few of the best hands. . . .[73]

As for trade unions, the workers joining them would put both owners and themselves out of business:

Dublin has some beautiful manufactures of poplin, velvet and glass; and there were once many more manufactories, but the workmen, not satisfied with good wages, refused to work at a lower price than they themselves should appoint, which the masters being unable to afford, the establishments were broken up, and the proprietors took their money elsewhere.[74]

The economic system was presented as being hard but fair. Examples of individuals who had risen from poverty to riches, through good character, individual exertion, and hard work were held up to the children. Their rise, mind you, was not automatic: "It is, of course, not to be expected that *many* poor men should become rich, nor ought any man to set his heart on being so; but it is an allowable and cheering thought, that no one is shut out from the hope of bettering his condition and providing for his children."[75]

The general tendency of lessons such as these is unmistakable: to inhibit the spread of ideas and attitudes that might encourage a restructuring of the economic order. Certainly in Ontario the introduction of the rhetoric and reasoning of political economy to justify this hands-off viewpoint was a cultural innovation, introduced from outside of the society, and can justifiably be labelled as an instance of attempted social control by means of the schools.

That said, one must step warily. It is impossible to say how well the medicine "took," if at all. Both children and teachers can be remarkable resistant to unwieldy lessons. Further, one really cannot say how this aspect of the "official" culture related to the everyday popular culture of the myriad local communities, and to prevailing views and beliefs as they evolved out of workaday life. It is possible that these school lessons ultimately facilitated the development of industrial capitalism in Canada, by retarding the growth of unions and by inhibiting governmental interference with the growing power of capital. Equally, it is possible that the school books had little or no effect, aside from introducing a new vocabulary for the discussion of economic matters. That is, at a less articulate, less technical level than that of the classical economist, the bulk of the Ontario population, overwhelmingly rural and mostly self-employed, may already have concluded from their own experience, or have believed from their own dreams, that individual initiative, free competition, and the unfettered right to accumulate capital were socially desirable. If so, then, the school texts merely taught the children new ways of expressing something that their parents already believed.[76]

Part II

(I)

Implicitly, the discussion thus far has indicated two signal aspects of the educational situation in nineteenth-century Ontario: that the school children and their guardians are not best understood as mere passive consumers of education, and, second, that, powerful though he was, Egerton Ryerson was not an autonomous force. In particular, Ryerson's freedom of action was limited by the fundamental characteristics of the educational structure that he imported from overseas. These transatlantic patterns implied central administrative problems and permitted only a narrow range of possible solutions.

At this point, it is appropriate to look at some aspects of the notorious "separate schools" question, for on that issue one can observe Ryerson's limited freedom of action, the "consumers'" refusal to accept passively his prescriptions, and one encounters once again the vexed matter of transatlantic cultural transfer.

Note two parallel cases.

In 1831, in his famous "Letter" Lord Stanley inaugurated a school system in Ireland that was intended to be non-denominational and thereby to bind the sectarian wounds that so weakened the Irish body politic. He intended that two practices would promote this eirenic result. First, at the local level, a strong preference would be given to applications for financial aid stemming jointly from Protestants and Catholics, and first preference of all should be given to applications put forward jointly by Protestant and Catholic clergymen. Second, in order that Protestant and Catholic children would be educated together, a clear and inviolable line between "literary instruction" and religious education was to be drawn. During regular school hours, when both denominations were in school together, no denominationally distinctive religious teaching was permitted, only the general lessons in Christian history and ethnics found in the school books. After school hours or on a separate day of the week, clergy could use the school for the denominational teaching of the children of their respective flocks.

In reality, and despite the appointment by Stanley of a strong board of commissioners of national education, his intentions were not honoured. Protestants and Catholics only rarely applied jointly to become school trustees and, simply to get the system operating, the Irish commissioners granted single-faith applications: by 1852 only 175 out of 4,795 Irish national schools were under ecumenical management. Protestant school managers appointed only Protestant teachers, and Catholic managers appointed Catholic teachers. Naturally, this made "mixed" schools (that is, schools where Catholics and Protestants studied side by side) unattractive to parents, for one side or the other would be under unfair pressure. The degree of potential mixing was further reduced by demographic factors (in parts of the west and south of Ireland there were very few Protestants) and by the Anglican Church's efforts from the 1830s through the 1850s to provide its own self-financing denominational school system. The ultimate result was an elementary school system that was non-denominational in theory but dual-confessional in practice; or, to use other terms, ecumenical in theory but segregated in practice.[77]

The second case is as follows. In 1846, Egerton Ryerson in his famous *Report* effectively inaugurated a mass school system in Ontario.[78] Ryerson, like Lord Stanley, wanted religious and civil amity — his key concept was harmony[79] — and, like Stanley, Ryerson intended that at the local level both Protestant and Catholic adults would support the local common school and would serve as trustees, that Protestant and Catholic children would be educated side by side, and that during the common hours of schooling only general Christian doctrine and general Christian ethics would be taught. Because a form of separate schools had existed in Ontario since 1841, Ryerson could not condemn them outright, but his views were clear: "Indeed, schools might be named," he wrote in 1846, "in which there is the most rigorous inculcation of an exclusive sectarianism, and where there is a deplorable absence of the fruits of both religion and morality."[80] He added slightly later that "In these remarks I mean no objection to Schools in connection with a particular religious community," but then continued:

> I refer not to the constitution and control of Schools or Seminaries, but to the kind of teaching which can be better understood than defined, — a teaching which unchristianizes four-fifths, if not nine-tenths, of Christendom, — a teaching which substitutes the form for the reality, — the symbol for the substance, — the dogma for the doctrine, — the passion for sect for the love of God and neighbours — a teaching which, as history can attest, is productive of ecclesiastical corruptions, superstition, infidelity, social disputes and civil contentions, and is inimical alike to good government and public tranquillity.
>
> I can aver, from personal experience and practice, as well as from a very extended inquiry on this subject, that a much more comprehensive course of biblical and religious instruction can be given, than there is likely to be opportunity for in Elementary Schools, without any restraint on the one side, or any tincture of sectarianism on the other, — a course embracing the entire *History of the Bible,* its *institutions, cardinal doctrines* and *morals,* together with the evidence of its authenticity.[81]

In other words, if provided with the appropriate curriculum, the common schools were more Christian than separate schools.

Nevertheless, Ryerson was saddled with legal precedents, and his 1846 Common Schools Act contained provisions for separate schools, although Ryerson was convinced that they would "die out, not by force of legislative enactment, but under the influence of increasingly enlightened and enlarged Christian relations. . . ."[82] The doleful reality of Ontario society, like that in Ireland, defeated the hopes of religious integration. In a series of pitched battles, between 1850 and 1863, the Roman Catholic hierarchy in Ontario attacked the common schools, and their victory, by 1863, was complete. In practice, they were given the right, wherever there had been enough Catholics to fill a primary school, to receive a share of municipal or provincial educational grants. As in Ireland, the chief restrictions on this dual-confessional system were a provincially limited choice of school texts, basic certification requirements for teachers, and the institution of government-approved inspectors.

From one perspective, what occurred first in Ireland and then in Ontario can be seen as separate and independent instances of the operation of a single paradigm. The initial term of that pattern was that:

1. The education authorities, religious leaders, and the general populace in each country agreed that secular education was unthinkable.[83]

Equally, they agreed:

2. that the religious system upon which their system would be based should be Christianity.

Then the trouble began, for:

3. although it was possible to compile sets of readings from religious writers and from the Bible that consisted only of the elements which the predominant Christian denominations held in common;

4. the Protestant denominations would not allow a specifically Roman Catholic gloss to be put on these common texts, and;

5. the Catholic authorities held that, unless these

readings were interpreted dogmatically and unless the entire school environment was under Catholic control, the schools were a danger to the Catholic faith.

Conceivably, either the Catholics or the Protestants could have given in and attended schools run under the guidelines established by their religious rivals, but, in fact:

6. each of the two major faiths was too strong politically to be crushed, so;

7. the school structure buckled: the educational authorities surrendered their dream of religious integration and accepted, instead, a form of religious segregation.[84]

Given the religious, ethnic, and political realities of Ontario, Ryerson's system, like Ireland's before it, would have been broken, no matter where his ideas had originated.

Although in the Irish and the Ontario cases the paradigms acted independently — like two identical stationary engines, fuelled by the same propellant, operating independently but virtually identically — there was transatlantic interaction: a number of the parts for that Ontario engine had been machined in Ireland before being exported and installed overseas. Even though Ryerson doubtless came, on his own, to be convinced of the undesirability of religious segregation of children, the mechanism by which he initiated the separate schools imbroglio came directly from Ireland: he held up as an example the way that the Irish system *seemed* to work:[85] "The proceedings of the National Board of Education in Ireland present an illustration of the extent to which there may be a cordial cooperation between even Roman Catholics and Protestants. . .," he declared in his *Report*[86] and followed this with a description of the Irish schools which made it appear as if united non-denominational education existed as the rule rather than the exception. Ryerson adopted the Irish vocabulary in dealing with united non-denominational schools — they were called "mixed schools"[87] — and, more important, Irish mechanisms. As he wrote to Bishop Charbonnel in a public letter in 1852, ". . . the very system which was thus established in Ireland in regard to books and religious instruction . . . is that which is established in Upper Canada, as I stated in my last letter to your Lordship, as may be seen by comparing our general School regulations with those which Dr. Murray and other members of the National Board of Education have established in Ireland. . . ."[88] To prove this point to Charbonnel, Ryerson enclosed both the Ontario and the Irish regulations. Section 2 of the official regulations on religious instruction were particularly revealing: ". . . the principles of religion and morality should be inculcated upon all the pupils of the school. What the Commissioners of National Education in Ireland state as existing in schools under their charge, should characterize the instruction given in each school in Upper Canada."[89]

The other important transatlantic contribution to the pattern as it operated in Ontario came through the massive Irish immigration of mid-century. The precise dimensions of the Irish immigrant flow to British North America in the Famine and immediate post-Famine years are impossible to determine, but certainly Ontario received over half of the settlers, and two-thirds is not at all an unlikely estimate.[90] Despite the common impression, this flow, as it affected Ontario, was not overwhelmingly, or even chiefly, Catholic. Indirect evidence suggests strongly that Protestants exceeded Catholics in the great migration to Canada by roughly a ratio of 2:1[91] One can argue about the precise figure: the relevant point for the present discussion is that *both* sides of the Irish ethnic community were bolstered by large groups of immigrants with a fresh and immediate experience of the Old Country, with its sectarian divisions. Moreover, by the mid-1840s, any alert persons who had lived for a time in Ireland would have known full well how the Irish national school system worked in practice — which is to say, knew that whatever the authorities in Dublin might pretend, on the ground the Irish schools were either Protestant or Catholic. That knowledge cannot have been irrelevant to the behaviour of the Irish immigrants and to that of their co-religionists when they settled in Ontario.

Anyone who knows the history of the British Isles reasonably well cannot help but have a sensation of *déjà vu* when surveying nineteenth-century Ontario's educational history, and this is not in the diluted sense of the phrase, as mere tedious repetition, but in the full original sense, of viewing something that uncannily, almost upsettingly, seems to have happened before. This unsettling sensation is caused by the way in which players in Ontario took places on the stage and responded to other figures in the drama as if they were reading from the same script that had been used in Ireland a few years, and, in some instances, a few months, earlier. In calling these similarities to the reader's attention, one is not engaged in an exercise in historical trivia. One is presenting once again, (a) a case of cultural congruence as between the Old World and the New, and, simultaneously, (b) another evidence of the influences of the Old upon the New.

Consider some of the *dramatis personae.* For either the Irish or the Ontario system to have any hope at all of surviving as a religiously integrated system of mass schooling, it was crucial that it have the backing of at least one influential Roman Catholic prelate. To have two or three would have been desirable; to have one was essential. In Ireland, this role was filled, from the system's founding in 1831 to his death in 1852, by Daniel Murray, the saintly Archbishop of Dublin. In Ontario, the figure was Michael Power, who had become Bishop of Toronto when the diocese of Kingston was split in 1842. In Dublin, Murray vetted all school books and all regulations in order to be sure that they did not offend Catholic interests. In Toronto, Bishop Power, who accepted the chairmanship of the Board of Education in July 1846, endeavoured to do the same. Neither Power nor Murray was a proponent of religiously mixed education, in the sense of favouring it in ideal circumstances over denominational schooling, but each was willing to accept it under existing circumstances as an alternative to no schooling at all. Each believed that the system could be rendered safe to Catholic religious interests and beneficial to the general welfare of their Catholic flocks.[92] As one would expect, Ryerson made considerable play of Power's adhesions to the board, and, in the 1850s, when fighting against Catholic critics, cited Power's adhesion: "Bishop Power not only acted with the Board of Education (a mixed Board) and presided at its meetings until the week before his death, but his name stands first of the six members who individually signed the first circular to the Municipalities of Upper Canada on the establishment of the Normal School — a mixed School. . . ."[93]

Crucially, Egerton Ryerson understood the analogy as between Bishop Power and Archbishop Murray, and he consciously tied the two together when making public arguments about the desirability of religious mixed schooling. In one of his early letters to Bishop Charbonnel, Ryerson said, after referring to Archbishop Murray's approval of the Irish system, "therefore, if your Lordship followed the example of the incomparable Dr. Murray, as well as that of the late Bishop Power, you would give your cordial support . . ." to the common school system.[94] Thus were the activities of Daniel Murray in Dublin brought to bear on educational controversies in Ontario.

Bishop Power died in the fall of 1847, as a result of his devotion to Christian duty: he contracted typhus while serving sick Irish immigrants. Archbishop Murray died in 1852. Both prelates were irreplaceable. In retrospect, it is clear that once they had left the stage, compromise between the Catholic church and the educational authorities on the volatile matter of religious integrated schooling no longer was possible.

The corresponding roles of the ranking Anglican prelates in Ireland and in Ontario were much less close, although fundamentally similar. In Ireland, Lord John George Beresford, Archbishop of Armagh and the ranking Irish ecclesiastic, led the majority of the Irish clergy in a fight against the national education system. Beresford desired, if possible, Anglican control over all education and, this being impossible, the full funding of denominational schools for

Anglicans. Eventually, in 1860, he surrendered, and suggested that those Anglican schools that were short of funds join the national school system.[95] His counterpart in Ontario, Bishop John Strachan, had fewer resources and considerably less social cachet than did Beresford, so his collapse was quicker. He followed the same path, however, moving from a desire for Anglican dominance over the entire school system to wishing to have full funding of all Anglican denominational schools, to a compromise whereby Anglican schools were merely permissible in cities and incorporated towns in cases where the school board (not the Anglican authorities) decided to establish such a school.[96] Ultimately, Anglican separate schools declined into virtual non-existence.[97] Self-important as each man was, Lord John George Beresford and John Strachan were only bit players in this particular drama.[98]

Pivotal to the Ontario and to the Irish dramas were two Catholic opponents of the respective mixed systems, men who were virtual theological clones: Paul Cullen and Armand Francis Marie, Comte de Charbonnel. Cullen, who became Archbishop of Armagh in 1849 and was translated to the archbishopric of Dublin in 1852, was probably the most influential Catholic cleric in the English-speaking world in the nineteenth century: he completely transformed the Roman Catholic church in Ireland, just at the time when Irish priests, following the great post-Famine diaspora of the Irish people, were becoming predominant in North America and Australasia. Cullen was unusual in the Irish priesthood in his being from a well-off grazier family, most of the Catholic gentry and aristocracy having been humbled during the Penal era of the eighteenth century. Also, unlike most Irish priests, he had spent his most formative years outside of Ireland, in Rome, where he eventually rose to become Rector of the Irish College, the channel of influence between the Irish bishops and the Pope. Thus, when, in 1849, Cullen returned to Ireland, he returned less as an Irishman than as a foreigner, and his ecclesiastical policy was thoroughly anti-indigenous. He was the very essence of ultra-montanism, and during his episcopacy he returned the previously idiosyncratic Irish Catholic church into a highly regimented body. Cullen was highly suspicious of Irish nationalism, equally distrustful of the civil state, vitriolically anti-Protestant, and very aggressive towards achievement of what he believed to be his church's rightful prerogatives. The mixed education of Protestants and Catholics was his special hatred and the commissioners of national education his particular target, for, though they had granted denominationalism in fact, they continued to articulate the theory of non-denominationalism. Eventually, in a tactically brilliant, albeit ruthless, series of moves, he forced in 1853 the resignation from the board of Richard Whately, the most prominent and committed proponent of religious integration.[99]

Bishop Charbonnel, even more than his Irish counterpart, was not cut from the common cloth; he was, after all, a French nobleman. Charbonnel, who acceded to the Toronto bishopric in 1850 and resigned it in 1860, was even more of a foreigner to his see than the highly romanized Cullen was to his archbishopric. Like Cullen, Charbonnel was an ultra-montanist in his views, albeit not nearly as efficient administratively as was Cullen. Charbonnel shared with the majority of bishops appointed by Pius IX a distrust of the state and of nationalism, and, in this perspective, even the mild attempt by Ryerson to form a British-Canadian identity through the schools could be seen as potential nationalistic danger to the faith. Charbonnel became as convinced as Cullen that the mixing of Protestants and Catholics in a united school system was wrong, and he fought with the same slashing style adopted by his Irish counterpart. His public war with Ryerson included statements such as the following, in which he compares the mixed system to: "a regular school of pyrrhonism, of indifferentism, of infidelity, and consequently of all vices and crimes."[100] And, because in practice the mixed schools were a danger to the faith of the Catholic children: "we, their temporal and spiritual parents, will act according to the doctrine of the God unknown to your schools, as he was in Athens: "if thy hand, foot, eye, is an occasion of sin to thee, cut it off, pluck it out, and cast it from thee."[101] Charbonnel believed that the common school system was a "cruel and disguised persecution" of Roman Catholics, and he threatened that, unless changes were made in the mixed schools so as to render them harmless to Catholics, it would be:

> forbidden to our faithful to send their children to these Schools, on pain of the refusal of the Sacraments, because the soul and heaven above everything; because the foot, the hand, the eye, occasions of sin ought to be sacrificed to salvation; because, finally, Jesus Christ has confided the mission of instruction which has civilized the world, to no others than the Apostles and their successors to the end of time .... [102]

Strong rhetoric, but effective. Ultimately, Charbonnel and his successor, John Joseph Lynch, won.[103]

Ryerson was aware of these parallels between Charbonnel and Cullen, acutely so. In his set of letters on "foreign ecclesiastics," he tellingly pointed out, in reference to Charbonnel, that the new Catholic doctrine of education in Ontario was: "first proclaimed by a Prelate who had drawn all his inspirations and sympathies from the continent of Europe, and has been most stoutly advocated by one of kindred inspirations and sympathies — the present Roman Catholic Archbishop of Dublin — who has spent twenty years on the Continent before his appointment .... "[104]

Even more shrewdly, Ryerson recognized that there was an interaction between Cullen and Charbonnel, based on Charbonnel's recourse to the decrees of the Synod of Thurles.[105] This bears comment, because that Synod's pronouncements on education, little noticed though they have been by historians outside of Ireland, became the basis for Catholic thinking about primary education in much of the English-speaking world, being taken abroad, as it were, by generations of Irish-trained priests. The Synod of Thurles had been convened by Paul Cullen in 1850 and made explicit in the English-speaking world the opposition to mixed education not only of the Irish bishops but, implicitly, of Pius IX. The Synod refrained from condemning the existing Irish national system of education with its theory of non-denominationalism but declared (Article I) that: "we deem it to be part of our duty to declare that the separate education of Catholics is, in every way, to be preferred to it."[106] The Irish bishops continued (Article VI): "We deem it dangerous for Catholic children to attend schools conducted by Protestants alone; and it is therefore necessary for their safe education, that, in every school frequented by them, there should be, at least, one Catholic schoolmaster or schoolmistress in attendance." Where the majority of children were Catholics, the Synod declared (in Article VI) that the head master or mistress should be a Catholic, and, most significantly, demanded that only Catholics who were approved by the bishop of the local diocese should be at the head of any school. This, manifestly, implied the superiority of the religious authorities over the civic authorities in appointing Catholic teachers. Further, the Irish bishops demanded that the local bishops have a veto over school books (Article VIII): "it is proper that, whether in common schools or in normal schools to which Catholics resort, the books used, even for secular instruction, should be approved by the ordinary. The bishops alone are to be regarded as the judges of the books used for the religious instruction of Catholic youth." When translated from Ireland to Ontario, these Catholic demands were perceived by Ryerson as a knife in the heart of his new system. In an enraged letter to Charbonnel's sideman in the school wars, Bishop Pinsoneault, Ryerson declared that:

> ... instead of appealing to facts the Bishop appeals to the Provincial Clerical councils of Baltimore and Quebec, and to the Council of Thurles in Ireland, which have declared against the principle of our Common Schools, and this declaration has been approved by Dr. Cullen, delegate of the Holy See, and, at length by the Sovereign Pontiff. "Hence it is (says the Bishop) that the Catholic body which believe in the *unerring authority* of the Church in all questions appertaining to *faith* and *morals* never will, because conscience forbids it, approve and countenance this Common School system, as now imposed on us in this section of the Province."

Here is the original — the recent origin of the warfare against our Common School system. And it is not wholly a foreign element? Here it may also be seen how "conscientious convictions" can be manufactured to order. Dr. Paul Cullen, after twenty years inhaling of foreign sympathies, comes to Ireland and proclaims a crusade against the National System of Education which his predecessor Archbishop Murray had aided to establish and build for eighteen years; then a Bishop from the continent, Bishop Charbonnel, comes to Toronto and commences a war against a National School system which his predecessor, Bishop Power, had aided to establish and build up during several years.[107]

Poor Ryerson! How perceptive an observer, how unfortunate a warrior. He, virtually alone amongst observers of educational developments, understood that in its structure and development the Ontario system operated as an independent Canadian simulacrum of the Irish structure and development and yet, simultaneously, overseas events, particularly those stemming from Ireland, could affect the situation in Ontario. These two insights, of course, are incompatible if one tries to hold them simultaneously, but, as in a true paradox, both perceptions are accurate. The situation is similar to that in modern subatomic physics, where it is accurate both to think of particles as physical entities and, alternately, to describe them in terms of waves. Each description is accurate in that each fits with observable phenomena. Yet the two descriptions cannot be employed simultaneously. A similar situation characterized events surrounding the Ontario common school system and, to his great credit, Ryerson recognized both forms of the educational reality with which he was dealing.

(III)

But where, in this strange drama of *déjà vu*, did Ryerson fit? Who was his prototype? In his great *Report* of 1846 Ryerson self-consciously made reference to Lord Stanley's "Letter" which established the Irish school system,[108] and in the course of events Ryerson's *Report* was to the Ontario system what Stanley's "Letter" was to the Irish one; but the role of an aloof English aristocrat was not one which Ryerson could, by any stretch of the imagination, assume in Ontario. In actual fact, Ryerson acted like a Canadian version of Archbishop Whately. That statement may at first seem strange, as it is hard to think of Ryerson as resembling a prelate of the Established Church, but the resemblance was uncanny. No man ever wore the mitre with less pretension than did Whately. He was a broad churchman, who loathed ecclesiastical faction fighting, who looked to the scriptures, not to tradition, as the chief source of Christian beliefs and morals, and was mildly liberal politically. He was a great talker, a virtual polymath, possessed of almost boundless energy, was insensitive to the finer points of manners and almost incapable of practising tact. Most important, he viewed himself as the schoolmaster of the Irish people, took great interest in the composition of the Irish national readers (parts of which series he wrote himself), and campaigned hard for non-denominational ("mixed") education. If one makes a slight adjustment for Egerton Ryerson's "high" Methodism, each of those attributes actually characterized Ryerson as well. The Irish archbishop had his understudy in Ontario's school superintendent.

Whately, of course, was an intellectual of international fame and Ryerson did not approach him in this regard, but he did learn from him. Whately's scholarly reputation was based primarily on two massive works, his *Logic* (1826) and his *Rhetoric* (1828). The former became the standard treatise on the subject in English, until displaced by John Stuart Mill's *System of Logic* (1843). The *Rhetoric* was a direct continuation of the *Logic* and discussed not only the various forms of argument, but how to be certain of the correctness of a given position before framing a fair and convincing argument addressed to others. Crucially, in its practical applications, the book was chiefly an eccelsiastical rhetoric, precisely the kind of volume that an intelligent Protestant clergyman, such as Ryerson, would have read and admired,[109] and Ryerson did, as was

shown by his approving references to the *Rhetoric* in his
1846 *Report*.[110] Whately's other work, on logic, also was
appreciated by Ryerson, albeit in its diluted form. In 1843,
Whately had put together a logic text for young people
called *Easy Lessons on Reasoning* and this was endorsed
by Ryerson in his *Report*[111] and the book found its way onto
the approved list for both elementary and high schools in
Ontario.[112]

Ryerson met Whately in Dublin during his educational
concourse in 1844–45, and clearly the Archbishop did
not hide his own light under a bushel: Ryerson, in his notes
summarizing the meeting, refers to having conversed
"with Archbishop Whately and other members of the
Board ... ," as if they were all an appendage to the
Archbishop; and Ryerson gained the (correct) impression
that not only had Whately been involved in various ways
in compiling the series of books for literary instruction but
the (erroneous) one that the Archbishop and Mrs. Whately
together had written all of the books of religious instruction
for the schools.[113]

The Irish education commissioners' books of non-
denominational religious instruction which were published
in addition to the basic Readers (which also contained a
great deal of religious material) were of three sorts: a volume
of religious poetry, a set of non-denominational extracts
from the Bible, and a special text on the evidence for the
truth of Christianity. Ryerson was convinced that these
religious books, when combined with the literary series of
Readers and with after-school catechetical instruction,
would be revolutionary:

> I am inclined to believe that there are few elementary schools
> in Great Britain — those of Scotland excepted — in which so
> much religious knowledge is imparted as in the 3,150 schools,
> containing 395,550 children, which have been established by
> the Board of National Education in Ireland. This great and
> good work must in the course of a few years, produce a marked
> change in the intellectual and social condition of Ireland.[114]

In trying to import this great putative revolution, Ryerson
imported the three sets of special religious publications

from Ireland, and in so doing he necessarily was drawing closer to his prototype, Richard Whately.

The volume of *Sacred Poetry*, compiled in Ireland by a Presbyterian divine, James Carlisle, and first published in 1837, was a minor volume and, though authorized for use in Ontario from 1846 onwards, was not central to Ryerson's plans.[115] Somewhat more important were the Irish commissioners' set of scripture abstracts, which had been endorsed in Ryerson's 1846 *Report* as "more literal and more comprehensive than Watt's Scripture History, or any of the many similar publications which have been most used in Schools."[116] The *Scripture Lessons* had a fairly complex publishing history, but in the final form, as Ryerson adopted them in Ontario in 1846, they involved four volumes, two of extracts from the Old Testament, two from the New.[117] The selection of extracts was made by James Carlisle, the Presbyterian divine mentioned above, but with considerable assistance. In particular, Richard Whately contributed to the second volume of Old Testament lessons, and Whately's close friend, Thomas Arnold, Headmaster of Rugby School, was engaged to compile the New Testament sections drawn from the Gospel of St. Luke and the Acts of the Apostles.[118]

Central to Ryerson's identification with Whately was what Ryerson called in his *Report* "an excellent and appropriate little book on the truth of Christianity."[119] He was referring, without citing authorship, to Richard Whately's *Lessons on the Truth of Christianity*, published by the Irish education commissioners. This book had grown out of a series of articles published in *Saturday Magazine* in 1837 and published in London in the same year as *Introductory Lessons on Christian Evidences*. Whately, a great promoter of his own works, immediately asked the Irish education commissioners to publish his book as a school text. Archbishop Murray objected, however, to Whately's first two chapters, as in them children were given evidence by which they might themselves judge whether or not Christianity was superior to paganism. The Reverend James Carlisle thereupon revised Whately's book, making it acceptable to the Catholic Archbishop, and, as published under a new title, it was intended to serve as an appendix to the *Fourth Book of Lessons*.[120] Ryerson had it placed on his first list of approved books.[121]

In assimilating to the Ontario school system Richard Whately's religious writing, Egerton Ryerson was directly transplanting cultural material. However, something more than that process was occurring, for, whether consciously or unconsciously, Ryerson eventually assumed positions and engaged in activities that could have been modelled on Whately. Consider the following coincidences, if such they are. (1) Whately, as has been noted, produced a book of *Lessons on the Truth of Christianity* that Ryerson admired and which was part of the approved (but not required) curriculum from 1846 until shortly after Ryerson retired in 1876; Ryerson himself introduced in 1871 a book entitled *First Lessons in Christian Morals for Canadian Families and Schools*[122] which was put on the approved books lists alongside Whately's and, like Whately's, was struck off only after Ryerson's retirement.[123] Ryerson's book did not overlap with Whately's and it is not hard to see the two as a set, the one dealing with the truth of Christian beliefs, the other with the belief in Christian virtues.[124] (2) Whately, it will be recalled, had written a special text on economics for children and most of that text had been reprinted in various books in the Irish Readers used in Ontario; Ryerson, in 1877, a year after his retirement from the education office, wrote an introductory book for the general public entitled *Elements of Political Economy*.[125] The symmetry here is striking. Whately and Ryerson had shared the economic material in the Irish school books. Whately's rudimentary knowledge of economics had gone into those texts, and, seemingly, Ryerson's equally elementary publication had come out. (3) Besides vetting all the Irish Readers, contributing to the Scripture extracts, writing his own book of Christian evidences for school children, his text on the art of reasoning and his own text on political economy for children, Whately was himself the author of two of the basic Irish

Readers: the *Sequel to the Second Book of Lessons* and the *Supplement* to the fourth book, each of which was needed to make easier the transition as between the preceding and following books in the series.[126] If not the father of the Irish school curriculum, Whately at least was the godfather, as was Ryerson in Ontario.[127]

(IV)

Given that we as historians are predisposed not to see repetitive patterns — history, we keep telling our graduate students, is a study of the unique — it must mean something when we begin to realize that, as in the case of the Ontario educational system, we have seen a pattern before.

I think that we have here an example of one form — and it is only one of several possible forms — of cultural transfer from the Old World. It is a commonplace to think of mid-nineteenth-century Canada as being a cultural colony, but that metaphor muddies the waters, because the concept of colonialization virtually precludes clear perception: "colonial" status is a value-loaded expression. Colonialization is opposed to Canadianization; colonial status is something that is naturally outgrown, a temporary and imperfect state. Instead of speaking of cultural colonialization, historians might well use a less-value-loaded concept and think of cultural transfer. The primary task should not be, as it is under the concept of "cultural colonialism" to chart the seemingly inevitable displacement of some alien trait with a Canadian one, but to ask dispassionately what cultural traits were brought over from the Old World and how did they develop?

Here, the development of linguistic dialects provides a useful analogy. Dialectologists do not waste time arguing whether or not the English language as spoken in Ontario was — or is — an example of cultural colonialism, but instead discuss what features changed, which ones stayed the same, and why. For our purposes, individual words provide the simplest examples of this way of thinking, although idioms and pronunciation, and grammatical structures would do just as well. For instance, one notes that most of the 500 or so most commonly used words in the British Isles in the mid-nineteenth-century were introduced into Canada and that most of these words are still in common usage, with their meanings basically unchanged in both countries since that time. These are words such as "mother," "father," "heat," "water," "air," and they have survived in Ontario in their mid-nineteenth-century meaning, not because of any cultural imperialism from the British Isles, but because they were a cultural transplant that fit efficiently with the social and physical realities of Ontario. Second, one finds that some words — "engine" is an example — were imported into Ontario from the British Isles, and that, in the twentieth century, these words in each country independently took on a new meaning, and these coincide with each other, being the results of similar but independent influences on the same original root. Thus, cultural imperialism was not involved in keeping the evolving Ontario meaning of "engine" in line with evolving British Isles meaning: each word changed meaning as technological developments reversed the concept of the dominant connotation of "engine," from a massive stationary power force, to a mobile one. Third, one can discover Ontario words which have no counterpart in the English language as spoken in the British Isles, as they had to be created or adopted from another language to deal with a reality that existed in Ontario, but not in the homeland — "jerky" and "pemmican" are instances. Fourth, Ontario inhabitants sometimes invested words from the British Isles with new meanings quite different from the original ones as a result of local developments unmatched by parallel ones abroad: "Grit" springs to mind, as does the change in the denominated major grain crop to which the word "corn" applies.

By analogy, one would like historians to develop a reasonably value-free taxonomy of possible cultural evolutions, beginning with their origins overseas. Ideally, this taxonomy would be able to cover a wide range of cultural phenomena — from material culture,[128] such as the evolution of agricultural tools, to language,[129] to patterns of political culture, such as the simultaneous evolution from the same roots of representative democracy in the British Isles and in Canada, to matters of intangible beliefs as expressed in religious practices and works of high art.

Continuing the linguistic analogy, the Irish educational system as imported into Ontario, was very much like a loan-word. It survived because it served a real need of the society. In its first quarter-century of development, the evolution of the Ontario common schools system was amazingly like the evolution of the Irish national school system because (similar to the word "engine" mentioned above) each school system encountered nearly identical pressures in its respective society. And, even while the Ontario process of educational importation and evolution was occurring, further secondary influences from the homeland were also affecting that evolution — in the same way that, in the twentieth century, the occasional new British phrase has been imported into Ontario as an overlay to the basic linguistic structure laid down in the previous century.[130]

Matters of cultural transfer are so complex, and those of subsequent evolution so confused by there being a myriad of variables, that one is tempted to take the easy route and to declare simply that everything that happened in Canada is "Canadian" and let it go at that. But that has no more validity than would a dialectologist's denominating the language spoken here as "Canadian" and refusing to look for its roots.

And our roots, as the case of mass education in Ontario in the nineteenth century shows, are deep and are found far, far, from these shores.

Chapter Seven
Conclusion:
Why So Easy?

(I)

The preceding chapter, on the possible patterns of transfer of popular culture from Ireland to central Canada, indicates that the evidentiary problems involved in assessing the impact of an ethnic group upon a national culture are immense. It is very hard to get the story right. On the other hand, it is dead easy to get it wrong. In part, this is because here, as in all exercises in historical writing, there are only a few ways of aligning a story and its supporting evidence properly, but virtually an infinity of ways of going astray.[1]

That admitted, easiness of a peculiar sort has characterized the historiography of the Irish in North America: readers and writers of that history have not so much become ensnarled in any of history's complex evidentiary tangles, as they have been remarkably easily fooled and at a very low level of complexity. The studies in this volume have shown that as producers of scholarship, historians who have dealt with the Irish in North America have been lax in their standards of evidence and have framed their basic story of the Irish in the United States and in central Canada on a remarkable paucity of solid evidence and upon a gross misreading of what evidence they actually have found.

Of course professional historians are both the producers

of historical writing and one of the largest groups of consumers — a scholar both does his own original work and assimilates that done by other people. Thus the operative question becomes: why was it so easy for Canadian and American historians to con themselves into buying an historical bill-of-goods that had a virtually non-existent evidentiary base?

I can only guess, but because this is a question of some importance in North American historiography, let me speculate openly.

Considering first the United States, one profitable avenue of interpretation is to discuss the dominant, if erroneous, beliefs concerning the Irish in the United States as historical realities in themselves. As was demonstrated in chapter three, the accepted description of the Irish in the United States is not derived from an exegesis of the data by historians, but is the product of eisagesis. That is, it is not the result of a reading-out of meaning inherent in the historical data, but of a reading-in of meaning derived from beliefs, values, and attitudes totally external to the available historical evidence. Thus, if one takes the generally accepted story of the Irish in the United States it can be analyzed as a set of accepted useful lies about the "Irish-Americans."* This accepted mythology can be evaluated for accuracy of historical content, as was done in chapter three, by comparing its tenets with the statements that one can validly draw with a reasonable probability of accuracy from the available historical evidence. The myth can also be analyzed as an entity which, whatever its accuracy, has a social function, just like any other religious or secular set of myths.

For whom has this mythology been operative? I know of no relevant study. One can, however, make two assertions with a reasonable degree of certainty: first, that the majority

---

*Although I will avoid the awkward device of putting "Irish-American" in quotation marks throughout this chapter, the reader should understand that by that term I am referring to that part of the wider population of Irish origin which was, and is, Roman Catholic in religion and is in some sense conscious of being of Irish background.

of people who have written the history of the Irish in the United States as an urban Catholic cohort are themselves of Irish Catholic background[2] and, second, that it is almost equally certain that the majority of professional historians who are serious consumers of this mythology are mostly of Irish Catholic background as well.[3] Hence, the primary producers of the mythology and the primary consumers almost certainly have been self-defined members of the Irish-American community. Of course, other historians of the United States have used the material which thus has been produced, but they have taken it at face value and have incorporated it into comprehensive depictions of the ethno-cultural striations that run through American culture.

Whether or not the generality of persons of Irish Catholic background in the United States who think of themselves as being in some sense Irish, ever read any historical writing concerning their group is not known, but *if* they read anything, perforce they will be reading the dominant mythology: there is no alternative in print. I would speculate further, however — and this is purely speculation — that the mythology produced by the historians of the Irish in the United States not only has been acceptable to the Irish-Americans as a group, but has served a vital social function. In fact, I suspect that what historians have propounded as the social history of the Irish in America is merely the articulation and codification at a relatively high intellectual level of a set of useful and protective folk-beliefs that the Irish-American community has evolved concerning itself.[4]

How could it be of any benefit for a group to have its agreed history so out of kilter with the actual evidence? For the Irish-Americans, the historical mythology seems to have served two functions. The first of these has been to make the past less of an alien time, less of a strange and foreign land, than actually is the case. A simple, absolutely pivotal distortion has blurred the difference between the Irish immigrants and their children who formed the basis of the Irish-American community in approximately the middle two quarters of the nineteenth century, and those who came thereafter. As discussed at length in chapter three, the Irish were *not* a city people in their formative years, but only became so later. The patently unjustified belief that they were a city people from the very beginning of their history in the United States has grafted a false sense of collective continuity into the accepted historical mythology of the Irish-Americans. The migration of the children and grandchildren of rural and small-town Irish persons into the cities during the later years of the nineteenth and during the twentieth centuries must have been as important and traumatic a break with the past for the Irish as for any other group. Yet, by covering over this disjuncture in the historical experience of the Irish-Americans as a group, the accepted historical mythology has allowed members of the group more easily to appropriate relevant meanings (true or false, it matters not) from what they hear of events of the middle of the last century, particularly the Famine era.

The second major attribute of the myths of Irish-American history is that they have created a false, but highly useful, collective baseline against which to measure the performance of members of the ethnic group in the twentieth century. Almost perversely, from the early years of the present century onwards, Irish-Americans have had a vested interest in bad-mouthing their forebears. Specifically, by propagating the myth that the Irish Catholic migrants to America were too technologically backwards and too financially incontinent to save enough money even to get into frontier farming, historians implicitly have made the twentieth-century Irish look good. After all, look at how far they have come since their great-grandparents' day.[5]

This false historical baseline, I would speculate, still is relevant today in the few remaining impacted areas of Irish-American settlement such as exist in Boston and New York City. As Lawrence McCaffrey has argued, "the Massachusetts Irish are historical fossils rather than typical members of the American-Irish community."[6] To individuals caught in the atypical residual ghettos, the myth that the Irish Catholic in America was destined from his earliest days to be an urban, and often a slum, dweller, is a point of potential continuity with the past and his own lack of upward mobility becomes less of a reproach.

Within the accepted mythology of Irish-American history lies embedded a demonology. The historical myth holds that the reason that the Irish-Americans were stuck in cities and were not able therefore to reap the bounties of the American heartland, was that the bastard-British forged shackles in the form of cultural and economic limitations that could not be shaken off, even in the New World. To an individual who was not making much of an economic success of his life in late nineteenth or early twentieth-century America, it must have been a great comfort to have been able to blame the old enemy rather than either the discriminatory structure of the American republic or one's own self.

An additional palliative for pain is involved. One of the most striking things about the Irish-Americans as a collectivity is that despite (or perhaps because of) their overall success in American society, they have undergone a great deal of distress and this has empirical referents. For example, a study of admissions to New York State mental hospitals for 1911 showed that the Irish-born had far and away the highest rate of admission for alcoholic and related disorders of any major immigrant group. A more sophisticated study for 1949–51 indicated that both the Irish-born and the second generation Irish-Americans were more apt to be hospitalized for mental reasons than were members of any other ethnic group.[7] Succeeding in America has exacted its price. To some Irish-Americans, the old demonology may provide a satisfactory explanation of why that price was so high.

The real test of any mythology is not its accuracy — that is irrelevant — but whether or not it works. To work, its components must fit together smoothly and without gross and unsettling internal contradictions, and the myth must serve a need, a function, in the community wherein it is believed. Considered as a system of myth, the accepted view of the Irish in America has served well. It worked.

Historians, though, should not so easily be led to confuse myth and history.

(II)

The situation in Canada has not been at all the same and thus the probable reasons that historians have been so easily misled have been quite different. Unlike the United States, there has been no tradition of historical writing about the Irish in Canada. As mentioned in chapter four, between 1878 and 1974 there was no major scholarly book (or even much in the ephemeral line) published about the Irish in central Canada, where most of them actually settled. Perforce, there was no mythology of the Irish in Canada as a separate ethnic group, merely disembodied historical misconceptions. Unlike the Irish in the United States, the people of Irish descent in Canada did not need a myth. For most of the nineteenth century, the Irish in Canada were the largest non-French ethnic group and their prepotence was particularly salient in the rich and (after mid-century) the most populace province, Ontario. The economic behaviour of the Irish, Catholic and Protestant, was not markedly different from that of the generality of their fellow "English-Canadians." Neither the Irish Protestants nor the Irish Catholics were a segregated minority, either geographically or socio-economically. Nor, as in the United States, was there a large twentieth-century residium who remained locked into the lower rungs of urban life after the majority of their fellows had passed upwards. Therefore, instead of requiring a separate ethnic mythology of their own, persons of Irish ethnicity shared the general cosmology of English-Canadianism — the Protestant Irish completely, the Catholics with some reservations. In a sense, the economic success of the Irish in Canadian society and their numerical prepotence amongst "English-Canadians" meant that they did not need an historical mythology as part of their survival equipment.

This absence of a collective ethnic mythology should have meant that Canadian historians were at a great advantage as compared to the Americans. They could have dealt with the Irish in Canada directly and accurately without having to cut through disturbing myths, such as those within which the Irish-American ethnic community wrapped itself. This task should have been especially easy to effect as the Canadian census data on ethnicity and on such related items as religion, occupation and place-of-residence are excellent, particularly as compared to the United States data. Given these advantages, and given the centrality of the Irish immigrants to nineteenth-century Canadian social life, a clear, well-documented historiography should have emerged.

Yet nothing of the sort happened. Instead, Canadian historians imported the Irish-American mythology, with scarcely a pause to relabel the package. The Irish Catholics in central Canada were declared to have been an urban group in the last century, the lowest strata in an industrializing society. Emphatically, we are not here viewing a case of United States cultural imperialism. Twentieth-century writers on the history of the Irish in the United States have shown a lack of interest in Canada, save concerning the Fenian raids, that borders on disdain and, indeed, an ignorance of relevant Canadian evidence that is virtually breath-taking. No, the mythology of the Irish-American was not forced upon Canadian historians, but instead was sought out by them and assimilated with an avidity that can only be taken as culturally diagnostic.

That taking the easy way — that is, assimilating the Irish-American mythology — was the wrong way for Canadian historians to proceed has been one of the major themes of this book. There is more behind the assimilation of the Irish-American mythology, however, than mere laziness and the buy-American reflex of Canadian social historians. As the essay on the work of H. Clare Pentland argued (chapter five), certain perduring slivers of Old World prejudice against the Irish Catholics have lingered well into our own time. The American line about the Irish Catholics being technologically backward, incapable of farming, and unable to amass capital, slipped across the border, into the work of H. Clare Pentland and Kenneth Duncan and into the canons of the "new" Canadian social history.

Ironically, this unconsciously racist view of the Irish Catholics meshed well with the ideological requirements of the new social history. One says "ironically" because the Marxist theoretical underpinnings of the new Canadian social history are admirably non-racist. Unhappily, though, many of the new social historians have jumped to accept the pronouncements of H. Clare Pentland, and with the same enthusiasm, that Archbiship Richard Whately leapt to accept George Combe's phrenological humbug. In the process they, like Whately, set aside their evidentiary principles and became not scholars, but marks.

Admittedly, if a Marxist-derived social history of Canada is to succeed, one needs, amongst other things, a clear description of the creation of a working class and of the relationship of that class to the dominant modes of industrial production. Because so much subsequent social history is contingent upon a formulation of how the working class came into being, it is tempting to hurry that job and to take short-cuts. That never works. In particular, as I have argued at length, kidnapping the Irish Catholics to form an industrial labour pool simply will not do.

To my mind, the most pressing item on the agenda for Canadian social historians — "old," "new," it matters not — is to merge the growing body of work on ethnicity in Canadian society with the equally rapidly expanding literature on the evolution of social class. At present, ethnic historians and social-class historians are engaged in a silent war; they ignore each other. Whereas many, probably most, historians of ethnicity view ethnic identity as primary and social class as, at best, tertiary affiliations, historians of class for the most part ignore ethnicity, treat it as a minor way-station on the path to proper class identity, or as an item of false consciousness that has inhibited the inevitable rise of class consciousness. Perhaps some few historians will be able to put aside what they want to believe and to look first, and last, at the primary evidence.

And, while doing so, they might cast a thought now and again to the parable of Archbishop Whately and his encounter with the subtle phrenologist and thence to the warning enhulled in that tale.

Notes

Notes to Chapter One

1. The only twentieth-century biography of Whately is Donald H. Akenson, *A Protestant in Purgatory: Richard Whately, Archbishop of Dublin* (Hamden, Conn.: published for the Conference on British Studies and Indiana University at South Bend by Archon Books, 1981). Unless otherwise cited, facts concerning Whately are taken from that study.

2. Ibid., p. 71.

3. David A. de Giustino, "Phrenology in Britain, 1815–1855: A Study of George Combe and His Circle" (Ph.D. thesis, University of Wisconsin, 1969).

4. Raymie E. McKerrow, "Whately's Theory of Rhetoric" (Ph.D. thesis, University of Iowa, 1974), p. 440.

5. Rev. Hercules Dickinson, quoted in William J. Fitzpatrick, *Memoirs of Richard Whately, Archbishop of Dublin, with a glance at his Contemporaries and Times* (London: 1864), vol. II, p. 287.

6. (Copy) George Combe to RW, 6 October 1831, National Library of Scotland (hereafter NLS), MS 7385; RW to Combe, 19 May 1832, NLS, MS 7229; (copy) Combe to RW, 6 June 1832, NLS, MS 7385; (copy) Combe to RW, 12 July 1832, NLS, MS 7385.

7. RW to George Combe, 19 May 1832.

8. RW to George Combe, 30 July 1831; RW to George Combe, 19 May 1832; RW to George Combe, 19 June 1832, NLS, MS 7229.

9. (Copy) George Combe to RW, 28 August 1832, NLS, MS 7385.

10. RW to George Combe, 2 September 1832, NLS, MS 7229.

11. (Copy) George Combe to RW, 6 September 1832, NLS, MS 7385.

12. RW to George Combe, 11 September 1832, NLS, MS 7229.

13. (Copy) George Combe to RW, 14 September 1832, NLS, MS 7385.

14. RW to George Combe, _____ October 1832, NLS, MS 7229; RW to Combe, 8 October, 1832, NLS , MS 7229; RW to Combe, 1 December 1832, NLS, MS 7229.

15. The letter of recommendation was published in the *American Phrenological Journal*, vol. I (1838), p. 47, and is quoted extensively by McKerrow, pp. 442–43.

16. On political economy and education, see de Giustino, pp. 246–96, and especially pp. 265–66.

For an interesting obituary see "Richard Whately, D.D.," *American Phrenological Review*, vol. 38 (December 1863), pp. 145–46.

17. RW to George Combe, 24 January 1833, NLS, MS 7231; (copy) Combe to RW, 24 January 1833, 26 January 1833, NLS, MS 7385; Mrs. Whately to Combe, 26 December 1835, NLS, MS 7236; RW to Combe, 11 January 1837, NLS, MS 7244; RW to Combe, 10 March 1838, NLS, MS 7248; RW to Combe, 4 September 1838, NLS, MS 7248.

18. RW to Mrs. Thomas Arnold, 9 March 1847, reproduced in Elizabeth Jane Whately [with Herman Merivale], *Life and Correspondence of Richard Whately, D.D., late Archbiship of Dublin* (London, 1866), vol. II, pp. 120–21.

19. Fitzpatrick, vol. II, p. 285.

Notes to Chapter Two

1. Forrest McDonald and Ellen Shapiro McDonald, "The Ethnic Origins of the American People, 1790," *William and Mary Quarterly,* 3d Ser., vol. 37 (1980), pp. 179–99, hereafter cited as McDonalds, "Ethnic Origins." Since the McDonalds' work appeared, another redaction of the ACLS *Report* has been published in David Noel Doyle, *Ireland, Irishmen and Revolutionary America, 1760–1820* (Dublin and Cork, 1981), pp 75–6. This work, done independently of the McDonalds' study, estimates the Irish element in the populations of the middle and southern states.

See also, Thomas L. Purvis, "The European Ancestry of the United States Population, 1790," *William and Mary Quarterly,* 3d Ser., vol. 41 (January 1984), pp. 85–101. Although Purvis's article deals chiefly with German, Swedish, Dutch, and French groups, it also presents a reassessment of the ethnic groups from the British Isles, employing a version of the surname-ratio method created by H.F. Barker and developed by the McDonalds. For comments on Purvis's work as it relates to European groups see below, note 15.

2. Published in the *Annual Report of the American Historical Association for the year 1931,* vol. I, *Proceedings,* pp 107–452, hereafter cited as *Report.*

3. On the committee members, see the various editions of *Who Was Who in America.*

4. *Report,* pp. 107–11.

5. That, as will be established later in the text, the ACLS committee and its consultants actually were unable to come up with ethnically unambiguous names, is here irrelevant. Their theory was as stated.

6. *Report,* pp. 111–12.

7. *Ibid.,* pp. 126–63.

8. The reader will have noted that in points (a) and (b) of the example, I say "England and Wales," but that in point (d) I refer to a conclusion for persons of "English" ancestry. This follows precisely Barker's method. He used separate Welsh and English name lists and related each of the names on the two lists to their occurrence throughout England and Wales and to the total population of England and Wales. Obviously, this invalidates his method as far as England and Wales are concerned. But for the moment, give Barker the benefit of the doubt by reading "English and Welsh" wherever he says "English" or "Welsh" separately.

9. I think that the most generous explanation for Barker's having used the number-per-1,000 rather than the more accurate and more easily understood ratios in their simplest form is that his method made the tedious arithmetical computations easier.

10. *Report,* p. 124.

11. That this is so is made clear by the respect given the data in Stephen Thernstrom's state-of-the-art compilation, the *Harvard Encyclopedia of American Ethnic Groups* (Cambridge, Mass., 1980) esp. pp 479, 503. The ACLS

Report furnishes the basis for the ethnicity estimates in the widely used text, *The Evolution of American Society, 1700–1815, An Interdisciplinary Analysis* by James A. Henretta (Lexington, Mass., 1973), pp. 122–25, and for the colonial estimates in the Bureau of the Census, *Historical Statistics of the United States. Colonial Times to 1790*. (See Bicentennial Edition, pt. 2, 1168).

12. The McDonalds' basic argument is that the "Celtic" element was underestimated by the procedures of the ACLS committee and its consultants. They may be right, but in my view they are arguing about where the mast should be placed on a boat whose hull is full of gaping holes. The vessel will sink the minute it comes down the slipway, in any case.

13. The 1870 U.S. census had asked whether or not one had foreign-born parents, but not where they came from.

14. Charles A. Price, "Methods of Estimating the Size of Groups," in Thernstrom, ed., pp. 1033–35, 1042.

Unfortunately, one fears that the 1980 ethnicity question also will be mishandled. The census authorities again allowed respondents to list multiple ethnic ancestries, not just their main ethnic identification, and 55 percent of the respondents listed more than one (*New York Times*, 16 May and 5 June 1983.)

15. *Report*, pp. 118–19, 124, 271–305. Again, I am providing only the central point of the obtuse explanation by Barker and by the ACLS committee.

Because the matter bears indirectly upon one's assaying of the Irish in colonial America, the matter of continental European groups bears further comment, particularly as Thomas Purvis's article "The European Ancestry of the United States Population, 1790," (see note 1, above), adopts Barker's method of estimating the German-American population and extends it to other European groups.

Purvis quite properly notes that Barker had no real idea of how many people of German ethnicity lived in Pennsylvania, but this is beside the point. *Even* if one knew the precise number of German-Americans in Pennsylvania in 1790, the surname-ratio method as proposed by Barker and adopted by Purvis would not work. Why? Both Barker and Purvis introduce a convenient fiction, namely, that for the purpose of calculating surname-ratios, Pennsylvania was a foreign country, a surrogate Germany. That is, one could use German names from Pennsylvania to develop a surname-frequency list as a surrogate for a surname-frequency list from the mother country. (This is said to be necessary because there is no direct surname data available for Germany). Whether or not this approach is even potentially legitimate is uncertain, for it introduces the difficult problem of second-level proxies: Purvis and Barker simultaneously use Pennsylvania as a surrogate for a foreign country and employ Pennsylvanian surname-data as a surrogate for ethnic data. What is certain, however, is that even if one puts aside the second-level proxy problem, one has a ratio as follows:

$$\frac{\text{Number of Persons in Pennsylvania with Certain German Names}}{\text{Total Population of German-Americans in Pennsylvania}} = \frac{\text{Number of Persons in Each State of the U.S. with Certain German Names}}{\text{Total Number of Persons of German Ethnicity in Each State of the U.S.}}$$

And this ratio can provide accurate conclusions only if one of the following two conditions obtains: (A) That there had been before 1790 such a high degree of geographic mobility by German-Americans as between Pennsylvania and *each* of the other states so that the German-Americans throughout the United

States were scattered entirely randomly as far as their family names were concerned. In that case, the Pennsylvanian-German surnames would be a simulacrum of the surnames of the German-Americans in each of the other states and the Barker-Purvis ratio would be valid. This degree of random geographic mobility cannot seriously be posited. (B) The alternative validating condition would be that the German population that settled in Pennsylvania was drawn from exactly the same sources as regards surnames as was the German population that settled in *each* of the other states. This is so inherently improbable as to have been virtually impossible: it would mean that there was no clustering in certain states of migrants from specific families, no bunching of persons from particular locations in Germany and no grouping of settlements in particular states of Germans from narrow economic or occupational strata in the old country (all three matters being ones that affect surname distributions). The existence of any significant degree of chain-migration would preclude these three characteristics holding; and if the Germans did not engage in chain-migration then they were totally unique not only in the New World, but in the known history of long-distance emigration.

The hard facts are that Pennsylvania cannot be used as a surrogate for Germany as far as surnames are concerned and that the surname-ratios derived from that state cannot be applied to other jurisdictions in the United States.

This conclusion holds, *mutatis mutandis*, for Dr. Purvis's calculations concerning the Dutch (wherein five countries and New York City are used as a surrogate for the Netherlands), the Swedes (for whom the Delaware Valley is employed as a proxy for Sweden) and the French (for whom, incredibly, three congregations of Hugenots in England are used as a surrogate for France).

16. *Report*, pp. 119–22, 360–97. Canadian readers may be particularly interested in Hansen's intuition concerning the French. "Perhaps a century from now when the Canadian conquest of New England is complete and the French-Canadian tongue, church, and mill worker are the dominant features of New England society, historians will center their studies upon that compact group of Quebec *habitants* from whom millions of Americans have sprung" (p. 380).

17. See McDonalds, "Ethnic Origins," p. 186, and *Report*, pp. 124, 187–88, 194–97.

18. *Report*, pp. 112, 164, 207, 232.

19. I assume that no elaborate documentation is required for the assertion that surnames were localized, rather than random, in the British Isles. The *Report* itself has nearly 200 pages of argument substantiating this fact. Surnames are shown to be centralized in the various countries in the British Isles, and there also is extensive documentation of localization within each country. That this fact — combined with the fact that certain areas experienced higher out-migration in the nineteenth century than did others — invalidated the *Report's* conclusions, was missed by the committee members.

The assertion that surnames were also specialized by social class requires even less demonstration, as anyone familiar with Burke and Debrett realizes.

20. *Report*, p. 111n5.

21. McDonalds, "Ethnic Origins," p. 185, and *Report*, pp. 218, 227–29.

22. In the discussion that follows I am ignoring entirely the highly problematical way in which missing or imperfect records for the states of New Jersey, Delaware, Georgia, Kentucky, Tennessee, and Virginia were treated.

23. *Report*, pp. 113, 209, 237.

24. Ibid. p. 230.

25. Ibid., p. 248.

26. Ibid., pp. 119–200, 209, 258–60.

27. Ibid., p. 113. *See also* pp. 165–67.

28. There was, of course, no English census in 1853. Presumably, the ACLS committee and its consultants used estimates derived from the 1851 census.

29. *Report*, pp. 113, 114.

30. I am laying aside entirely the problem that was introduced by the evolution of Irish names. This was not merely orthographical. The entire method of establishing surnames changed considerably between the end of the eighteenth century and the late nineteenth.

31. *Report*, p. 115.

32. Ibid., pp. 117, 252.

33. Although they said "1860" in their *Report*, presumably the ACLS committee and its consultants were using the 1861 census of Scotland.

34. Whether this was a conscious attempt to offset the anti-Free State bias involved in the equation of historic Ulster with Northern Ireland is unclear. To complicate matters further, the tendency to overestimate Irish Catholics was somewhat reduced by the fact that the census chosen, that of 1821, was artificially low, as it had been the first full Irish census and the populace met it with hostility and therefore the population was underenumerated. On this and related matters, see Joseph Lee, "On the Accuracy of the pre-Famine Irish Censuses," in J.M. Goldstrom and L.A. Clarkson, eds., *Irish Population, Economy, and Society: Essays in Honour of the Late K.H. Connell* (Oxford, 1981), pp. 37–56.

35. *Report*, p. 265.

36. See table 34, p. 165, "Irish Religious Distributions, 1834," in Donald H. Akenson, *The Church of Ireland: Ecclesiastical Reform and Revolution, 1800*–1885 (New Haven, Conn. 1971). Even if one subtracts the Diocese of Meath (in Leinster) from the calculation, the Presbyterian proportion still is less than 23 percent.

37. *Report*, p. 267.

38. Given that the procedures of Barker and of the ACLS committee tended to raise artificially the numbers of persons of all three Irish ethnic subgroups, it would be intriguing to know where the compensatory subtraction was made: in English and Scots representation in the final ethnicity figures for the U.S., or in those for European groups.

39. *Report*, p. 263.

40. McDonalds, "Ethnic Origins," p. 181. I hope that in disagreeing with the McDonalds as to the chances of doing a valid redaction of the ACLS *Report* on the 1790 census, I am not obscuring my gratitude for their pioneering work in calling some of the *Report's* problems to public attention. That said, there are problematic aspects of the McDonalds' work, other than the methodological ones cited in the text. The McDonalds' article on the ethnic origins of the American people, 1790, is part of an interpretative agenda to which they allude in that article. This agenda is being carried out under the auspices of the Center for the Study of Southern History and Culture at the University of Alabama, most notably by the McDonalds and by Professor Grady McWhiney. This may be labelled, not unfairly, the Celtic Vision of the American Past. In addition to the McDonalds' article in the *William and Mary Quarterly*, see: Forrest McDonald and Grady McWhiney, "The Antebellum Southern Herdsman: A Reinterpretation," *Journal of Southern History*, vol. 41 (May 1975), pp. 147–66; Forrest McDonald and Grady McWhiney, "The Celtic South," *History Today*, vol. 30 (July 1980), pp. 11–15; Forrest McDonald and Grady McWhiney, "The South from Self-Sufficiency to Peonage: An Interpretation," *American Historical Review*, vol. 85 (December 1980), pp. 1095–1118; Forrest McDonald, "The Ethnic Factor in Alabama History: A Neglected Dimension," *Alabama Review*, vol. 31 (1978), pp. 256–65; Grady McWhiney and Perry D. Jamieson, *Attack and Die. Civil War Military Tactics and the Southern Heritage* (University of Alabama: University of Alabama Press, 1982).

The Celtic Vision as yet is not fully unfolded, but as adumbrated so far it suggests:

1. that those persons in colonial America whose origins were in the British Isles, but who were not English in the narrow sense, were "Celtic." That is, the "Highland and Lowlands Scots, Welsh, Irish, and Scotch-Irish" were a single cultural-racial group and comprised "the Celtic elements in the American population" (McDonalds, "Ethnic Origins," p. 181; cf McDonald and McWhiney in *AHR*, p. 1108*n*31, where it is admitted that the various Celtic groups were not identical, "but after a great deal of study we have concluded that it is legitimate to consider them as a single general cultural group ..."). Elsewhere, the Cornish are also included as Celts, despite most aspects of Cornish culture being dead before the era of Cornish migration to colonial America. (*See Attack and Die*, p. 172.);

2. the Celts, as defined above, are believed to have been underrepresented in most estimates of the ethnicity of the American population, both in the colonial era and later;

3. similarily, the economic, cultural, and social institutions of the Celts have either been ignored or downplayed by American historians. In particular, it is suggested that the pastoralist (and allegedly Celtically-derived) aspect of American agriculture largely has been ignored;

4. many, if not most, of the cultural, economic, and institutional differences between the north and the south are said to be ascribable to the differing proportions of Celtic and English elements in the populations: "By 1850, then, the South was three-quarters or more Celtic, New England and the upper Middle West were three-quarters or more English, and the border areas between were mixed." ("The Celtic South," p. 11).

Whether or not the holders of the Celtic Vision are correct in suggesting that American historiography is too Anglophillic is something that American historians necessarily must settle for themselves. It is important to note, however, that as far as the field of Celtic studies is concerned, the holders of the Celtic Vision are much more certain about what "Celtic" means than are scholars who spend their life in the field. Ever since Herodotus mentioned the Danubian tribe, the Keltoi, scholars have wondered who the Celts really are. In the eighteenth and nineteenth centuries, it is very hard to distinguish a Celt from a non-Celt, both in the Old Country and in the New.

Here historians are on a cleft stick. If one uses "Celtic" as a linguistic term, then one cannot lump together, for example, the Gaelic-speaking Scots Highlanders and the English- or Lallans-speaking Scots Lowlanders, or, from the beginning of the nineteenth century, include most of the Irish, as they had become largely English-speakers. One can, of course, substitute racial-physiological definitions of Celticness based on certain empirically-derived data (e.g. a high incidence of 0 blood type, high forehead, long head, high incidence of skin cancer), but this sort of definition carries with it no cultural connotations — and the reason that historians such as the McDonalds wish to study the Celts is to determine their impact upon the cultural matrix of the United States, broadly defined.

Certainly, few scholars of the Celtic countries in the seventeenth-nineteenth centuries would accept that the inhabitants of Ireland, Scotland, and Wales all practised a single, traditional form of pastoral agriculture. Equally few would accept the Celtic Vision's emphasis upon the direct continuity of aspects of Celtic behaviour from earliest times to the mid-nineteenth century. (The assertion reaches its extreme of absurdity in *Attack and Die* wherein the aggressiveness and tactical prodigality of the Confederacy is explained by their being Celts, and a direct line of military behaviour is suggested, from Celtic warfare as practised in 225 B.C. right down to the middle of the American Civil War. See pp. 174ff).

41. Washington, D.C.: Government Printing Office, 1907–08.

42. Ibid., 1909.

Notes to Chapter Three

1. The agreed explanation which follows in the text is derived from my reading of the work of the fifty-odd authors of general works on the Irish as set forth in *The Irish-American Experience. A Guide to the Literature* by Seamus P. Metress (Washington, D.C.: University Press of America Inc., 1981, pp. 1-5), and of most (but certainly not all) of the more specialized studies done in the last forty years. In choosing to quote from specific works of synthesis in the text which follows, I am using those volumes which are either best known and widely read, or most respected in the scholarly community. This is not to say that the authors of those synthetical works always have read accurately the specialized studies on which their general expositions are based, but that is irrelevant: the generally-agreed explanation has become an historiographic reality in itself.

More recently two articles have appeared which, though less comprehensive than Metress's work, are valuable: R.A. Burchell, "This Historiography of the American Irish," *Immigrants and Minorities*, vol. 1, (November 1982), pp. 281-305, and David Noel Doyle, "The Regional Bibliography of Irish America, 1800-1930: a Review and Addendum," *Irish Historical Studies*, vol. 23 (May 1983), pp. 254-83.

2. William V. Shannon, *The American Irish* (New York: MacMillan, 1963), p. 27.

3. Lawrence J. McCaffrey, *The Irish Diaspora in America* (Bloomington: Indiana University Press, 1976), p. 62.

4. Carl Wittke, *The Irish in America* (New York: Russell and Russell, 1956), pp. 26-27. The importance to the synthesizing historians of Oscar Handlin's *Boston's Immigrants. A Study in Acculturation* (Cambridge: Harvard University Press, 1941) and to a lesser extent, of Stephan Thernstrom's *Poverty and Progress* (Cambridge: Harvard University Press, 1964) is so obvious as not to require comment, except to note that one cannot fairly hold against either author the fact that their findings often have been over-generalized by later synthesizers. Each author made the limits of his data clear.

5. McCaffrey, p. 63.

6. Shannon, p. 27.

7. John B. Duff, *The Irish in the United States* (Belmont, California: Wadsworth Publishing Co., 1971), p. 16.

8. George Potter, *To the Golden Door. The Story of the Irish in Ireland and America* (Boston: Little Brown and Co., 1960), p. 171.

9. This letter, taken from the *Belfast News-Letter* of 17 April 1821 was first printed in William Forbes Adams' monograph *Ireland and Irish Emigration to the New World from 1815 to the Famine* (New Haven: Yale University Press, 1932), and is quoted directly in Wittke (p. 62), Duff (p. 16), and Shannon (p. 27). In each of the last three instances, it is employed to help to explain the post-Famine behaviour of the Irish Catholic migrants to America, a usage which loses some of its force when one considers that the letter was written a full quarter century before the Famine and was quite probably written by a Protestant. (At that time, the *News-Letter* was a rabidly anti-Catholic paper, and its columns were not generally open to Roman Catholics.)

Rather more apposite would be the very revealing book of poems by a Kansas priest who had been a curate in Wicklow: Thomas Butler, *The Irish on the Prairies and Other Poems* (New York: D. and J. Sadlier and Co., 1874).

10. McCaffrey, p. 63.

11. See, for example, the ingenious attempt to tie together Catholicism, Gallic linguistic patterns, and Irish-American economic behaviour by Kerby A. Miller, with Bruce Boling and David N. Doyle, "Emigrants and Exiles: Irish Cultures and Irish Emigration to North America, 1790-1922," *Irish Historical Studies*, vol. 22 (September 1980), pp. 97-125.

12. The accepted view of the Irish in Canada was most clearly defined in articles by two influential scholars. One of these was Kenneth Duncan whose "Irish Famine Immigration and the Social Structure of Canada West," became something of a classic. Originally published in the *Canadian Review of Sociology and Anthropology* (1965), pp. 19–40, it was reprinted in *Studies on Canadian Social History*, edited by Michiel Horn and Ronald Sabourin (Toronto: McClelland and Stewart, 1974), pp. 140–63 and in *Canada: A Sociological Profile* (Toronto: Copp Clarke, 1968), p. 1–16, edited by W.E. Mann.

The other scholar was the highly influential social historian H. Clare Pentland, whose views of the Irish were clearly articulated in "The Development of a Capitalistic Labour Market in Canada," *Canadian Journal of Economics and Political Science*, vol. 25 (November 1959), pp. 450–61. His Ph.D. thesis "Labour and the Development of Industrial Capitalism in Canada (University of Toronto, 1960) contained a long discussion of the Irish and was an influential work, as it was adopted as something of an underground classic by the radical social historians of the 1970s' generation. Pentland's thesis, only slightly modified, has been published posthumously as *Labour and Capital in Canada, 1650–1860* (Toronto: James Lorimer, 1981), edited by Paul Phillips.

Duncan's work is discussed in detail in chapter four of the present volume and Pentland's in chapter five.

13. A Gordon Darroch and Michael D. Ornstein, "Ethnicity and Occupational Structure in Canada in 1871: the Vertical Mosaic in Historical Perspective," *Canadian Historical Review*, vol. 61 (September 1980), pp. 305–33. The one exception to the general pattern of Irish Catholics being farmers was Nova Scotia, because of the existence of a large group of urban Catholics in Halifax.

14. Donald H. Akenson, "Ontario: Whatever Happened to the Irish?" *Canadian Papers in Rural History*, vol. 2 (1982), pp. 204–56. *See also*, Akenson, *The Irish in Ontario: A Study in Rural History* (Montreal and Kingston: McGill-Queen's University Press, 1984).

15. By roadblocks, I mean facile suggestions such as: that the U.S. and Canadian cases are not comparable because there was a higher proportion of Protestants amongst the Irish migrants to Canada than to the U.S.; that those Irish Catholics who came to Canada were "loyalist" in politics, as compared to those who went to the south; and that the Irish Catholics who moved to Canada were in some ways culturally advantaged.

Concerning the first of these objections, it is true that the Catholics were indeed fewer than the Protestants — roughly one-third of the Ontario Irish cohort was Catholic — but the size of the total Irish Catholic group certainly is large enough to permit them to be studied as a separate sub-group: an aggregate of several million persons when considered over the entire run of census data. Presumably this group would be comparable to the Irish Catholics in the U.S. (I am assuming that the suggestion that association with Irish Protestants in some way made the Irish Catholics in Canada better farmers and more able to stand rural loneliness is not an idea that anyone would seriously put forward.)

As for the objection that the Irish Catholics who came to Canada were in some way not real Irishmen, because they settled under the Crown, it is very hard to see how "loyalism" of this sort made a person a more effective pioneer than did the "republicanism" of the U.S. Irish. Certainly, the idea that republicanism and success in a rural environment are not compatible would have come as a shock to successive governments of the Irish Free State and the Republic of Ireland. (In any case, I doubt if the political attitudes which the Irish Catholics brought with them to Canada were significantly different from those held by migrants to the United States. The core of Thomas N. Brown's seminal study,

Irish-American Nationalism (Philadelphia: Lippincott, 1966), is that the extreme nationalism of the Irish Americans was a response to their problems in American society, not a set of beliefs brought from the homeland.)

As for the third point, I find no evidence that the abilities of the Irish-American Catholics were any less than those of the Irish-Canadian Catholics (or of the Irish-Canadian Protestants, for that matter). At heart, any suggestion that the Canadian experience is an inappropriate comparison to the American one, must come down to an assertion (suitably disguised to make it palatable to American social historians) that amongst the Catholic migrants to North America, Canada received the winners and the United States the losers. That is, Canada received those who were able to adapt to forms of agricultural technology unknown in the home country, who had the character to overcome the insecurity of living in isolation in the countryside, in addition to having the tenacity to amass enough resources to enter commercial farming. Manifestly, this is hard to accept, but unless one is willing to argue that the difference between Canada and the United States in regard to Irish Catholics was simply the difference between winners and losers, and unless one can also specify the set of mechanisms that resulted in such an efficient social sorting as between the two countries in the New World, then one must agree that the two groups are legitimately comparable, and look for specific mechanisms in the New World that explain their alleged divergences.

16. The matter of legitimacy-of-comparison aside, I will argue later in the text that historians of the Irish in the United States must study the Canadian situation because Canadian government records hold certain crucial pieces of evidence lacking in American sources.

17. This terminology, stemming as it does from American melting-pot ideology is somewhat misleading, for is implicitly minimizes the degree of cultural transfer and of resistance to assimilation by the foreign-born, by simply re-defining the foreign-born as "American."

18. That certain historians have labelled as "second generation" not only the American-born children of the foreign-born, but also children who were very young when the immigrants arrived in the United States and thus were educated almost entirely in the States, confuses matters somewhat. This labelling further diminishes the apparent "foreigness" of the foreign-born children so denominated, and implies a greater degree of subsumation by the dominant American culture than usually is justified.

19. The methodology of the ACLS re-study of the 1790 census is treated in detail in chapter two of the present volume.

20. The problem was that persons returning more than one ethnic origin were lumped into an "other" category which embraced roughly half the population! See Charles A. Price, "Methods of Estimating the Size of Groups," in Stephen Thernstrom (ed.), *Harvard Encyclopedia of American Ethnic Groups* (Cambridge: Harvard University Press, 1980), pp. 1033–34.

21. Unfortunately, it appears that the mistake of 1970 was repeated for the 1980 census. Individuals were again allowed to list multiple ancestries, rather than a single dominant one, so that 55 percent listed two or more. (*New York Times*, 16 May 1982). *See also* Ibid., 5 June 1983.

22. Price in Thernstrom (ed.), p. 1040.

23. For a fascinating discussion of this fear of collecting religious data, and especially of the trouble which arose when it was proposed to include religion on the 1960 census, see William Petersen, "Religious Statistics in the United States," *Journal for the Scientific Study of Religion*, vol. 1 (1965), pp. 165–78. This article also discusses the Census Bureau's suppression (!) of the data it had collected in the 1957 voluntary-sample study.

24. Lawrence J. McCaffrey, "A Profile of Irish America," in David N. Doyle and Owen D. Edwards (eds.) *America and Ireland, 1776–1976. The American*

Identity and the Irish Connection (Westport, Conn: Greenwood Press, 1980), p. 82.

25. A very useful version of that census was compiled by J.D.B. Debow, superintendent of the U.S. census, *A Statistical View of the United States ...* (Washington, D.C.: Beverley Tucker, Senate Printer, 1854).

26. Niles Carpenter, *Immigrants and their Children. A Study based on Census Statistics relative to the Foreign born and the Native Whites of the Foreign or Mixed Parentage* (Washington D.C., Census Monographs VII, Government Printing Office, 1927) p. 2.

Although the U.S. Census Bureau's collections of ethnic data went no further than the immigrant and his offspring, it is of course possible to do extrapolations of the gross number of persons in the third generation. This was attempted by the Census Bureau for the 1920 census (See Carpenter, p. 92) and, further, amateur demographers were always willing to try to establish the total strength of the Irish ethnic group from the limited knowledge available concerning the first two generations in the United States. Michael J. O'Brien, historiographer of the American-Irish Historical Society, surveyed some of the early attempts and shrewdly, if tiredly, remarked that "to form any reliable estimate of the numerical strength of the Irish and their descendants in the United States would, I believe, be a hopeless task and while several have attempted to do so, I am of the opinion that all such estimates should be discarded as mere conjecture." Michael J. O'Brien, "The Irish in the United States," in *The Glories of Ireland* (Washington D.C.: Phoenix, Ltd., 1914), edited by Joseph Dunn and P.J. Lennox, p. 208.

27. Derived from U.S. Immigration and Naturalization Service *Annual Report, 1975*, as found in Patrick J. Blessing, "Irish," in Thernstrom (ed.), p. 528. For each year's figures, see *Reports of the Immigration Commission, Statistical Review of Immigration 1820–1910 ...* (Washington, D.C.: Government Printing Office, 1911), pp. 14ff.

28. The example in the text is simplified for expository purposes. If one wishes to try to calculate the "ethnic multiplier" for the first and second generation, one can try to relate these two facts: that in 1880 there were 1,854,571 persons in the United States who had been born in Ireland; and in the same year, 4,529,523 persons in the U.S. reported having (either dead or alive) an Irish-born father and 4,448,421 having an Irish-born mother. See *Compendium of the Tenth Census (June 1, 1880) compiled pursuant to an Act of Congress approved August 7, 1882* (Washington: Government Printing Office, 1883), vol. 1, p. 485 and vol. 2, pp. 1407–08.

Actually, it is reasonable to suggest that the multiplier was higher for those who arrived earlier in the nineteenth century than for those who arrived later. It has been shown that the number of children under five years of age per 1,000 persons (a crude indicator of family size) dropped from 976 in 1810 for the entire U.S. white population to 835 in 1840 and then declined regularly during the nineteenth century, ending at 541 in 1900. (The figure for 1930, to give a twentieth-century example, was 386). See Yasukichi Yasuba, *Birth Rates of the White Population in the United States, 1800–1860* (Baltimore: Johns Hopkins Press, 1962), pp. 26–27.

Further, Yasuba's study suggests that fertility rates were higher in places where new land was easily available and lower where it was not. Which is to say that, if the Irish followed the national pattern, those who arrived earlier and were more apt to settle into pioneer agriculture were more apt to have larger families and thus to be a disproportionately larger segment of the ethnic group than their immigrant numbers would suggest (see Yasuba, p. 186–87).

29. Compiled from: DeBow, p. 117, *Population of the United States in 1860* (Washington: Government Printing Office, 1864), vol. I, p. xxix; *The Population of the United States ... 1870* (Washington D.C.: Government Printing

Office, 1872), vol. I, p. 340; *Completion of the Tenth Census* ..., vol. I, p. 485; *Twelfth Census of the United States, 1900* (Washington, D.C.: Government Printing Office, 1903), vol. I, p. xix.

30. Arnold Schrier, "Ireland and the American Emigration, 1850–1900," (Ph.D., Northwestern University, 1956), p. 231.

31. See census rate in the text, above. The drop in the rate of decennial increase was from 67.5 percent for the decade 1850–60, to 5.2 percent for the decade 1860–70.

32. Carpenter, p. 79; Schrier, p. 231.

33. Taken from U.S. Immigration and Naturalization Service, *Annual Report, 1975*, as found in Patrick J. Blessing, "Irish," in Thernstrom (ed.), p. 528.

34. Computed from *The Population of the United States* ... *1870*, vol. I, pp. 704–5.

35. See table 2–1, p. 53, in David Ward, *Cities and Immigrants* (New York: Oxford University Press, 1971).

36. Carpenter, Table 130, p. 286. On the likely median age of arrival, see p. 38*n*12.

37. The residency question is discussed at great length in Carpenter *passim*.

38. My comments here are intended for American historians. Similar remarks on the utility and superior quality of the Canadian census data have been directed towards historians of the British Isles by C.J. Houston and W.J. Smyth, "The Irish Abroad: Better Questions through a Better Source, the Canadian Census," *Irish Geography*, vol. 13 (1980), pp. 1–19.

39. For convenience, I am using modern terminology, referring to Canada and not to British North American, to Ontario, rather than Upper Canada, and so on.

40. E.P. Hutchinson, "Notes on Immigration Statistics of the United States," *American Statistical Association Journal*, vol. 53 (December 1958), pp. 968–79.

I am here leaving aside entirely the problem involved with the counterflow from the U.S. to various foreign countries. *Net* migration data are what one requires, but in the absence of records on alien departures from the U.S. there is no way of measuring net immigration before 1908. (Carpenter, p. 3).

41. Estimate found in J.D.B. DeBow, *The Industrial Resources Statistics etc. of the United States* (New York: Appleton, third ed., 1854), vol. 3, pp. 396 and 424, cited in Hutchinson, p. 975.

42. Edward Jarvis, "Immigration," *Atlantic Monthly*, vol. 29 (April 1872), p. 456, quoted in Hutchinson, p. 976.

43. Compare tables 1 and 2 in Akenson, "Ontario: Whatever Happened to the Irish?" Migration from non-British Isles sources to Canada was proportionately so small in the 1815–50 period as not to affect the conclusion that almost certainly a majority of the foreign-born cross-border migrants to the U.S. were Irish-born.

44. I am here avoiding the virtually insoluble question of how great was the counter-flow of British Isles born persons who shipped to the U.S. and came from thence to Canada. Undoubtedly, it was much less than the flow from Canada into the U.S., but whether it was 2 percent or 20, 3 percent or 30, no one really knows (see Hutchinson, p. 976).

45. Ibid., pp. 974–75, 980–81.

46. Computed from Ibid., p. 981.

For instance, the Irish-born constituted 4.81 percent of the U.S. population in 1870, while in 1871 the Irish-born constituted 6.2 percent of the Canadian population. Compare the text above, section IV (2), with *Seventh Census of Canada, 1931* (Ottawa: Kings Printer, 1936), vol. I, p. 517.

47. Compiled from General Register Office, *Studies on Medical and*

Population Subjects, No. 6. External Migration. A Study of the Available Statistics, 1815–1950 by N.H. Carrier and J.R. Jeffery (London: HMSO, 1953), p. 95. For a discerning discussion of the limits of the data, see pp. 137–39.

48. Compiled from *Commission on Emigration and Other Population Problems, 1948–1954. Reports* [Pr. 2541] (Dublin Stationery Office, 1954), pp. 314–16. The quotation above in the text is from p. 316*n.*

49. William Forbes Adams, *Ireland and Irish Emigration to the New World from 1815 to the Famine* (New Haven: Yale University Press, 1932). See especially his appendix, "Statistics of Irish Emigration, 1815–1845," on which my comments in the text are largely based. Adams' work is often paid lip-service, but its substance generally is ignored, largely, one conjectures, because it runs against the grain of the present concensus amongst historians of the Irish in America. That is, Adams' work implicitly affirms three points: first, that the central episode in the history of the Irish in the New World begins not with the Famine, but in 1815; second, that one must deal with all of North America if one is to come to terms with the Irish in the U.S.; and, third, that no matter how difficult the task, one must work with the available demographic data and, in particular, have an explicit understanding of the limits of that data. That fifty years after Adams' work, I am having to argue explicitly what Adams accepted implicitly is not entirely heartening.

50. Compiled from Leon E. Truesdell, *The Canadian Born in the United States. An Analysis of the Statistics of the Canadian Element in the Population of the United States 1850 to 1930* (New Haven: Yale University Press, 1943), tables two and seven, pp. 10 and 19, and from the sources detailed in notes 30 and 32.

Despite the author's wide reading, Marcus Lee Hansen's posthumous volume, *The Mingling of the Canadian and American Peoples* (New Haven: Yale University Press, 1940) has very little in the way of statistical evidence.

51. The precise date is problematical. The Irish were the largest Canadian ethnic group in 1881, but the English had surpassed them by 1901. Unfortunately, the 1891 census did not yield ethnicity data in a form comparable to that provided by the censuses of 1881 and 1901, so one necessarily must be vague. For the data, see *Seventh Census of Canada, 1931*, vol. I, p. 710.

52. On the inferences concerning the Irish which one can draw from the Ontario census of 1842, see chapter four.

53. See the "Editor's Introduction," by E.R.R. Green in *Essays in Scotch-Irish History* (London: Routledge and Kegan Paul, 1969), pp. ix–xi.

54. James G. Leyburn, *The Scotch-Irish. A Social History* (Chapel Hill: University of North Carolina Press, 1962), p. xi.

55. The two classic books on the subject which set the framework for the continuing emphasis on the eighteenth century and upon a virtually racialist view of the differences as between the Ulster Scots and the Irish Catholics were: Charles A. Hanna, *The Scotch-Irish, or, The Scot in North Britain, North Ireland, and North America* (New York: Knickerbocker Press, 1902), 2 vols., and Henry Ford Jones, *The Scotch-Irish in America* (Princeton: Princeton University Press, 1915).

In a summary of his own book, written for a popular audience, James G. Leyburn stated categorically that "there was almost no further influx from northern Ireland after the Revolutionary war." ("The Scotch-Irish," *American Heritage*, vol. 22, December 1970, p. 99).

The major dissentient from the concensus view that the Ulster Scots were a significant group in the eighteenth, but not the nineteenth, century, is Maldwyn A. Jones, whose "Scotch-Irish" in Thernstrom (ed.), *Harvard Encyclopedia of American Ethnic Groups*, pp. 895–908, is a succinct, but dramatically revisionist, view that deserves to be widely read amongst American ethnic historians.

For a revisionist view concerning the eighteenth century, see David Noel Boyle, *Ireland, Irishmen, and Revolutionary America, 1760–1820* (Dublin: published for the Cultural Relations Committee of Ireland by the Mercier Press, 1981).

The substance of R.J. Dickson's *Ulster Emigration to Colonial America 1718–1775* (London: Routledge and Kegan Paul, 1966) is a dispassionate, thorough, and convincing monograph. The author's introduction, however, repeats the assertion that there were two distinct groups of people who emigrated from Ireland to the United States: "the hundreds of thousands of Irish emigrants to colonial America who have been overshadowed by the millions who emigrated from Ireland in the second half of the nineteenth century (p. ix).

56. One of the more engaging discussions of the Ulster–Scot as a rural phenomenon was provided by the late Estyn Evans, Ireland's pioneering historical geographer, in the "The Scotch-Irish in the New World: An Atlantic Heritage," *Journal of the Royal Society of Antiquaries of Ireland*, vol. 95 (1965), pp. 39–49.

Rather broader recent interpretations of the same agreed-phenomenon are: Forrest McDonald and Grady McWhiney, "The Antebellum Southern Herdman: A Reinterpretation," *Journal of Southern History*, vol. 41 (May 1975), pp. 147–66; Forrest McDonald, "The Ethnic Factor in Alabama History: A Neglected Dimension," *Alabama Review*, vol. 32 (1978), pp. 256–65, and Forrest McDonald and Grady McWhiney, "The Celtic South," *History Today*, vol. 30 (July 1980), pp. 11–15.

The counter-tradition — that is, the presentation of the Ulster–Scot as an urban settler is thin indeed. Its two poles, chronologically, are set by Joel Tyler Headley's journalistic history of the New York Orange riots of 1870 and 1871 (in his *The Great Riots of New York, 1712–1873*, New York: E.B. Treat, 1873) and, by Christopher McGimpsey's "Internal Ethnic Friction: Orange and Green in Nineteenth-Century New York, 1868–1872," *Immigrants and Minorities*, vol. 1 (March 1982), pp. 39–59.

57. This use of census data, admittedly quite crude, is loaded *against* suggesting that the Irish Protestants emigrated quite frequently: presumably the Catholics, being overly represented in the pauper class, more frequently starved or died of Famine-related diseases than did the Protestants; therefore, much of their population loss was from those causes, not solely from emigration.

58. The residual population in each year's figures consists of Other Protestant Dissenters (especially Methodists), Jews, Atheists, and Unknown.

Sources: *Derived from First Report of the Commissioners of Public Instruction, Ireland*, pp. 9–45 [45], H.C. 1835, xxxii, and from *Report and Tables relating to Religious Profession, Education and Occupations of the People*, p. 28 [3204-III], H.C. 1863, lix. The 1834 data were later "corrected" by various governmental authorities and not always convincingly, yet not to such an extent as to change by more than a few tenths of a percentage point the figures taken from the primary document.

Religious percentages in Ireland before 1834 are highly problematical. For a sensible, although not definitive, attempt to deal with the earlier situation, see "Appendix B, Statistics of Religious Affiliation in Ireland in the Eighteenth and Nineteenth Centuries," in S.J. Connolly, *Priests and People in Pre-Famine Ireland, 1780–1845* (Dublin: Gill and MacMillan, 1982), pp. 281–83.

59. *Census of Ireland, 1901*, part II, *General Report* p. 50 [Cd. 1190], H.C. 1902, cxxix.

60. For example, one might hypothesize that the drop in the Protestant population came from a lowering of their family size (and thus of religious-specific fertility), while the Catholic drop in population came chiefly from emigration. Actually, however, the opposite is most likely to have happened.

That is, the brunt of the Famine having fallen on the Catholic poor, the limits on marriage that developed in the post-Famine era (described for example in Conrad M. Arensberg and Solon T. Kimball, *Family and Community in Ireland*, Cambridge: Harvard University Press, second edition, 1968), probably fell most severely on the Catholics. Again, I am presenting the census data in such a way as to minimize the possibility of our having to accept the idea of large-scale Protestant emigration; and even so, that hypothesis emerges as one most needful of being tested.

61. As David Fitzpatrick points out in "Irish Emigration in the Later Nineteenth Century," *Irish Historical Studies*, vol. 22 (September 1980), pp. 127–28, from 1851–76 the data are wobbly, but not without worth. In 1876 the method of making the count was revamped to abolish local anomalies in the collection method.

This is the appropriate point to call attention to a remarkable series of articles by the historical geographer S.H. Cousens. Taken together, these suggest that for the period 1812–61, inclusive, migration from Ireland was especially sharp from north-central Ireland, that is from Ulster and the neighbouring countries of Connaught and Leinster, and from certain localized pockets of Protestants, such as small textile communities in the south of Ireland. Cousens' view is that the dissolution of the link between the poorest Catholic peasantry of the south and west of Ireland and the land occurred quite late, roughly in the last quarter of the nineteenth century. This coincides quite well with the point made earlier in this text, that, from approximately the middle 1870s the Irish immigrants to the United States exhibited basic patterns of behaviour in occupation and residence similar to that of the "new immigrants," who in origin were mostly drawn from similar groups amongst the European peasantry.

Cousens' most important articles are: "The Regional Variation in Emigration from Ireland between 1821 and 1841," *Institute of British Geographers, Transactions* no. 37 (1965), pp. 15–30; "Regional Death Rates in Ireland during the Great Famine, from 1846 to 1851," *Population Studies*, vol. 14 (1960–61), pp. 55–73; "The Regional Variation in Mortality during the Great Irish Famine," *Proceedings of the Royal Irish Academy*, vol. 63, sec. C, pp. 127–49; "The Regional Pattern of Emigration during the Great Irish Famine, 1846–51," *Institute of British Geographers Transactions*, vol. 28 (1960), pp. 119–34; "Emigration and Demographic Change in Ireland, 1851–1861," *Economic History Review*, 2 ser., vol. 14 (1961–62), pp. 278–88.

For a useful table covering 1846–55, based primarily on some of Cousens' data, see Oliver MacDonagh, "The Irish Famine Emigration to the United States," *Perspectives in American History*, vol. 10 (1976), pp. 419–20.

62. The table does not include 110,668 emigrants whose origin in Ireland was unspecified. My suspicion is that these emigrants of unspecified origin belonged mostly to the years 1851 and 1852, before the improvement in record-keeping introduced in 1853.

Derived from data in *Commission on Emigration and Other Population Problems, 1948-1954*, pp. 315–16, and 325. One has to derive the figures indirectly as the Republic's governmental commission that produced this study apparently did not wish to highlight the high proportion of overseas emigration which came from what is now Northern Ireland.

63. W.E. Vaughan and A.J. Fitzpatrick (eds.), *Irish Historical Statistics, Population, 1821-1971* (Dublin: Royal Irish Academy, 1978), p. 59.

64. Derived from the same source as note 62 above.

65. See Vaughan and Fitzpatrick, pp. 311–32.

66. Akenson in *Canadian Papers in Rural History*, vol. III, pp. 222 and 231, and chapter four of the present study, pp. 82, 84.

67. Darroch and Ornstein, table 1, p. 312.

68. Jones in Thernstrom, pp. 904–05.

69. I am grateful to Dr. Cormac O'Grada of University College, Dublin, for passing on his knowledge of the immigration archives.

For an example of an interesting use of the immigration archives, see C.J. Erickson, "Who were the English and Scots emigrants to the United States in the late nineteenth century?" in D.V. Glass and Roger Revelle (eds.), *Population and Social Change* (London: Edward Arnold, 1972), pp. 347-81.

70. For example, Bruce Elliot of Queen's University is completing a major study of several hundred Tipperary families, from their Old World locale to their several successive locations in Ontario. Each individual's personal background and movement is precisely data-linked on both sides of the Atlantic.

An excellent example of the standard of evidence and of documentation required when making transatlantic geographic linkages is J. Richard Houston's *Numbering the Survivors: A History of the Standish Family of Ireland, Ontario, and Alberta* (Agincourt, Ontario: Generation Press, 1979).

71. The most impressive example of which I am aware is that done by Professor Darrell A. Norris of the State University of New York, Geneseo, who has done work on the "family paths" of a considerable number of individuals who at one time or another passed through Euphrasia township, Ontario. The largest cohort in this group consisted of Irish Protestants. See Darrell A. Norris, "Migration, Pioneer Settlement, and the Life Course: the first Families of an Ontario Township," in Donald H. Akenson, ed., *Canadian Papers in Rural History,* vol. IV (1984), pp. 130-52.

72. Most notably by R.W. Widdis of the Department of Geography, of Queen's University.

73. These three categories are the ones used in Carpenter's study (see, for example, p. 23), an official census monograph.

74. The data on the fifty cities is found in *The Population of the United States ... 1870,* vol. I, pp. 388-89.

75. *Historical Statistics of the United States (1975),* series A203.

76. The specific case of the Irish aside, Carpenter's study of the 1920 census data may be relevant: it showed that throughout the population there was an inverse relationship between recency of migration and propensity to live in the countryside. "It is probably due mainly to the presence, in the rural areas, of sons and daughters of an earlier generation of immigrants who settled on the land more numerously than is the case at present, but may be due also to the moving out from city to country of sons and daughters of later immigrants." (p. 22)

77. As late as the 1920 census, the Canadians were being cited (together with the Mexicans) as being the "outstanding exceptions" to the generalization that immigrants always have been heavily represented in the cities. Carpenter, p. 147.

78. Ward, p. 56.

79. Jay P. Dolan in *The Immigrant Church: New York's Irish and German Catholics, 1815-1865* (Baltimore: Johns Hopkins University Press, 1975) presented a comparative study of German and Irish parishes immediately after the Famine migration. He found that in both groups the majority of immigrants left New York City within ten years of arrival. Most interestingly, the tendency to remain in the city was greater among Germans than among Irish (pp. 40-41). His total number of cases was necessarily small, as he was engaged in a set of micro-studies; replicating his work on a large scale would be most instructive.

80. The standard volume on the work force in the U.S. in the nineteenth century is Stanley Lebergott, *Manpower in Economic Growth: The American Record since 1800* (New York: McGraw Hill Book Co., 1964). Unfortunately, it appears that the matter addressed in the text — concerning a multiplier that

could be applied to agricultural occupations as defined in the nineteenth century census in order to obtain the size of the comprehensive rural economic sector, including not only farmers and agricultural workers, but smiths, millers, coopers and so on — has yet to be dealt with by economic historians. The difficulty is two-fold. Farmers support local blacksmiths, millers and coopers, but the millers and coopers also demanded the services of blacksmiths (and so on) so how does one partition them? Secondly, there is a problem of location. A variable amount of grain, for example, could have been sent overseas to be milled in Liverpool, depending on communication access to the sea and the state of overseas geopolitical relations.

During the 1950s and 60s regional economists did a fair bit of work on the "local employment multiplier" which essentially asked, for example, how many local jobs would be created if one created one additional farm job. The answers, unhappily, were highly variable, their multiplier running from 1.3 to about 9.0. Twentieth-century estimates of the national employment multiplier for the U.S. would place the multiple in the range of three or four. By using a multiple of two in the text, then, I am probably underestimating the number of Irish persons who were actually employed in the rural economy. (I am grateful to the economic historian Marvin McInnis for sharing with me on this point his wide knowledge of agricultural history.)

81. The chief exception to the ignoring of the Irish in agriculture in major general studies of the American Irish is Carl Wittke's chapter VII, "The Irish as Farmers," pp. 62–74. He argues that the Irish who distributed themselves on farms from coast to coast were a minor element in the total Irish immigration (p. 63), and explains in detail why they could not have been successful farmers.

One unpublished study, an exception to the usual view of the Irish as urban labourers, is Kieran Denis Flanagan, "Emigration, Assimilation, and Occupational Categories of the Irish-American in Minnesota, 1870–1900" (M.A., University of Minnesota, 1969). This bears special note. It shows that even prior to the Catholic colonization movement in Minnesota, the Irish were strongly *over*-represented amongst farmers. In 1870, 53 percent of the Irish-born in Minnesota were farmers, as against a 42 percent total population average. This was a proportion higher than that for any other immigrant group. In 1890 the Irish proportion was 40 percent against a general average of 31 percent. Interestingly, the 1900 census showed that the second generation of Irish in Minnesota had a lower than average propensity to farm (See especially pp. 224ff). Which is to say that in the case of the Minnesota Irish, the first generation experienced an extreme attack of farming fever and that the second underwent an equally extreme case of rural depopulation.

Also useful is Patrick J. Blessing, *The British and Irish in Oklahoma* (N.P.: University of Oklahoma Press, 1980), which illustrates the step-wise migration of the Irish into a region of rural employment.

For sidelights on the Irish as farmers, see Elfrieda Lang, "Irishmen in Northern Indiana before 1850," *Mid-America*, ser. 1, vol. 36 (1954), pp. 190–98; Alice E. Smith, "The Sweetman Irish Colony," *Minnesota History*, vol. 9 (1928), p. 331–46; Philip L. White (ed.), "An Irish Immigrant Housewife on the New York Frontier," *New York History*, vol. 48, April 1967, pp. 182–88. Joseph A. King, *The Irish Lumberman-Farmer: Fitzgeralds, Harrigans, and others* (Lafayette, Cal: privately printed, 1982).

Historians of the American-Irish are not the only scholars who have ignored the rural component of their ethnic group. Indeed, it can fairly be argued that the entire field of American ethnic studies is based on a series of urban models which have little explanatory value in dealing with rural groups. On this point, see the discerning article by Kathleen Neils Conzen, "Historical Approaches to the Study of Rural Ethnic Communities," in Frederick C.

Luebke (ed.), *Ethnicity on the Great Plains* (Lincoln: University of Nebraska Press, 1980), pp. 1–18.

82. Computed from *The Population of the United States ... 1870*, vol. I, pp. 704–05.

83. Actually, one would expect the Irish population in agriculture to more likely triple, rather than double, as between the immigrant generation in 1870 and the native-born of Irish extraction in 1870. This is because the national pattern would dictate a doubling-and-a-half, and also because the Irish figure should exceed that national percentage: as discussed earlier in the text, the Irish of the immigrant generation were underrepresented as farmers as compared to other immigrant groups up through 1870, so that any shift as between the second and third generations will increase the multiplier much more than in the case of, say, the Swedes or Germans, who were farmers to begin with.

Essentially, I am here loading the case against overstating the proportion of the Irish in agriculture. If one wanted to push, one could easily suggest that as high as one-third of the first immigrant generation were in the rural economic sector broadly defined, and that up to three-quarters of the U.S. born persons of Irish extraction (the second, third, and fourth generations) were in the rural economic sector, broadly defined, in 1870.

84. The reader may have noticed that I have not employed the data collected by the U.S. immigration officials on the occupations declared by immigrants upon arrival on the U.S. shores. This is because the reporting was very incomplete (ranging from 40 to 56 percent in the nineteenth century), but was in any case valueless. Asking an immigrant what his occupation will be in the New World produces only information on what he thinks the "right" answer is, when faced by an immigration official, or on what misinformation he has been fed before migrating. For examples of credulity concerning these data, see: Robert E. Kennedy, Jr., *The Irish. Emigration, Marriage and Fertility* (Berkeley: University of California Press, 1973), pp. 75–76, and Richard A. Easterlin, "Immigration: Social Characteristics," in Thernstrom (ed.), table 6, p. 482.

85. For the exact figures for 1834 and 1861 see the estimate above, p. 62.

86. Maldwyn Jones (in Thernstrom, p. 905) estimates that Ulster Presbyterians (who comprised roughly one-half of the Irish Protestant population) constituted roughly 10 percent of the Famine exodus from Ireland.

The reader may think that I have inadvertently ignored the fact that the Protestants were overrepresented in the emigration to Canada, and thus presumably underrepresented in the United States so that the percentage of Protestants in the U.S. Irish cohort would be below the Irish national average. This possibility is counteracted, however, by two factors: (1) Almost certainly the Irish Protestants had a higher propensity to migrate than did the Catholics in Ireland. This can be inferred from the census data on pp. 62–3, and also from that fact that they tended to be higher on the economic scale and thus less likely to be poverty-immobilized paupers. (2) The flow of migrants from Ireland to the U.S. by way of Canada was so large that even if Protestants were overrepresented in Canada, they were perforce overrepresented in their secondary migration to the States.

Jones' suggestion concerning the importance of Protestant migration during the Famine period is given credence by Cormac O'Grada's study of American immigration records, which show that in 1847–48 40.6 percent of the Irish migrants to the U.S. via New York City were from Ulster. "Across the Briny Ocean: Some thoughts on Irish Emigration to America 1800–1850," paper given at the second conference of Scottish and Irish Social and Economic Historians, University of Strathclyde, September 1981), p. 18.

87. See data in the text, pp. 62–4.

Undoubtedly, dealing with the Anglican migrants to the U.S. will be very difficult because of their near-invisibility in U.S. society. Similar problems were encountered by R.T. Berthoff in his study of British immigrants and his monograph will repay study. Rowland Tappan Berthoff, *British Immigrants in Industrial America, 1790–1950* (Cambridge: Harvard University Press, 1953).

88. Kerby A. Miller, with Bruce Boling and David N. Doyle, "Emigrants and Exiles: Irish Cultures and Irish Emigration to North America 1790–1922, *Irish Historical Studies*, vol. 22 (September 1980), p. 105.

89. In a late-addition final footnote to his article (p. 125n83), Miller notes the Darroch and Ornstein article and suggests that their work confirms his thesis. Only a massive misreading of the Darroch and Ornstein study could lead to this conclusion.

90. Irish historiography being what it is, one can at this point become lost in a dizzying infinite regression. Someone might suggest that the reason the Protestants had a higher occupational-economic profile in the Old Country was because they had persecuted the Catholics under the eighteenth century penal laws. But then, someone else might suggest (à la Froude) that the Protestants obtained this coercive power over the Catholics by view of their peculiar culture. And so on. To break out of the spiral, one would do well to experiment with the usage of class and occupation in the Old World as independent variables and with occupation and residence in the New World as dependent variables.

Notes to Chapter Four

1. One preparatory point must be re-emphasized. This is the seemingly obvious one (discussed in detail in chapter three) that, in the case of every non-indigenous people, there is a crucial distinction between an *immigrant* cohort and an *ethnic* group. The former consists of people who were born abroad but who eventually settled in this country. Often they are referred to as "first generation" Canadians. An ethnic group, in contrast, is a multi-generational entity, comprised of the children, grand-children and later descendants of the original immigrants. Ethnicity is an enduring characteristic and has empirically demonstrable referents in religion, politics, and family patterns, often long after later generations have ceased to feel consciously their ethnic heritage.

2. The source for the official unrevised estimate of total United Kingdom migrants and of migrants from Ireland is N.H. Carrier and J.R. Jeffery, *External Migration. A Study of the Available Statistics, 1815–1890* (London: Her Majesty's Stationery Office, 1953), p. 95. The revised data come from William Forbes Adams, *Ireland and Irish Emigration to the New World from 1815 to the Famine* (New Haven: Yale University Press, 1932), pp. 413–14.

The reader may notice that for 1825 and 1826 Adams' revised estimates of Irish migrants to British North America exceeds the unrevised official emigration figures for all of the British Isles. It would be natural — but quite wrong — to see this as indicative of a flaw in Adams' procedures. Actually, Adams made allowances for children and for illegal migrants, which the official version of the figures did not do. A "true" version of the official figures would have to include the same compensations to figures for all of the British Isles which Adams made only for the Irish.

3. The sources for table 2 are Carrier and Jeffrey, p. 95, and for the revised estimates I have employed Adams' formula. See Donald H. Akenson, "Ontario: Whatever Happened to the Irish?" *Canadian Papers in Rural History*, vol. 3 (1982), pp. 228, and 251–52n51. The source of supplementary data necessary for the making of these calculations is specified p. 252n51.

4. Source for table 3: Carrier and Jeffrey, p. 95. From 1853 onwards, the

quality of the official data was high enough to obviate the need for revisions of the sort that Adams has made.

5. The data from which table 4 is derived are found in *Census of Canada, 1870-71*, vol. IV, *Censuses of Canada, 1665-1871*, pp. 132, 136, 148, 166, 174, 182, 206, 246, 258, 290, 334, 346, 362.

6. Figure 1 is based on data from the 1870-71 dominion census. The data are conveniently available in *Census of Canada, 1831*, vol. I, *Summary*, p. 710.

7. A Gordon Darroch and Michael D. Ornstein, "Ethnicity and Occupational Structure in Canada in 1871: The Vertical Mosaic in Historical Perspective," *Canadian Historical Review*, vol. 61 (September 1980), table 1, p. 312.

8. Ibid.

9. Table 5 is derived from data found in *Census of Canada, 1931*, vol. I, pp. 710-23.

10. Darroch and Ornstein, table 7, p. 326.

11. I am grateful to Professor R. Marvin McInnis for sharing his data from the Canada West Farm Survey, 1861, with me. As it appertains to persons of Irish birth, the material is summarized in Donald H. Akenson, *The Irish in Ontario: A Study in Rural History* (Montreal and Kingston: McGill-Queen's University Press, 1984), pp. 339-44.

12. Darroch and Ornstein, passim, but especially pp. 314, 325-26.

13. Table 6 is derived from raw data found in: *Census of Canada, 1931*, vol. I, pp. 710-23; *Eighth Census of Canada, 1941*, vol. IV, pp. 334-441; *Ninth Census of Canada, 1951*, vol. I, table 32; *Census of Canada, 1961*, series 1.2, *Ethnic Groups*, pp. 34-1 — 36-12.

After 1961 the census authorities began lumping the Irish, Welsh, English, and Scots together as a single ethnic group, so the data-base on the Irish ends in 1961.

14. The sources for table 7 are the same as for table 6.

15. Table 8 is derived from: M.C. Urquhart and K.A.H. Buckley, *Historical Statistics of Canada* (Cambridge: Cambridge University Press, 1965), pp. 23 and 27; Carrier and Jeffrey, p. 96; and for 1960ff, from the successive *Canada Yearbooks* and successive *Canadian Statistical Reviews*. There is some discordance in the sources, but the data are solid enough to support the weight put upon them in the text.

16. For example, compare the data on the Irish-born in Canada in this chapter (table 4) with that on the Irish-born in the United States as given in chapter three, (note 46).

17. The 1842 census is found in *Appendix (F.F.), Journals of the Legislative Assembly, 1843*. It is reprinted in altered form, in *Census of Canada, 1870-71*, vol. IV, *Censuses of Canada, 1665 to 1871*, pp. 134-40. The reprint is preferable, as arithmetical errors in the original are corrected in the reprint. The differences, however, are relatively small.

18. The two relevant estimates are those by Michael Smith, of 95,000, and of Joseph Bouchette, of 135,000 which, though published three years apart, can be taken as co-equal in time, as they both deal with the situation before heavy trans-Atlantic immigration began. (Michael Smith, *A Geographical View of the Province of Canada* ..., 1813, and Joseph Bouchette, *Topographical Description* ..., 1815). Most observers have taken the lower estimate as the more likely to be closer to the truth.

19. I am here following the procedure and, in the absence of Upper Canadian figures, the usage of a rate of natural increase taken from the United States, as found in H.M. Johnston, *British Emigration Policy, 1815-1830* (Oxford: Clarendon Press, 1972), p. 1n1.

20. Because of the arithmetical corrections necessary in the 1842 census, one cannot accept their proportional distribution of the "unknown" category, but must do it oneself.

21. Census of 1848, in *Census of Canada, 1870–71*, vol. IV, *Censuses of Canada, 1665–1871*, p. 164. The multiplier obviously is low, but I suspect that any error is self-correcting. Many widows and widowers probably were tallied (incorrectly) as being married, even though they had no spouse. Thus, the married figure probably is artificially high, and the multiplier artificially low. The final result of the estimates of total families, however, should be reasonably accurate.

22. *Census of Canada, 1851–52*, vol. I, p. 308, shows 152,336 families, comprising 863,971 members actually resident and an additional 13,651 family members temporarily absent, for a total of 877,622 family members.

23. For a useful formulation of Ravenstein's laws in modern terms, see D.B. Grigg, "E.G. Ravenstein and 'the Laws of Migration'," *Journal of Historical Geography*, vol. 3 (1979), pp. 41–54.

24. On the various forms of migration, see 'A General Typology of Migration," by William Peterson, *American Sociological Review*, vol. 23 (June 1958), pp. 256–66.

25. Everett S. Lee, "A Theory of Migration," *Demography*, vol. 3 (1966), p. 56.

26. Adams constructs a set of interesting tables on emigration ports in the years immediately after the Napoleonic Wars (pp. 420–25). On later emigration to Upper Canada from specific Irish ports, see: *Report on Canadian Archives, 1900* ("Emigration," pp. 58–59); *Second Report from the Select Committee on Emigration from the United Kingdom*, H.C., 1826–27 (237), v, p. 70; *Emigration. Return ...*, 1833, H.C., 1833 (696), xxvi, p. 3; *Emigration. Return ...*, H.C., 1839 (536–I), xxxix, p. 34.

27. S.H. Cousens, "The Regional Variation in Emigration from Ireland between 1821 and 1841," *Institute of British Geographers. Transactions*, no. 37 (December 1965), pp. 15–30.

28. Alexander Macdonnell to Lord Durham, 22 June 1838, reproduced in Lord Durham's *Report on the Affairs of British North America*, vol. III, *Appendixes*, edited by C.P. Lucas (Oxford: Clarendon Press, 1912), p. 20.

29. Two points: (1) one employs the number of native-born French Canadians as given in the 1842 census, without any redaction for first-generation immigration. (This is not a methodology incompatible with Revisions B and C, as it is assumed that the first-generation ethnic populations all were tallied in the census as part of the non-French, native-Canadian category); (2) the French-Canadian native-born numbers must be slightly augmented, however, to distribute the "unknown" category, as was done in estimating the total ethnic population.

30. Here let me re-emphasize the need for humility in interpreting the data and also the necessity of keeping in mind the arithmetic of the formula employed. As discussed below, the Catholic percentages employed are highly problematical, but they deal with a very small percentage of sub-categories of the total population so that the effect of any error in the data would be very small on the final result.

That said, one is dealing in each instance with speculation, albeit of an informed sort. Intentionally, I have probably somewhat overestimated the Catholic percentage of the non-French second-generation Canadian-born population. That a number as high as 3 percent is even within the bounds of possibility rests on the fact that amongst the earliest settlers (whose descendants by 1842 often were second-generation born in Canada) were the considerable numbers of Glengarry Fencibles.

The probable overestimation should compensate for any underestimation of the Catholic proportion of the Scots-born and first-generation Scots, for I have opted for the low end of the possibility range in dealing with the Scots Catholics. Unfortunately, the only data on Scots which I can find indicates that in 1871 (a late date for my purposes), 10 percent of the Scots throughout Canada were Roman Catholics (Darroch and Ornstein, p. 312). This figure can be taken as the top edge of the possibility range for Upper Canada in 1842. But I am loath to project a national figure for the 1870s onto this province for the 1840s, especially in view of the relatively large communities of Scottish-derived Catholics in various parts of the maritimes.

What do the contemporary data for Upper Canada suggest? Unfortunately, one cannot deal with data on Scottish religious persuasion by reference to the Upper Canada census data of 1842. It would be temptingly simple to determine the actual number of Scots Catholics by subtracting the number of adherents of the Church of Scotland from the Scots ethnic total (taken to be the average of that given in Revisions B and C in the text). However, because of adhesions from other ethnic groups in Canada, the membership of the Church of Scotland in 1842 *exceeded* the Scots ethnic population!

Thus, we must turn to religious data from the home country. This is such a vexed matter that even Flinn's massive work on Scottish demography virtually avoids the entire religious question. The earliest information we have comes from the religious census of 1851, with its well-known shortcomings and double-counting.

But, our problem is even worse, as we know that the Scots who emigrated did not form a representative profile of the entire population, and, in particular, one needs to know more about the position of highlanders' emigration (for, as Bishop Macdonnell suggested, highland Catholics were an important element of his flock).

"Which part of Scotland supplied the most emigrants?," Scotland's most distinguished demographer recently has asked. His reply: "On this point the available records are at their most intransigent." (Flinn, *Scottish Population History*, p. 453).

The most careful and useful studies are by James Cameron. His Ph.D. thesis (University of Glasgow, 1970) is summarized as "Scottish Emigration to Upper Canada, 1815–55: a study of Process," in W. Peter Adams and Frederick Helleiner (eds.), *International Geography 1972* (Toronto: University of Toronto Press, 1972), vol. I, pp. 404–06. See also Cameron's "The Role of Shipping from Scottish Ports in Emigration to the Canadas, 1815–55," in Donald H. Akenson (ed.), *Canadian Papers in Rural History*, vol. 2 (1980), pp. 135–54. If one takes Cameron's data on emigration from Scottish ports to the St. Lawrence for 1831–37, inclusive, and also takes into account the proportion of highlanders sailing from the Clyde, then it appears that roughly (very roughly), 44 percent of those emigrating in that period were highlanders. (Derived from Cameron, in *Canadian Papers in Rural History*, vol. 2, figures 2 and 3.) For an array of non-statistical data, see *First Report from the Select Committee on Emigration. Scotland*, H.C. (82), 1841, vi and *Second Report from the Select Committee on Emigration, Scotland*, H.C. 1841 (333), vi. Also helpful is Ronald Sunter's "The Scottish Background to the Immigration of Bishop Alexander Macdonnell and the Glengarry Highlanders," *Study Sessions 1973, The Canadian Catholic Historical Association*, pp. 11–20.

Now, if one tallies the number of attendants at public worship on Sunday, 31 March 1851, and assumes that because the Protestant practice in many parishes of holding two services a day led to a one-third over-counting of Protestants, one finds that the proportion of Catholics in the highlands was approximately 5.5 percent (calculated from *Census of Great Britain, 1851. Religious Worship and Education. Scotland* [1764], H.C., 1854, lix, pp. 6–20).

Juxtaposing this with Cameron's data, and assuming that all the Catholic Scots came from the highlands, then a reasonable estimate is that 2.4 percent of all Scots emigrants were Catholic.

Unfortunately, for our purposes, the Catholics were not distributed evenly over the population, but were found in pockets. Moreover, Scottish emigration was noted for being highly localized, large numbers of whole parishes emigrating together or within a year or two of each other. Upper Canada was especially attractive to some of these groups. Thus, in employing 3 percent, I am trying to minimize any underestimating of the numbers of Scots Catholics. Further, in cognizance of Darroch and Ornstein's work, I have built in further compensation for possible under-estimation of the Scots Catholics when dealing with the second-generation non-French cohort born in Canada (see above).

31. In all the calculations above, the ethnic estimates used are the mean of those shown in Revisions B and C in the text.

32. The 1871 religious estimate is based on data in the *Census of Canada, 1870–71*, vol. I, pp. 142–44, 280–81, 364–65.

Of necessity, the religious-ethnic proportions are derived differently than those for 1842, but the data and procedures are sufficiently comparable to support strongly the conclusion argued in the text. The 1871 census was the first to provide data, not only on place of birth but on the ethnic origin of all respondents. This was basically a self-definition item, and as such, it defined ethnicity in a manner that varied according to each individual's perception; thus, for example, a third-generation Scot might define himself as Scots, while a first-generation individual of another ethnic group might refuse any ethnic label at all. This apparent messiness was actually the strongpoint of the ethnicity census, for it employed self-definition rather than arbitrary and imposed external criteria.

As for the calculation, it was derived by (1) taking the total Roman Catholic population as a starting figure; (2) subtracting the number of French-derived ethnicity, under the presupposition that the French Canadians were overwhelmingly Catholic; and (3) assuming that whatever number of French Canadians had turned Protestant were equalled by Catholics in the English, American, and Continental European-derived population; then (4), as was done in the calculation for 1842, assuming that 3 percent of the Scots in Canada were Catholic and subtracting from the previous total. This leaves 188,912 Catholics amongst a total Irish ethnic population of 559,442.

My figure of 33.8 percent is close to that of William J. Smyth, who calculated that, in 1871, "thirty-six per cent represents the absolute maximum proportion of Irish who could have been Catholics." (William J. Smyth, "The Irish in mid-Nineteenth Century Ontario," *Ulster Folk Life*, vol. 23 (1977), p. 100.

In their valuable recent book, *The Sash Canada Wore. A Historical Geography of the Orange Order in Canada* (Toronto: University of Toronto Press, 1980), Houston and Smyth estimate that there were in 1871, 182,000 persons in Ontario of Irish Catholic background (p. 186n27). This estimate, which equals 32.5 percent of the Irish ethnic population, well may be more accurate than mine as my formula may have underestimated the number of Scots Catholics and, unlike the case in 1842, there is no item in the 1871 formula to compensate for such underestimation. This said, my point in the text is buttressed, not weakened, by Houston and Smyth's work as, if they are accurate, it would mean that there were slightly fewer Catholics than I posit. And if true, my point that the post-Famine migration to central Canada was not composed wholly, or even chiefly of Catholics, is strengthened.

33. University of Toronto, 1961.

34. Vol. 25 (November 1959), pp. 450–61.

35. Vol. 29 (September 1948), pp. 255–77.

36. Pentland, "The Lachine Strike of 1843," p. 257n4.

37. 1965, pp. 19–40.

38. Reprinted in *Studies in Canadian Social History*, edited by Michiel Horn and Ronald Sabourin (Toronto: McClelland and Stewart, 1974), pp. 140–63. The article is also reprinted in *Canada. A Sociological Profile*, edited by W.E. Mann (Toronto: Copp Clarke, 1968), pp. 1–16.

39. Michael Cross, "Recent Writings in Social History," in *Re-Interpreting Canada's Past*, edited by J.L. Granatstein and David Flint (Toronto: The History and Social Science Teacher Pamphlet Series, no. 2, 1982), pp. 3–4.

40. Duncan in Horn and Sabourin (eds.), p. 153.

41. Ibid., p. 144.

42. Ibid., p. 146.

43. Ibid., p. 147.

44. Ibid., p. 157.

45. Ibid., p. 146.

46. Computed from *Census of the Canadas, 1851–52*, vol. I, pp. 4–37, and from *Census of the Canadas, 1860–61*, vol. I, pp. 48–80, and cf. pp. 128–60.

47. Ibid. The concept of an urban-rural breakdown of population data is a relatively new one and was not used by the census authorities for the three censuses (1851, '61, and '71) with which I deal in Part II. In employing incorporated cities, towns, and villages as the unit whereby to compute "urban" populations, I am following the example of the historical analysis done in the 1920s and published in *Seventh Census of Canada, 1931*. (See vol. I, pp. 81, 154, for a justification of this procedure.) This procedure will underestimate all urban percentages to the extent that (a) urban areas were unincorporated or (b) the extent whereby two separately incorporated areas merge physically into each other but remain distinct municipal entities. Point (b) is a serious problem in evaluating twentieth-century census data, but had little import in the nineteenth. And, although there were unincorporated towns of 2–3,000, the inclusion of villages as small as 4–500 as urban, more than offsets the potential underestimation of this account.

I should warn any reader who wishes to do a similar calculation for another ethnic group of a vexing problem: one cannot relate one's totals for the cities, towns and villages as shown in the 1851 and 1861 enumerations to the overall figures of urban life as given in the historical sections of the 1931 census. The reason is that the census authorities, in doing their historical work, "corrected" the 1851 and 1861 returns (but did not indicate where, why, or how they did this). As a result, the urban total given in the historical section of the 1931 census (see vol. I, p. 366) is higher than that reported district-by-district in 1851, but lower than 1861. Fortunately, in many cases for 1851, and in most for 1861, one can infer what the 1931 investigators did, and proceed according to their pattern. Even so, the figure one derives for 1851 is 3.5 percent less than that in the historical section of the 1931 census, and that for 1861 is one-tenth of one pecent higher. Because returns for cities seem to have been unambiguous and thus not needing "corrections" by the historical census workers for the 1931 volume, it is clear that most of the changes were made in the figures for the towns and villages.

For the purpose of the argument put forward in the text, the possible under-enumeration of "urban" Irishmen is not serious: it amounts only to a possible 3.5 percent in 1851 and then consists almost entirely of individuals who lived in small towns and villages, whose claim to be urban would be dubious at best.

For those working on other ethnic groups, however, it means that they must (as I have done in this study) calculate not only the city, town and village components of their respective population, but must also calculate by exactly the same criteria the total urban segments of the entire population of the province so that valid comparisons can be made to the general population. If the 1931 data is used as a shortcut, the comparisons will be invalid.

48. *Manual containing "The Census Act" and Instructions to Officers employed in taking the First Census of Canada (1871)* (Ottawa: Queen's Printer, 1871), p. 23.

49. *Census of Canada, 1870–71*, vol. I, pp. 86–145, cf. 252–81.

50. The source of the raw data is the *Census of Canada, 1870–71*, vol. I, pp. 86–145.

Because the basic argument of this section is that most Irish Catholics did not live in cities and were not socially acclimatized in Ontario in the same urban experience as is often held to have occurred in the United States, the formula used to estimate the number of Irish Catholics in cities, towns and villages is biased so as to err, if at all, in the direction of *over-estimating* their urban numbers: in particular, it may do so by underestimating the number of Scots Catholics. In other words, the case against the Irish Catholics being an urban people could easily have been made even stronger.

The formula is as follows: Irish-born urban Catholics = total of urban Catholics – 100 percent of urban French Canadians – 3 percent of urban Scots.

This is the same formula used for the general population. See note 32, above.

Note that this formula should be used only with aggregate populations and not to calculate the Irish Catholics in any specific municipality.

51. For purposes of comparison, the reader may wish to note the residential pattern of the Protestants of Irish descent for 1871:

Protestants of Irish descent living in cities (average size: 26,517)	6.9 percent
Protestants of Irish descent living in towns and villages (average size: 2,148)	9.9 percent
Total urban of Protestants of Irish descent (including all cities, towns and villages, average size: 3,266)	16.8 percent
Total Protestants of Irish descent living in rural areas	83.2 percent

Notes to Chapter Five

1. *Labour/Le Travailleur*, Autumn, 1982, p. 297.
2. The English edition employed here is the complete edition, translated by Ralph Mannheim, introduced by Professor D.C. Watt (London: Hutchinson, 1969), which follows the first German edition. Helpful as background is Werner Maser's *Hitler's Mein Kampf*, translated by R.H. Barry (London: Faber and Faber, 1970).
3. *Canadian Historical Review*, vol. 63 (June, 1982), pp. 227–30.
4. Toronto: James Lorimer and Co., 1981.
5. This reputation is based largely, but not solely, on his magisterial volume, *The Making of the English Working Class* (London: Victor Gollancz, 1963).
6. Palmer, in *CHR*, p. 230.
7. Ibid., p. 228.
8. *Mein Kampf*, p. 208.
9. Ibid., p. 213.
10. Ibid.
11. Ibid.
12. Ibid., p. 214.
13. Ibid., p. 215.
14. Ibid., p. 218.
15. Ibid., p. 216.
16. Ibid., p. 221.
17. Ibid., p. 231.
18. Ibid., p. 211.

19. Ibid., p. 226.

20. I am not here arguing either (a) that all racial, ethnic, and religious groups are the same, or (b) that there are not dysfunctional aspects of the social-religious systems of every group. Historians need to respect the integrity of racial, religious, and ethnic groups and, simultaneously, to paint them accurately, warts and all. When describing negative characteristics, it is especially important that the very highest evidentiary standards be employed and that one indicate very clearly to what proportion and strata of the given group the negative characteristics apply.

21. Pentland, p. 176.

22. It is not irrelevant that his initial Ph.D. thesis topic was "A History of Labour in Canada to 1867." This later was changed to "A Study of Canadian Labour (Organized and Unorganized) in the Period 1830–1860," and then to "The Irish Labourers on Canadian Canals and Railways, 1830–1860." The final title was "Labour and the Development of Industrial Capitalism." (Phillips, "Introduction," pp. ix–x).

23. Pentland, p. 24.

24. In the original unpublished thesis, Pentland called this a "feudal" system, a use of the term unknown to European historians. In a phrase of lapidary tactfulness, G.S. Kealey noted that "Pentland's use of 'feudal' is unique." (Gregory S. Kealey, "H.C. Pentland and Working Class Studies," *Canadian Journal of Political and Social Theory*, vol. 3, spring-summer 1979, p. 92, *n.* 15.

25. Pentland, p. 25.

26. Ibid., p. 24. This concept of "overhead," of course, should not be confused with the same word as used by micro-economists and accountants.

27. Ibid., p. 17.

28. Ibid.

29. Ibid., p. 24.

30. That Pentland equated the labour market of industrial capitalism with the "free" market of classical economics is indicated in various places, especially p. 26 ("... the free labour market of industrial capitalism ...") and pp. 211–12, *n* 1: "In practice this system [that of "classical and neo-classical economic theory"] can scarcely emerge or operate unless the demand for employment is usually greater than the demand for workmen. A labour reserve is necessary for its sanctions to operate effectively."

31. This is implied in his very definition of the labour market of industrial capitalism being "abundant." Paul Deprez states that "the creation of an abundant labour market was viewed by Pentland as a necessary pre-condition to capitalism ..." ("Pentland's Scarcity of Labour and the Industrial Revolution," *Canadian Journal of Political and Social Theory*, vol. 3, spring-summer, 1979, p. 96).

Pentland here had a logical problem that is more apparent than real: he described the abundant labour market as being both a precondition of the rise of industrial capitalism and a result of that rise. The apparent contradiction can be resolved without doing violence to his meaning by suggesting that an abundant labour *supply* is necessary to the rise of industrial capitalism, but that the labour *market* of abundance is the result.

32. See, for example, Pentland, p. xlvii. "In the nineteenth century, a new condition, relative abundance of labour (unskilled and skilled) invited the replacement of personal arrangements by new ones that approximated more and more to the industrial capitalist methods developed elsewhere."

33. That Pentland was working this way, inferring the surplus of labour from the large immigration flow is illustrated in his statement that: "The immense overseas immigration of 1847 was officially numbered at 90,000 persons, but probably was much larger. Coinciding with economic recession, it was bound to produce overabundance of labour everywhere." (p. 117)

There is a possible variant interpretation of alternative "ii," namely that Pentland did not infer the abundance of labour from the immigrant flow, but simply assumed that it existed and used the immigrant flow to explain where the assumed surplus came from. It could be argued that his mind worked this way:

Major premise: that industrial capitalism inevitably involves an abundant supply of labour

Minor premise: that central Canada became an industrial-capitalist economy

Therefore, an abundant labour supply existed.

The major premise, of course, is virtual canonical Marxism. Although (as Paul Phillips and Bryan Palmer both note), Pentland was not a Marxist in the strictest sense, there is no doubt that he was heavily indebted to the Marxist tradition. In particular, one sees in his book a Canadian version of the classical five-steps — (1) primitive communism, (2) slave ownership, (3) feudalism, (4) capitalism, and (5) socialism evolving into communism. Points (1) and (5) are outside of his time frame, but (3) and (4) are the ones that form the centrepiece of his book: in his thesis the chapter on personal labour relations was about "feudalism." Further, the only explanation for his peculiar chapter one, on slavery in Canada (which contributes nothing to his main argument), can only be its being derivative from the canonical sequence.

That said, one cannot conclude that Pentland was necessarily so strongly influenced by Marxist views that he merely assumed, rather than inferred, the abundant labour pool. As noted earlier, Pentland took his view of the labour market from classical economics, and, as his footnotes showed, was particularly indebted to Sir John Clapham for his view of the labour market as it concerned the Irish. (Especially Clapham's "Irish immigration into Great Britain in the nineteenth century." *Bulletin of the International Committee of Historical Sciences*, V, part III, no. 20, July 1933, pp. 598–602.) Thus, it is best to be generous and to accept the (admittedly slight) evidence that Pentland was inferring a labour surplus from migrant flow, not merely assuming it before he even began his investigation.

A very useful test of Pentland's surplus-labour theory would be for scholars to study the several discrete labour markets that existed in mid-nineteenth-century Canada and the degree to which, in each, it can actually be shown that labour was over-supplied.

34. Pentland, p. 62.
35. Ibid., p. 53.
36. Ibid., p. 77.
37. Ibid., p. 55.
38. Ibid., p. 80.
39. Ibid., p. 90.
40. Ibid., pp. 93 and 94.
41. Ibid., p. 94.
42. Ibid., pp. 94–95.
43. Ibid., p. 99.
44. Ibid., p. 102.
45. Ibid., p. 104.
46. Ibid., p. 96.
47. Ibid., pp. 104–5.
48. Ibid., p. 104.
49. Ibid., p. 104.
50. Ibid., p. 109.
51. Ibid., table II, column 3, pp. 82–83.
52. London: Her Majesty's Stationery Office, 1953.
53. Dublin: Stationery Office, 1954.
54. Ibid., p. 62. See also, p. 226, *n.* 5.

55. Carrier and Jeffery, table D/F/G (I), p. 95.

56. Pentland, p. 101. Of course, "after 1815" is not an operationally valid time period.

57. Ibid., pp. 79–80.

58. Ibid., p. 102.

59. Ibid., p. 226, *n*. 5. My guess is that Pentland actually was referring to the 1860–61 censuses of Canada East and Canada West which asked the birth place of all persons, not just of the "British born" (by which, incidentally, Pentland means not British-born, but British Isles born).

60. Pentland, pp. 64, 104.

61. Ibid., p. 236, *n*. 40.

62. Ibid., p. 236, *n*. 40. Note here the influence of Sir John Clapham on Pentland's thinking about labour markets and the Irish. Pentland says that the concept of the "effective Irish" was "used by Clapham, in consideration of Irish resistance to assimilation."

63. Ibid. How Pentland arrived at his number for the "effectively Irish" in 1871 is a conundrum that so far has resisted my attempts at analysis. I have tried, rather like the scientists who cracked the code of Stonehenge, to rearrange the statistical data available to Pentland into a variety of formulae, but none of them works. The one thing certain, however, is that he used quite different measures of the "effectively Irish" for 1825–61 and for 1871. In the previous years, he claims that the effectively Irish were the Irish-Catholic immigrants and their first-generation children (that he does not reveal how he knows these items is beside the point at present). Then, for 1871, he uses as his basic population (which he divides into Protestants and Catholics) the multi-generational data concerning origin generated by the 1871 census.

64. For a treatment of the Ontario data — the same material available to Pentland — see Donald H. Akenson, "Ontario: Whatever Happened to the Irish?" *Canadian Papers in Rural History*, vol. 3 (1982), pp. 204–56.

65. Another relatively harmless bit of creativity was Pentland's dismissal of the Welsh: "Statistics of racial origin, and commentaries, indicate that very few Welsh came to Canada." (p. 232, *n*. 111) Certainly, the Welsh could not in any case have been a major part of his putative abundant labour pool, but, still, one would like to know what "statistics of racial origin" he meant. The pre-Confederation census lumped the Welsh with the English when tallying place-of-birth, and the Dominion censuses lumped them with the English when doing place-of-birth and national-origin tallies.

66. Pentland, p. 261, *n*. 29.

67. Ibid., p. 205, *n*. 73. See also p. 81, where he argues that so many persons going to the U.S. was "simply a measure of the limited capacity of the Canadian labour market." In other words, all the people leaving could not possibly cause a labour shortage in Canada, but can only be taken as an indication of a surplus!

68. Ibid., pp. 89 and 90. See also p. 226, *n*. 5.

69. Ibid., p. 88.

70. Ibid., p. 90.

71. E.P. Hutchinson, "Notes on Immigration Statistics of the United States," *American Statistical Association Journal*, vol. 53 (December 1958), pp. 974–75, 980–81.

72. A. Gordon Darrach and Michael D. Ornstein, "Ethnicity and Occupational Structure in Canada in 1871: the Vertical Mosaic in Historical Perspective," *Canadian Historical Review*, vol. 61 (September 1980), table 7, p. 326.

73. Pentland, p. 101. Pentland also asserted that (p. 101) during the 1816–35 period there may have been a number of immigrants to Canada by way of New York equal to one-third of the number of those lost by out-migration. Not only is this claim not documented, it is undocumentable: the passes issued

by the British consul-general for travel to Canada have not survived in sufficient numbers.

74. Pentland, p. 99.

75. Derived from *First Report of the Commissioners of Public Instruction, Ireland*, pp. 9–45 [45], H.C. 1835, xxxii; and from *Report and Tables relating to Religious Profession, Education and Occupations of the People*, p. 28 [3204–III], H.C. 1863, lix. The 1834 data were later "corrected" by various governmental authorities, but not always convincingly. I have reported the original figures. In any case, the latter "corrections" were less than a few tenths of a percentage point, and therefore not significant for the case being here made.

76. See *Report and Tables relating to Religious Profession, Education and Occupations of the People*, p. 62.

The 1871 census, whose categories were more precise than those of the 1861 census, showed that Anglican males were seventeen times more likely to be farmers and graziers than landed proprietors and 11.75 times as likely to be farm servants as to be landlords. Computed from *Census of Ireland for the Year 1871*, p. 24, [C. 1106–vii], H.C. 1874, lxxiv, pt. ii.

77. It is, of course, a logically distinct operation to infer that the Anglo-Irish were a significant portion of the Irish emigrant stream and another one to infer that they necessarily were part of the stream that came to Canada. However, given the strong loyalism of the Anglo-Irish to the Crown and to the United Kingdom constitution, it is not unrealistic to suggest that they came to Canada at least proportionately as frequently as they went anywhere else.

This inference is indirectly confirmed by Darroch and Ornstein's data which showed that in 1871 in the four original provinces of the Dominion, 22.6 percent of the persons of Irish ethnicity were Anglicans, making them much the largest Protestant group among the Irish (table 1, p. 312). Mind you, these data were collected after, not before, the migration to Canada and it is possible in theory that the Anglican numbers in Canada were inflated by large numbers of Ulster Presbyterians and their children converting to Anglicanism in the New World. That, however, seems less likely than the suggestion that the large Anglican population was the product of a large migration by the Anglo-Irish to Canada.

78. Pentland, p. 96.

79. Ibid., p. 103.

80. Ibid., p. 106.

81. Ibid., p. 107.

82. For Pentland's purposes, he would have found most illuminating Cousen's "The Regional Pattern of Emigration during the Great Irish Famine, 1846–51," *Institute of British Geographers' Transactions*, vol. 28 (1960), pp. 119–34, but reading of each or any of the following articles of S.H. Cousens would have indicated to him that his own views of Irish migration were almost totally untenable: "The Regional Variation in Emigration from Ireland between 1821 and 1841," *Institute of British Geographers, Transactions* no. 37 (1965), pp. 15–30; "Regional Death Rates in Ireland during the Great Famine, from 1846 to 1851," *Population Studies*, vol. 14 (1960–61), pp. 55–73; "The Regional Variation in Mortality during the Great Irish Famine," *Proceedings of the Royal Irish Academy*, vol. 63, sec. C, pp. 127–49; "The Regional Pattern of Emigration during the Great Irish Famine, 1846–51," *Institute of British Geographers' Transactions*, vol. 28 (1960), pp. 119–34; "Emigration and Demographic Change in Ireland, 1851–1861," *Economic History Review*, 2 ser., vol. 14 (1961–62), pp. 278–88.

83. Pentland, p. 104.

84. Ibid.

85. Ibid., p. 106.

86. Akenson, "Ontario: Whatever Happened to the Irish?" p. 233.
87. Darroch and Ornstein, table 4, p. 320.
88. Pentland, pp. 104–5.
89. Ibid., p. 106.
90. Darroch and Ornstein, table 4, p. 320 and p. 325.
91. For example, Phillips, in his "Introduction," pp. xxviii–xxix.
92. John Le Carre, *Tinker, Tailor, Soldier, Spy* (New York: Bantam Books, 1975), p. 315.
93. For a highly relevant discussion of racism in Canada, see "Combatting Racism" by Heribert Adam, *Queen's Quarterly*, vol. 89 (Winter 1982), pp. 785–93.
94. See Pentland, p. 72.
95. See ibid., pp. 98, 68, and 66, respectively.
96. Ibid., p. 105.
97. Ibid. p. 108.
98. See ibid., pp. 66–69, and 107–9.
99. Ibid., p. 107.
100. Phillips, "Introduction," pp. vii–viii.
101. I am not here generalizing without data. That these attitudes were common amongst Ulster-Scots of the weaver-cottier class in the relevant period is documented by a massive literature. As an introduction to Ulster-Scots culture, the reader might consult my study of a County Antrim Presbyterian community, *Between Two Revolutions, Islandmagee, Co. Antrim, 1798–1920* (Dublin: Academy Press; Hamden, Conn.: Archon Books; Toronto: P.D. Meany Co., 1979).
102. Toronto: New Hogtown Press, 1981.

Notes to Chapter Six

1. "School Readers as an Educational Force (A Study of a Century of Upper Canada)," *Queen's Quarterly*, vol. 39 (November 1932), pp. 688–703.
For more recent discussions of the Irish national school books, see Harvey J. Graff, *The Literacy Myth. Literacy and Social Structure in the Nineteenth-Century City* (New York: Academic Press, 1979), pp. 42–48, or James H. Love, "Cultural Survival and Social Control: The Development of a Curriculum for Upper Canada's Common Schools in 1846," *Histoire Sociale/Social History*, vol. 15 (November 1982), pp. 357–82.
2. Although this article is concerned only with elementary education, there is some material of interest in Robert Falconer's "Irish Influence on Higher Education in Canada," *Proceedings and Transactions of the Royal Society of Canada*, 3 ser., vol. 29, sec. II, pp. 131–43.
3. The standard biography is C.B. Sissons, *Egerton Ryerson. His Life and Letters* (Toronto: Clarke, Irwin and Co., Ltd., 1947), 2 vols. See also: John H. Putnam, *Egerton Ryerson and Education in Upper Canada* (Toronto: Morang, 1903); Gordon T. Stubbs, "The Role of Egerton Ryerson in the Development of the Public Library Service in Ontario," (M.A., University of British Columbia, 1965); Sylvia Carlton, "Egerton Ryerson and Education in Ontario, 1844–1877," (Ph.D., University of Pennsylvania, 1950); Clara Thomas, *Ryerson of Upper Canada* (Toronto: Ryerson Press, 1969).
"The Story of my Life," by the late Rev. Egerton Ryerson, D.D., Ll.D. (Toronto: William Briggs, 1883) was not only edited by J. George Hodgins but in part written by him.
The context of Ryerson's work is treated analytically in several of the essays in Neil McDonald and Alf Chaiton (eds.), *Egerton Ryerson and His Times* (Toronto: Macmillan, 1978).

In "Egerton Ryerson's Philosophy of Education: Something Borrowed or Something New?" *Ontario History*, vol. 61 (March 1969), pp. 77–86, David Onn argues convincingly against there having been much American influence on Ryerson. Onn does not consider seriously the possibility of European, British, or Irish influences on Ryerson, but instead sees "the ideas working in this man" as the driving force in shaping the Ontario educational system.

4. Technically, Ryerson's appointment in 1844 was as assistant superintendent of education. In practical terms, however, Ryerson was in charge. In 1846 his title was raised to reflect his actual powers and he became superintendent of education for the province.

5. The data for these assertions are found in Donald H. Akenson, "Ontario. Whatever Happened to the Irish?" *Canadian Papers in Rural History*, vol. III (1982), pp. 204–56.

6. Derived from *Census of Canada, 1931*, vol. I, table 35, p. 716.

7. Ryerson to Lord Stanley, 27 November 1844, quoted in J. George Hodgins (ed.), *Documentary History of Education in Upper Canada, from the passing of the Constitutional Act of 1791 to the close of the Reverend Doctor Ryerson's Administration of the Education Department in 1876* (Toronto: Warwick Bros. and Rutter, 1897), vol. V, p. 120.

8. Edward G.G.S. Stanley (1799–1869), fourteenth Earl of Derby (1851) and Prime Minister of the United Kingdom 1858–59 and 1866–68.

9. On Stanley's activities in creating the Irish school system, see Donald H. Akenson, *The Irish Education Experiment. The National System of Education in the Nineteenth Century* (London: Routledge and Kegan Paul, and Toronto: University of Toronto Press, 1979), p. 59, and especially pp. 107–22. Although Stanley's letter is easily found in the U.K. parliamentary papers, the versions differ, so it is best to consult that variorum edition in *The Irish Education Experiment* ..., pp. 392–402.

10. Ryerson to Stanley, 27 November 1844, quoted in Hodgins, vol. V, p. 120.

11. *Report on a system of public elementary Instruction for Upper Canada by the Reverend Egerton Ryerson, D.D.* (Montreal: Lovell and Gibson, 1847). The *Report* is dated 27 March 1846.

One hardly needs to remind the reader that popular education in Ontario did not being with Ryerson. He adopted and moulded to his own interest pre-existing educational structures, especially those set up by the school acts of 1841 and 1843. For useful background, see Susan E. Houston, "Politics, Schools and Social Change in Upper Canada," *Canadian Historical Review*, vol. 53 (September 1972), pp. 249–76, and J. Donald Wilson, "Education in Upper Canada: Sixty Years of Change," in J. Donald Wilson, Robert M. Stamp, and Louis-Phillipe Audet, *Canadian Education: A History* (Scarborough: Prentice-Hall, 1970), pp. 190–213. The latter article has been reprinted under the title of "The Pre-Ryerson Years," in McDonald and Chaiton (eds.), pp. 9–42.

12. Ryerson to unnamed (probably J.M. Higginson), [late 1845], quoted in Hodgins (ed.), vol. V, p. 246.

13. *Report*, p. 44. Not accidentally, on the same page Ryerson included a direct quotation from Lord Stanley's "Letter" of 1831.

14. *Report*, p. 174.

15. See section III of the 1846 Common Schools Act.

16. Ryerson to Robert Baldwin, 1849, quoted in *"The Story of my Life"*, p. 425.

17. "... There is little evidence that their advice [that of the members of the board of education] was sought on a regular basis or that they had any influence in the decision-making process." Neil McDonald "Egerton Ryerson and the School as Agent of Socialization," in McDonald and Chaiton (eds.), p. 102.

18. On these and ancillary functions of the trustees of the school section, see 1846 Act, section XXVII.

19. The following articles are very useful: D.A. Lawr and R.D. Gidney, "Who Ran the Schools? Local Influence on Education Policy in Nineteenth-century Ontario," *Ontario History*, vol. 72 (September 1980), pp. 131–43; R.D. Gidney and W.P.J. Millar, "Rural Schools and the Decline of Community Control in Nineteenth-century Ontario," Fourth Annual Agricultural History of Ontario Seminar, *Proceedings*, pp. 70–91; R.D. Gidney, "Making Nineteenth-century School Systems: The Upper Canadian Experience and its Relevance to English Historiography," *History of Education*, vol. 9, no. 2 (1980), pp. 101–16; R.D. Gidney, "Centralization and Education: the Origins of an Ontario Tradition," *Journal of Canadian Studies*, vol. 7 (1972), pp. 33–47; R.D. Gidney and D.A. Lawr, "The Development of an Administrative System for the Public Schools: the First Stage, 1841–50," in McDonald and Chaiton (eds.), pp. 160–83; R.D. Gidney and D.A. Lawr, "Bureaucracy vs. Community? The Origins of Bureaucratic Procedure in the Upper Canadian School System," *Journal of Social History*, vol. 13 (Spring 1980), pp. 438–57.

20. Wilson, in Wilson, Stamp, and Audet (eds.), p. 221.

21. The structure and evolution of the Irish national system of education is detailed in *The Irish Education Experiment*. ... For a précis, see Donald H. Akenson, "National Education and the Realities of Irish Life, 1831–1900," *Eire-Ireland*, vol. 4 (Winter 1969), pp. 42–51.

22. During its first two decades, the "board" in Ireland, that is, the commissioners of national education, had relatively more power in Ireland than did Ryerson's board in Ontario. This changed quickly in the 1850s, especially after the resignation of Archbishop Whately in 1853, and, increasingly, the resident commissioner of national education came to occupy a position vis-à-vis his board equivalent to that which Ryerson held in relation to his Ontario board.

23. At the local level, the primary difference between the Irish and the Ontario systems was that the Irish school managers had no powers of taxation, whereas, under the education acts of 1847 and 1850, it was possible (although not compulsory) for school boards to strike a rate. Significantly, Ryerson minimized the differences as between the two systems. In 1853 he wrote:

The elected Trustees of Schools in Canada, sustain the same relation to our Common Schools that the local "patrons" sustain to the National Schools in Ireland. The sole difference, therefore, between the National Schools in Ireland and in Upper Canada, in respect of the control of religious instruction is that with us, the Trustees or Patrons of the school are periodically elected by the freeholders and householders at large — which is not the case in Ireland.

("Note by the Chief Superintendent of Schools for Upper Canada," a footnote to a reproduction of the Regulations of the Commissioners of National Education in Ireland, found in *Correspondence between the Roman Catholic Bishop of Toronto and the Chief Superintendent of Schools on the Subject of Separate Common Schools in Upper Canada*, Toronto: Thomas Hugh Bentley, 1853, pp. 25–26).

24. In addition to Akenson, *The Irish Education Experiment* ... , pp. 143–46 and 279–81, see Eustas O'Heidan, *National School Inspection in Ireland: the Beginnings* (Dublin: Sceptre, 1967), passim.

25. *Report*, p. 177.

26. Ibid.

27. See 1846 School Act, section VI, and 1847 Common Schools Act, section V, sub-section 4.

28. In point of fact, the power of local district councils (which became the county councils) to appoint and to dismiss school superintendents (who, later, were renamed "inspectors") actually continued until 1930 when the

Department of Education finally acquired the full responsibility both for their appointment and their salary (Sissons, *Egerton Ryerson* ... , vol. II, p. 101, *n.*1).

29. R.D. Gidney and D.A. Lawr, "The Development of an Administrative System for the Public Schools: The First Stage, 1841–50," in McDonald and Chaiton, pp. 173–74.

30. Akenson, *The Irish Education Experiment* ... , pp. 146–49; J.M. Goldstrom, *The Social Content of Education, 1808–1870. A Study of the Working Class School Reader in England and Ireland* (Shannon: Irish University Press, 1972), pp. 88–89.

31. Ryerson to unspecified (probably J.M. Higginson) [late 1845], in Hodgins (ed.), vol. V, p. 244.

32. Ibid.

33. *Report*, p. 148.

34. See 1846 Common Schools Act, sections V and XIII, sub-sections five and six, and section XXXIV.

Interestingly, in his first set of school regulations, in the section "Duties of Trustee," Ryerson called special attention to the care needed in the trustees' appointing teachers and, as the ideal definition of a desirable teacher for the Ontario schools, gave them one developed by the commissioners of national education in Ireland. (See *Special Report of the Measures which have been adopted for the Establishment of a Normal School*, Montreal: Lovell and Gibson, 1847, p. 56.)

35. "Minutes of the Commissioners of National Education in Ireland" (National Library of Ireland, Dublin), 5 November 1846, 4 March 1847, and 3 June 1847; Hodgins (ed.), vol. V, p. 246.

36. The context of Rintoul's being offered the Toronto headmastership is revealing. On 24 July 1846 Ryerson wrote to the secretaries of the commissioners of National Education in Ireland as follows: "It is the desire of the Canadian Board of Education to profit by the successful labours of the commissioners of National Education in Ireland, and to introduce a similar system of Schools, as far as the circumstances of Upper Canada will enable us to do so, and especially the Dublin system of Normal School instruction and the series of School Books which have been published under the sanction of the Irish Education Board." Consequently, Ryerson stated, "It is very desirable that the first Master of the Canadian Normal School should have the sanction of the Commissioners of National Education in Ireland...." (Copy) Archives of Ontario, RG 2, series B, vol. 1). See also Love in McDonald and Chaiton (eds.), p. 115; *Special Report of the Measures which have been adopted for the Establishment of a Normal School* ... , pp. 4–5.

37. "Minutes of the Commissioners of National Education in Ireland," 29 July 1847; Akenson, *The Irish Education Experiment* ... , p. 145; Nicholas Flood Davin, *The Irishman in Canada* (London: Sampson, Low, Marston and Co., 1877), p. 643; Sissons, *Egerton Ryerson* ... , vol. II, p. 149, *n.*1 and *n.*2.

Viola E. Parvin, *Authorization of Textbooks for the Schools of Ontario, 1846–1950* (Toronto: University of Toronto Press, 1965), pp. 34–35.

38. During Ryerson's educational tour, the Hodgins family (now back in Ireland) had provided Ryerson with "the kindest attentions," and young Hodgins' uncle, said Ryerson, "was also to me the warmest of friends." And Hodgins' mother now was a widow. All these were reasons, in addition to young Hodgins' ability, put forward by Ryerson for his appointment. Ryerson to MacNab (draft), 31 March 1845, quoted in Sissons, vol. II, p. 87.

39. Footnote by Hodgins in Hodgins (ed.), vol. V, p. 119.

Hodgins' testimonial of competence by the Irish education authorities was given by a letter of Professor Robert Sullivan, 13 May 1846 (reproduced ibid., p. 119.)

40. Akenson, *The Irish Education Experiment* ..., pp. 130, 132.

41. Hodgins (ed.), vol. V, 149 *n*.

42. Certain ancillary personnel also came from Dublin. For instance, Col. Henry Goodwin, a County Tyrone Catholic and retired from the Royal Horse Artillery, emigrated to Canada in 1850, and Lord Elgin convinced Ryerson to engage him as a teacher of gymnastics, fencing and "general deportment" in the normal school. He taught from 1853 to 1877 (Davin, p. 621).

Rather less peripheral to the education enterprise was the Rev. J.W. McGauley, the Professor of Natural Philosophy in the normal school in Dublin. Ryerson, when he met him in 1845, adjudged McGauley to be "an accomplished Scholar, and a man whom it is really a treat to hear — from the elegant simplicity and correctness of his language, the clearness of his conception and the thoroughness of his knowledge...." McGauley (who became a personal friend of J.G. Hodgins during the latter's Dublin training stint) took up an appointment as a teacher in Toronto in 1856, and then moved to London, Ontario, where he opened a private school. He was appointed a professor in London, England, in the early 1860s and lived the rest of his life in the Old Country. (See *DNB* and Hodgins, especially vol. V, pp. 119 *n* and 245–46.)

Although not directly related to central administrative appointment policies, the ethnicity of local school teachers through the province warrants investigation. The 1871 census would make a study of this sort possible. I suspect that a cross-tabulation of ethnicity with the occupation of school-teaching would show (1) that the most common ethnic background of common school teachers was Irish and (2) that, moreover, the Irish were disproportionately high amongst teachers. I found that pattern in my own study of the social history of Leeds and Lansdowne Township in eastern Ontario (admittedly a non-representative area in many ways), and, more important, Willard Francis Dillon may have found the same in western Ontario. See Dillon, "The Irish in London, Ontario, 1826–1861," (M.A., University of Western Ontario, 1963), pp. 85–106.

43. The most thorough discussion of the content and methods of the Irish national readers is found in Goldstrom, *The Social Content of Education, 1808–1870,* passim. The books are discussed in Akenson, *The Irish Education Experiment* ..., pp. 225–74. They are also discussed in the articles by Fox, Love, and Graff, mentioned above (see note 1). Aside from the Fox, Love, and Graff items, however, one gains the distinct impression that few Canadian educational historians have based their impressions of the books upon a full set of readers. This is understandable, as a complete set is very hard to come by. My own set (incomplete) is now housed in the Center for International Education Documentation of the Northeastern University Library, Boston, Mass. The most complete set, including the various revisions, is found in the National Library of Ireland, Dublin.

44. *Digest of Evidence before the committees of the Houses of Lords and Commons in the year 1837 on the national system of education in Ireland* (London: 1838), p. 29.

45. J.M. Goldstrom, "Richard Whately and Political Economy in School Books," *Irish Historical Studies,* vol. 15 (September 1966), pp. 136–37.

46. Quoted in *Royal Commission of Inquiry into Primary Education (Ireland),* vol. I, part I, *Report of the Commissioners,* p. 117 [C. 6], H.C., 1870, xxvii, part i.

47. Ryerson to unnamed (probably J.M. Higginson) [late 1845], quoted in Hodgins (ed.), vol. V, p. 246.

48. My own subjective opinion, from reading both sets, is that the Irish

readers were much more coherent, better organized, and would have been much more satisfactory from which to teach. William Sherwood Fox's observation is pertinent (pp. 693–94):

> Before me are copies of these Irish books printed in Canada and ranging in date from 1846 to 1863. *A Sequel to the Second Books of Lessons* [written by Archbishop Richard Whately], issued in 1859, is one of the most remarkable common school text-books I have ever seen. As everybody knows, it is difficult to present real ideas in readable form to boys and girls of the Second and Third Reader stage; yet the author of this little work has been eminently successful in attaining his aim. Balance, sanity, clarity and simplicity are the outstanding marks of this book. Like his predecessors and contemporaries, he has retained current moral religious teachings, but he has added to their effectiveness by delicately reducing the bald and offensive obviousness with which such teachings are usually presented. This sense of restraint is, in the main, characteristic of all the Irish Readers and is in glaring contrast to the method of the McGuffey Series. Possibly we can see in them the origin of a certain moderation which has become one of our Canadian traits . . . The making of this book was really a notable achievement.

49. *Report*, p. 174.

50. 1846 Common Schools Act, sections II (6) and III (2).

51. As Ryerson's original "General Regulations and Instructions" said, "The series of Readers and Other School Books published by the National Board of Education in Ireland, and recommended by the Canadian Board, are doubtless the best, and will be the cheapest series of Canadian School Books sold in Canada, as may be seen by referring to the list of prices in the Appendix to these Forms and Regulations." (Regulation reproduced in *Special Report of the Measures which have been adopted for the Establishment of a Normal School . . .*, p. 56.

52. It is not clear if the Irish commissioners were selling abroad at cost-price or with a mark-up, and I suspect that they did not know themselves, as their accounting methods were rudimentary. In 1840 they claimed that the price they received for sale other than to Irish national schools "always yields a profit to us on the transaction." (*Seventh Report of the Commissioners of National Education in Ireland for the Year 1840*, p. 5 [246], H.C., 1840, xxviii.) Later, however, they intended to sell at cost-price overseas: "Ordered, that in future the National Schools Books be sold to the Colonies at cost-price with 10 per cent added to cover incidental expenses." ("Minutes of the Commissioners of National Education in Ireland," 26 November 1846.) The indisputable point is that the books were being made available to Canada at a very small margin above the cost-price (the 10 percent handling charge).

53. See letter of Ryerson to the Textbook Publishers of Canada, 6 January 1847, reproduced in *Brockville Recorder*, 14 January 1847.

54. See Parvin, p. 42.

55. Love, p. 368.

56. Wilson, in Wilson, Stamp, and Audet (eds.), p. 220.

57. Parvin, p. 29. Another ninety failed to report.

58. [Alexander Marling] *A Brief History of Public and high School Text-Books authorized for the Province of Ontario, 1846–1889, prepared by the Education Department* (Toronto: Warwick and Sons, 1890), p. 10.

59. On Ryerson's reluctance to abandon the Irish readers, see Neil McDonald, "Canadianization and the Curriculum: Setting the Stage, 1867–1890," in E. Brian Titley and Peter J. Miller (eds.), *Education in Canada: An Interpretation* (Calgary: Detselig Enterprises Ltd., 1982), p. 97.

60. Ryerson quite openly noted the relationship to the previous Irish readers. See ibid., p. 97.

61. Marling, pp. 8 and 32; Parvin, pp. 53–54, 68, 149.

62. *First Book of Lessons for the Use of Schools* (Dublin and Toronto, 1847), p. 20.

63. Akenson, *Irish Education Experiment* ... , pp. 236–37.

64. Ibid., p. 235.

65. Scott N. Stokes, secretary to the Roman Catholic Poor School Committee in Great Britain, to the secretary, English Committee of Council on Education, 1 August 1851, reproduced in *Eighteenth Report of the Commissioners of National Education in Ireland, for the Year 1851*, pp. lvi–lvii [1582], H.C. 1852–53, xlii.

66. Many Irish Anglican clergy opposed the system of national education for its first three decades, not because of any problems with the textbooks, but because, being clergy of an established church, they did not wish to share control of education with the secular authorities. By the 1860s most Anglicans were reconciled to the national system.

67. Wilson, in Wilson, Stamp, and Audet, p. 224.

68. The standard nineteenth-century lives of Whately are: E.J. Whately (with Herman Merivale), *Life and Correspondence of Richard Whately, D.D., late Archbishop of Dublin* (London: 1866), 2 vols.; and William J. Fitzpatrick, *Memoirs of Richard Whately, Archbishop of Dublin, with a glance at his Contemporaries and Times* (London: 1864) 2 vols. The modern life is Donald Akenson, *A Protestant in Purgatory. Richard Whately, Archbishop of Dublin* (Hamden: published for the Conference on British Studies Biography Series and for Indiana University, by Archon Books, 1981).

69. Akenson, *A Protestant in Purgatory* ... , p. 18.

70. Goldstrom, "Richard Whately and Political Economy in School Books, 1833–1880," pp. 133–35.

71. Ibid., p. 137.

72. *Supplement to the Fourth Books of Lessons* (p. 30), quoted in Goldstrom, *The Social Context of Education* ... , p. 73.

73. *Fourth Books of Lessons*, pp. 209–10, quoted in Goldstrom, "Richard Whately and Political Economy in School Books, 1833–1880," pp. 140–41.

74. *Fourth Book of Lessons*, p. 54, quoted in Goldstrom, *The Social Context of Education* ... , p. 75.

75. *Fourth Book of Lessons*, p. 225, quoted ibid., p. 74.

76. There is an ancillary issue that also should be left open: the motives of those who determined the school curriculum. This is important, as much of the historical literature on social control in education suffers from the frequent confusion of effect with cause by assuming that, because the school system in a given case had a given effect, achieving this specific effect was the intention of those who set up and governed the system. This causual linkage demands proof, not mere assertion. Further, one must avoid the Manichean disposition that runs through much of the social control literature: the motives of those who control the curriculum are often viewed as being dark and oppressive. Again, this sort of judgement demands proof.

In the case of Richard Whately, one finds not a rampant capitalist, nor a cynical manipulator of the working class, but a gifted teacher and a lifelong proponent of their welfare as he understood it. Whately chaired the monumental Irish poor law investigation of 1833–36 and fought very hard, but unsuccessfully, against the imposition of the notorious English poor law upon the Irish people. Instead of the English poor law, he advocated a widespread relief system, massive public works, and assisted emigration. His farsighted system for developing backward areas in Ireland presaged by nearly a century the creation of regional development plans in Great Britain. (See Akenson, *A Protestant in Purgatory* ... , pp. 125–30.) My own opinion (and it is no more than that) is that Whately's chief motive in writing the political economy lessons was that he believed that the universe worked in the way that the economists said it did, and that it was only justice and kindness to let the children of the working class learn it, just as it was appropriate to teach them how the physical universe worked.

As for Ryerson, he was strongly convinced of the need to reinforce the political loyalism of the people of Ontario and also hoped to teach them literacy and to inculcate in them Christian virtues. Whether or not he cared much about the lessons in political economy, I do not know, although, as will be shown in part 2, section 3, he was sufficiently devoted to the doctrines of political economy later to write his own textbook. But even in doing that, his motives are not clear.

77. Akenson, "Irish Education and the Realities of Irish Life, 1831–1900," pp. 42–51.

78. The details of the development of a dual confessional school in Ontario are complex. Especially helpful is Franklin A. Walker's impressive monograph, *Catholic Education and Politics in Upper Canada. A Study of the Documentation Relative to the Origin of Catholic Elementary Schools in the Ontario System* (Toronto: J.M. Dent and Sons, 1955). Also very useful are: C.B. Sissons, "Ontario," in *Church and State in Canadian Education. A Historical Study* (Toronto: Ryerson Press, 1959), pp. 1–125, and Wilson, in Wilson, Stamp, and Audet, pp. 231–38.

79. For a perceptive comment on the importance of "harmony" in Ryerson's outlook, see Houston, pp. 264–65.

80. *Report*, p. 22.

81. Ibid., pp. 23–24.

82. [Editor unspecified; not prepared by Ryerson himself] *Dr. Ryerson's Letters in reply to the Attacks of Foreign Ecclesiastics . . .* , (Toronto: Lovell and Gibson, 1857), p. 8, date of original 24 April 1852.

83. For Ryerson's view on the "evils of a godless system of education," see *Report*, p. 24.

84. The applicability of this paradigm is not limited to the nineteenth century. In the 1920s, shortly after the partition of Ireland, the Northern Ireland Minister of Education, the Marquis of Londonderry, tried to do what Lord Stanley and Egerton Ryerson before him had attempted, establish a religiously integrated system of primary education. His failure followed almost precisely the same pattern. See Donald Akenson, *Education and Enmity. The Control of Schooling in Northern Ireland, 1920–1950* (Newton Abbot and New York: published for the Institute of Irish Studies of the Queen's University of Belfast, by David and Charles and by Barnes and Noble Books, 1973).

85. By the time Ryerson visited Ireland, the Irish system was in fact a dual confessional one in practice, and ecumenical only in theory. It took Ryerson a long time — until 1857 (see Sissons, *Egerton Ryerson*, vol. II, p. 357) — to admit that the Irish reality was different. Either Ryerson was dissembling greatly when, in 1846, he held up the Irish system as an example of religiously united education, or, more likely, he was a remarkably uncritical observer of foreign educational phenomena. As I will suggest later, I suspect that he came under the influence of Richard Whately, one of the great talkers of the nineteenth century.

In the first set of school regulations issued under the 1846 Common Schools Act, Ryerson referred extensively to the Irish system as a pattern to follow on religious matters. For instance, he stated that "in schools which are composed both of Roman Catholic and Protestant children, the Commissioners of National Educational in Ireland have made the following regulations which are worthy of imitation wherever desired and practicable in Canada" (he then quoted the Irish commissioners for half a page on doctrinal religious instruction being given only on separate days or at special times). Two other lengthy extracts were also taken from the Irish rules, and, finally, Ryerson concluded: "The foregoing quotations (which might be greatly extended) from the Irish Commissioners' Reports, are made, because their system may be considered as the basis of the Canadian system ... That system is Christian, but not sectarian." (Quotations from the General Regulations and Instructions, as reprinted in *Special Report of the Measures which have been adopted for the Establishment of a Normal School* ... , pp. 60–61.)

86. *Report*, p. 43.

87. Not to be confused with twentieth-century Irish usage, wherein "mixed" means co-educational schools.

88. Ryerson to Charbonnel, 12 May 1852, reproduced in *Correspondence between the Roman Catholic Bishop of Toronto and the Chief Superintendent of Schools, on the Subject of Separate Common Schools in Canada* (Toronto: Thomas Hugh Bentley, 1853), p. 16.

89. Ibid., p. 24. Note the phrase "What the Commissioners of National Education in Ireland state as existing...." Ryerson was beginning to admit the possibility of a dissonance between what the Irish commissioners claimed, and what actually was the case. This stands in contrast to the summary of Irish education given in 1868 in Ryerson's *A Special Report on the Systems and State of Popular Education on the Continent of Europe, in the British Isles, and the United States of America, with Practical Suggestions for the Improvement of Public Instruction in the Province of Ontario* (Toronto: Leader Steam Press, 1868). By then he wanted to put as much distance as possible between himself and the Irish system. He gave it only three out of 198 pages. Clearly, the scales had fallen from his eyes concerning the Irish system. He laconically reported that "while the original non-denominational object of the system is still avowed, the great majority of the schools have become denominational." (p. 94)

90. In 1871, 66.1 percent of those persons of Irish ethnicity living in the four original provinces were found in Ontario. This obtained even after the peak Irish flow of 1846–52. (See chapter four, table 6).

91. That this is a reasonable estimate (but no more than an estimate) of the composition of the Famine flow is indicated from the data in Akenson, "Ontario: Whatever Happened to the Irish?" pp. 220–21, and 230–31.

92. On Power, and the educational context in which he operated, see Walker, pp. 36–55. On Murray, see Akenson, *The Irish Education Experiment* ... , passim.

93. Ryerson to Bishop Pinsoneault, 24 February 1857, reproduced in *Dr. Ryerson's Letters in reply to the Attacks of Foreign Ecclesiastics* ... , p. 99.

94. Ryerson to Charbonnel, 12 May 1852, in *Correspondence between the Roman Catholic Bishop of Toronto and the Chief Superintendent of Schools* ... , p. 16.

95. On Beresford and on the Church Education Society, see Akenson, *The Irish Education Experiment* ... , especially pp. 197–201, and 286–94. Manifestly, if Archbishop Beresford opposed the national school system and Archbishop Whately favoured it, there was great tension in the church. The loose administrative structure that made this sort of squabbling possible is analyzed in Donald H. Akenson, *The Church of Ireland: Ecclesiastical Reform and Revolution, 1800–1885* (New Haven: Yale University Press, 1971).

96. See Ryerson to W.H. Draper, 12 April 1847, reproduced in Sissons, *Egerton Ryerson* ... , vol. II, pp. 135–36, and Walker, pp. 66–68. For general background, see J.L.H. Henderson, ed., *John Strachan, Documents and Opinions* (Toronto: McClelland and Stewart, 1969), especially pp. ix, 116–27.

97. By 1896 there were only ten Protestant (read Anglican) separate schools

in operation, by 1938 four, and by 1967 just two; which is to say that in practical terms "separate school" became a synonym for "Roman Catholic school." See Wilson, in Wilson, Stamp, and Audet, p. 237.

98. Because in Part II of this chapter I am concentrating on the major cultural issue of religious segregation vs. integration, I am setting aside another set of wars that bedevilled both the Ontario and the Irish systems: in each case, booksellers and book publishers, seeing huge potential profits in the expanding school networks, but kept out by the authorities' policy of publishing at very low costs (in the Irish case) and of importing very cheap editions (in the Ontario case), attacked vigorously. In each instance, they used a version of the Gospel of Free Trade as the ideological Trojan horse inside of which were hidden, if they succeeded, high prices for school books, and profits of themselves.

The Ontario situation is presented, albeit less than analytically, in Stubbs (pp. 29–34) and Parvin (pp. 41–46). Quite illuminating is *The School Book Question: Letters in Reply to the Brown-Campbell Crusade against the Educational Department for Upper Canada* (Montreal: John Lovell, 1866). The Irish battle has not yet been dealt with in the historical literature, but the basic primary sources are: the Minutes of the Commissioners of National Education in Ireland (National Library of Ireland, Dublin) especially 1850–52, and the Irish commissioners' printed *Reports* for 1848 [1066]; 1849,, 2 vols. [1231, 1231–II]; 1850 [1405], Appendix to 1850 [1405–II]; 1851 [1582], and in the *Royal Commission of Inquiry into Primary Education* (Ireland), vol. I, part I [C. 6].

99. There is no adequate biography of Cullen. The four volumes by Peadar MacSuibhne (Naas: Leinster Leader, 1961–74) border on hagiography. On Cullen on national education, see Akenson, *The Irish Education Experiment* ..., pp. 254–74, passim. The vanquishing of Whately is dealt with in more detail in Akenson, *A Protestant in Purgatory* ..., pp. 192–204. For a recent discussion of Cullen, Desmond Bowen, *Paul Cardinal Cullen and the Shaping of Modern Irish Catholicism* (Dublin: Gill and MacMillan, 1983).

100. Charbonnel to Ryerson, 24 March 1852, reproduced in *Dr. Ryerson's Letter in reply to the Attacks of Foreign Ecclesiastics* ..., p. 4.

101. Ibid., p. 5.

102. Charbonnel to Ryerson, 1 May 1852, reproduced ibid., p. 21. For some indication of the context in which these episcopal statements were made, see Dennis O'Driscoll, "Divergent Images of American and British Education in the Ontario Catholic Press, 1851–1948," *Study Session 1976. Canadian Catholic Historical Association*, pp. 5–22.

103. One must say "ultimately," because by the 1863 act the Catholic right to separate schools was established, but the dispersed nature of the population in Ontario meant that in many areas it often was a generation or more before a separate school was built.

104. Ryerson to Bishop Pinsoneault, 24 February 1857, reproduced in *Dr. Ryerson's Letters in reply to the Attacks of Foreign Ecclesiastics* ..., p. 101.

105. Ibid., p. 102.

106. The decrees of the Synod of Thurles are most conveniently available in [James Kavanagh], *Mixed Education, the Catholic Case stated* ..., (Dublin, 1859), pp. 412–15.

107. Ryerson to Pinsoneault, 24 Feb. 1857, reproduced in *Dr. Ryerson's Letters in reply to the Attacks of Foreign Ecclesiastics* ..., p. 102.

108. *Report*, pp. 43–44.

109. On the *Logic* and the *Rhetoric*, see Akenson, *A Protestant in Purgatory* ..., pp. 54–62. The *Rhetoric* is of more than historical interest in the development of education. The textbooks and methods used in America state university courses in Speech are to this day stongly Whatelian, and their fundamental precepts of discourse can be traced directly to him.

110. For quotations from Whately's *Rhetoric*, see *Report*, pp. 79 and 90.

111. "The Archbishop of Dublin has written an admirable Elementary work on *The Art of Reasoning,* which has been published by the Irish National Board, and is now used in the Irish Schools." (*Report*, p. 143)

112. Marling, pp. 36 and 43. The book was approved for use in Ontario by its proper title, *Easy Lessons on Reasoning,* not Ryerson's gloss, given above. The volume probably was too advanced for all but the best pupils in the common schools. It seems to be of a level appropriate for a grade 12 or 13 student of today. The volume was quite popular outside the schools. By 1852 its commercial publishers had it in a third American and a fifth English edition.

113. Ryerson to unnamed (probably J.M. Higginson), [late 1846], quoted in Hodgins (ed.), vol. V, p. 246.

114. *Report*, pp. 45–46.

115. Marling, p. 7, Parvin, p. 144. On the contents of the volume, see Akenson, *The Irish Education Experiment 2..*, pp. 240–42.

116. *Report*, p. 45.

117. Marling, p. 7; Parvin, p. 144.

118. Akenson, *The Irish Education Experiment* . . . , pp. 244–45; Akenson, *A Protestant in Purgatory* . . . , pp. 262–63.

119. *Report*, p. 45.

120. Akenson, *The Irish Education Experiment* . . . , pp. 242–43. Akenson, *A Protestant in Purgatory* . . . , pp. 186–87.

121. Marling, p. 7, Parvin, p. 144.

122. Toronto: Copp, Clark and Co., 1871.

123. Marling, pp. 8–9.

124. I am grateful to Dr. William Westfall of the Canadian Studies Programme, York University, for pointing out to me another link to Whately. As Ryerson freely admitted, his *First Lesson in Christian Morals* was founded in substance on William Paley's *Evidences of Christianity.* Richard Whately was strongly indebted to Paley as well, and, more important, in 1859 had published the standard nineteenth-century annotated edition of Paley's *Moral Philosophy.* (On Ryerson's indebtedness to Paley see "The Story of My Life," pp. 430–31, and United Church Archives, Ryerson Papers, vol. 1, file 3.)

125. *Elements of Political Economy; or, how individuals and a country become rich* (Toronto: Copp, Clark and Co., 1877). The book is in the form of questions and answers. Ryerson does not mention Whately in the preface, but acknowledges Nassau Senior. It is not, I think, accidental that Ryerson's book was intended for use by fourth and fifth class pupils (Robert M. Stamp, *The Schools of Ontario, 1876–1976,* Toronto: University of Toronto Press, 1982, p. 10.) This was the same level for which Whately's book on Christian evidence was intended.

126. Akenson, *The Irish Education Experiment* . . . , p. 231 *n* 24.

127. Ryerson also wrote, published, and had sanctioned for the schools a production entitled *First Lessons on Agriculture; for Canadian Farmers and their Families.* Of the edition which I have seen (second ed., Toronto: Copp, Clark and Co., 1871), roughly two-fifths is highly abstract, but the remainder is good sound practical advice. Without practical instruction to accompany it, however, the book must have been of questionable value. This calls to mind the similar publication in Ireland, *The Agricultural Class Book,* published in 1850, which rarely was accompanied by practical work, and it was said by school inspectors that the best results from studying this volume were achieved by Belfast street children who rarely if ever had been near a real farm.

To the parallels between Ryerson and Whately mentioned in the text must be added the melancholy fact that each man continued to be vilified by religious opponents long after his death. As late as 1924–25 Fr. E.J. Quigley published a six-part series in the *Irish Ecclesiastical Record* mostly given over to vilifying Whately and to justifying Cardinal Cullen. In the June 1969 number of *Culture* (pp. 93–113), an article on "Catholics and Secular Culture. Australia and Canada Compared," by Dr. Timothy Suttor of the University of Windsor, waxed apoplectic about a "destroyer" who "came in the wake of Durham's report of 1840" and attempted to destroy the Catholic schools of Ontario. "The destroyer's name was Ryerson, a Methodist who in character, policy, durability and political influence resembled his Australian coevals like Hartley and Wilkins." (p. 105)

128. For a promising start in dealing with the evolutionary pattern of material imported from the British Isles, see John J. Mannion, *Irish Settlements in Eastern Canada. A Study of Cultural Transfer and Adaptation* (Toronto: University of Toronto Press, 1974).

129. For innovative work on language see Ian Pringle, "The Concept of Dialect and the Study of Canadian English," *Queen's Quarterly* (Spring, 1983), pp. 100–21, and also Enoch Padolsky and Ian Pringle, "Demographic Analysis and Regional Dialects Surveys in Canada: Data Collection and Use," in Donald H. Akenson (ed)., *Canadian Papers in Rural History*, vol. IV (1984), pp. 240–75.

130. The secondary transplantations of the Irish system into those parts of western Canada that adopted versions of the "Ryersonian system" would be well worth tracing in detail. For preliminary work, see: Alan H. Child, "The Ryerson Tradition in Western Canada, 1871–1906," in McDonald and Chaiton, pp. 279–301.

Notes to Chapter Seven

1. The now-classic *Historians' Fallacies. Toward a Logic of Historial Thought* by David Hackett Fisher (London: Routledge and Kegan Paul, 1971) repays several readings; it is both highly instructive and very entertaining.

2. For example, if one takes the fifty authors of general books or articles on the Irish in the United States listed by Metress, forty of them have distinctly Irish surnames and, probably, Catholic backgrounds. For the list of authors, see Seamus P. Metress, *The Irish-American Experience. A Guide to the Literature* (Washington D.C.: University Press of America Inc., 1981), pp. 1–5. Lest anyone think that I am falling into the "ACLS fallacy" of over-reading surnames as evidence, let me emphasize that I am here not making a precise demographic statement but only giving rough evidence for the notion that the history of the Irish Americans has been written largely by members of their own group. The actual proportion of historians of the Irish-Americans who have an Irish background is probably considerably higher than the 80 percent indicated above, as inter-marriage with other ethnic groups has resulted in a large number of people having some Irish background, but a surname that is not distinctively Irish.

3. Specifically, forty-five of the seventy-one persons on the rolls of the American Committee for Irish Studies in 1978 who were professional historians had surnames that usually denominate Irish Catholics. The proportion with some Irish background inevitably is much higher. Again, I am not pressing this point as a statistical statement, but merely as an indication that in the United States most of those who read and teach Irish history as part of their professional duties come from Irish Catholic roots.

4. That there is a reciprocal relationship between the scholars and the general ethnic community bears note. Although the academics effectively have been articulating at a scholarly level what are essentially communal folk-beliefs, their versions of the Irish-American mythology filter into the general community and become in themselves components of the Irish-American communities' definition of itself.

5. This denigration of the generation who migrated from Ireland as technologically and culturally limited, would run against the grain of filial piety except for one thing: as noted below in the text, the alleged backwardness of the Irish migrants to America is blamed on the English. Granted, the English were no great blessing as governors and landlords, but as emphasized in chapters three, four, and five, despite their handicaps in the Old Country, the Irish Catholic migrants to the New World were neither technologically backward nor commercial fools. Quite the opposite: they were extraordinarily adaptable to a variety of technical and economic environments and, considering that they started with virtually nothing, very sharp at amassing capital.

6. Lawrence J. McCaffrey, *The Irish Diaspora in America* (Bloomington: Indiana University Press, 1976), p. 183.

7. Nancy Scheper-Hughes, *Saints, Scholars, and Schizophrenics. Mental Illness in Rural Ireland* (Berkeley: University of California Press, 1979), tables 11 and 12, pp. 72 and 73.

Index